PENGUIN BOOKS

THE STORY OF THE SCROLLS

Geza Vermes was born in Hungary in 1924. He studied in Budapest and Louvain, where he read Oriental History and Languages and in 1953 obtained a doctorate in Theology with a dissertation on the Dead Sea Scrolls. From 1957 to 1991 he taught at the universities of Newcastle and Oxford. His pioneering work on the Dead Sea Scrolls and the historical figure of Jesus led to his appointment as the first Professor of Jewish Studies at Oxford, where he is now Professor Emeritus. Since 1991 he has been director of the Forum for Qumran Research at the Oxford Centre for Hebrew and Jewish Studies. Professor Vermes is a Fellow of the British Academy and of the European Academy of Arts, Sciences and Humanities, the holder of an Oxford D.Litt. and of honorary doctorates from the universities of Edinburgh, Durham, Sheffield and the Central European University of Budapest.

His books, published by Penguin, include *The Complete Dead Sea Scrolls in English* (most recent edition, 2004), *The Changing Faces of Jesus* (2000), *The Authentic Gospel of Jesus* (2003), *Who's Who in the Age of Jesus* (2005) and his trilogy about the life of Jesus, *The Passion* (2005), *The Nativity* (2006) and *The Resurrection* (2007), republished in one volume as *Jesus: Nativity – Passion – Resurrection* in 2010. His pioneering work, *Jesus the Jew* (1973; most recent edition, 2001) and his autobiography, *Providential Accidents* (1998) are available from SCM Press, London.

GEZA VERMES

The Story of the Scrolls

The Miraculous Discovery and True
Significance of the Dead Sea Scrolls

PENGUIN BOOKS

PENGUIN BOOKS

Published by the Penguin Group
Penguin Books Ltd, 80 Strand, London WC2R 0RL, England
Penguin Group (USA) Inc., 375 Hudson Street, New York, New York 10014, USA
Penguin Group (Canada), 90 Eglinton Avenue East, Suite 700, Toronto, Ontario, Canada M4P 2Y3
(a division of Pearson Penguin Canada Inc.)
Penguin Ireland, 25 St Stephen's Green, Dublin 2, Ireland
(a division of Penguin Books Ltd)
Penguin Group (Australia), 250 Camberwell Road, Camberwell, Victoria 3124, Australia
(a division of Pearson Australia Group Pty Ltd)
Penguin Books India Pvt Ltd, 11 Community Centre, Panchsheel Park, New Delhi – 110 017, India
Penguin Group (NZ), 67 Apollo Drive, Rosedale, North Shore 0632, New Zealand
(a division of Pearson New Zealand Ltd)
Penguin Books (South Africa) (Pty) Ltd, 24 Sturdee Avenue, Rosebank, Johannesburg 2196, South Africa

Penguin Books Ltd, Registered Offices: 80 Strand, London WC2R 0RL, England

www.penguin.com

First published by Penguin Books 2010

2

Copyright © Geza Vermes, 2010
All rights reserved

The moral right of the author has been asserted

Set in 12/14 pt Monotype Garamond
Typeset by Rowland Phototypesetting Ltd, Bury St Edmunds, Suffolk
Printed in England by Clays Ltd, St Ives plc

ISBN: 978-0-141-04615-0

www.greenpenguin.co.uk

Contents

Preface

Graham Greene, my favourite novelist, used to call his lighthearted stories such as *Our Man in Havana* 'entertainments'. Taking from him my inspiration, I would define *The Story of the Scrolls* as an *entertainingly* informative account of my lifelong entanglement with Qumran. After recounting the old saga, I will set out briefly and neatly conclusions reached in the course of sixty years of wrestling with the Dead Sea Scrolls and share with the readers my mature views on their true significance.

G.V.

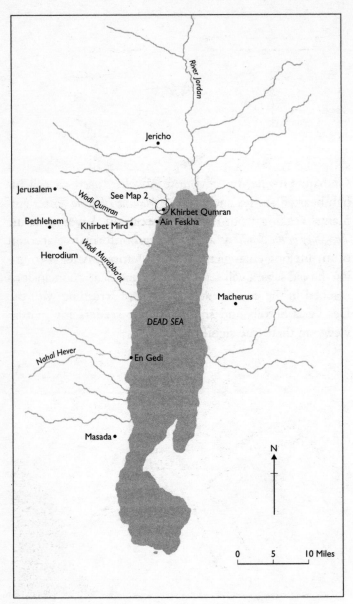

The area surrounding the Dead Sea, showing Qumran

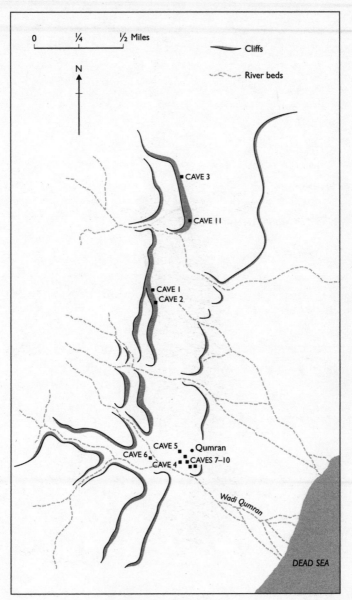

The Caves of Qumran

Part One

I

The State of Biblical Studies before Qumran

Old age carries with it a plethora of nuisances, but it possesses unique advantages too: long memories. Events and their context, about which younger generations only learn from hearsay or read in books, belong to their elders' personal experience. Images are engraved in the mind; they can still be seen, their pristine reality perceived, felt and tasted. Incidents of years ago seem as though they had happened yesterday. Memory, it is true, often plays small tricks which tend to embellish or to distort the past. But events that made a profound impact on one's mind frequently retain much of their original and authentic import and flavour. Having lived through them makes all the difference. For me, these considerations are especially true for my obsession with the Qumran Scrolls.

By accident or by grace, for over more than half a century I have had the good fortune to be actively involved in the saga of the Dead Sea Scrolls. I have watched the story unfold before my eyes. This is why the reader needs to be acquainted with my credentials.

In 1947, when the first scrolls were discovered at Qumran, I was an undergraduate of twenty-three, with horrible experiences of the war behind me, entailing the loss of my parents in the Holocaust. But I was also fired with curiosity and desperately longed for intellectual challenge and adventure. When I began to write this book in 2007, the sixtieth anniversary year of the first Scrolls find was being celebrated the world over: from Ljubljana in Slovenia, a rather unlikely place for the International Organization of Qumran Studies to foregather, followed by conferences in Britain and Canada, and ending with the mammoth international jamboree of the Society of Biblical Literature and the greatest ever exhibition of original Dead Sea Scrolls in the Natural History Museum in San Diego on the Pacific coast of the United States. Not to be outdone by the rest of the world, the Israeli confraternity of Qumran academics was preparing another sumptuous gala in 2008 to mark, I suppose, the start of the seventh decade of the era of the Scrolls. It was followed by another congress in Vienna and a further one was scheduled in Rome in 2009.

Between 1947 and the present day much water has flowed under the bridges of the many cities where biblical research is pursued. As a result, the Dead Sea texts have lost the novelty they enjoyed in the early days. They have become matter-of-fact reality, something that is imagined to have *always* been there. Indeed, they had been there before most of the people alive today were born. Also, the then stateless young man, who in 1948 dreamed of becoming one day a recognized Qumran expert, is now the author of *The Complete Dead Sea Scrolls in English* in the Penguin Classics series and an Emeritus Oxford professor, though under the 'has been' sounding title – 'emeritus' is often mistranslated as 'former' – continues to lurk much writing and a fair amount of lecturing activity. As for the Scrolls, they have ceased to be 'the *recently discovered* manuscripts' as we used to refer to them in the 1950s. Bit by bit, they have found their niche in the curricula of higher education on all the continents, as well as in the pigeon-hole of 'Church conspiracy' within the modern myth and folklore created by the international media. Even today, if the proverbial opinion pollster were to inquire in the street about the Dead Sea Scrolls, he would hear half of his clients mutter: 'The Scrolls ... Hmm ... Aren't they old manuscripts kept locked away in the Vatican?' Readers of this book, if they persevere to the end, will surely know better. They will also learn that 2009 has marked the completion of the publication of all the Qumran texts.

1. The Portrait of the Story-teller

To provide real background for this chronicle, let me summarily introduce myself. My unusual first name (not to mention my accent, which remains undeniable even after more than fifty years of life in England) reveals that I hail from Hungary. I was born in 1924 in an assimilated Jewish family. Shortly before my seventh birthday in the – as it turned out – mistaken belief that it would secure a better future for me, my journalist father and school-teacher mother decided to convert to Roman Catholicism. The three of us were baptized in the town of Gyula in south-east Hungary by the parish priest, the Reverend William Apor, a baronet, scion of a very old aristocratic family, who is now heading towards canonization in the Catholic Church, having been beatified in 1997 by the saintmaker *par excellence*, Pope John Paul II. From the late 1930s the increasingly oppressive Hungarian anti-Semitic legislation, taking no notice of the family's baptismal certificates, deprived my father of his livelihood, made my life difficult at my Catholic school and, above all, denied me access to higher education except via a Church-run theological seminary, which I entered in 1942. In March 1944, on Hitler's order, the half-hearted Germanophile Magyar government was replaced by enthusiastic puppets of the Nazi Reich, and all hell was let loose on the Jews of Hungary. My parents were deported and joined the millions of innocent victims of the Holocaust. Protected by providence, the Church and a great deal of sheer luck, I managed to survive until the arrival of the Red Army in Budapest on Christmas day, 1944. During the previous seven months I was crossing and recrossing the country (fortunately without ever being challenged to identify myself) and ended up with the help of my former parish priest, William Apor, by then bishop of Győr in western Hungary, in the Central Theological Seminary of Budapest. My saintly protector soon had to pay with his life for his constant generosity towards people in need: he was shot dead by drunken Russian soldiers, whilst gallantly trying to shelter a group of women who had sought refuge in the episcopal residence.

Waiting for news from my parents, confused and depressed, I stuck for another eighteen months with my studies in theological college in Nagyvarad. By that time (1945–6), this city (renamed Oradea) and the whole of Transylvania were reoccupied by the Romanians. When by 1946 it became obvious that my parents had perished, I decided to turn my back on the country of my birth, which tolerated, and partly even engineered, the horrors of 1944. I migrated westwards in search of freedom, knowledge and enlightenment. To achieve my dream, I sought admission into the French religious society of the Fathers of Zion (*Pères de Sion*). Despite the totally unreliable postal service between Romania and the West in 1946, my application was received in Paris, but it was a near miracle that the letter informing me of my acceptance and the duty to present myself in early October at the training establishment of the order in Louvain (now Leuven in Belgium) reached me on 2 June, the date on which I planned a clandestine night-crossing from Romania to Hungary. If that precious envelope had remained in transit just for another twenty-four hours, it would probably never have caught up with me as no postal connection existed in those days between the two unfriendly countries, Romania and Hungary. I distinctly remember keeping a protective hand on the pocket which contained the letter from Louvain to ensure that this virtual passport to freedom would not be lost in the fields where I was trying to evade the Romanian frontier guards.

A few months later, in September 1946, I had again to opt for the illegal crossing of the frontier separating Hungary from Austria. I was faced with the proverbial Gordian knot or a Catch-22. To leave Hungary I needed a Russian exit permit. No such permit could be obtained without a Belgian visa in my passport, indicating that I had somewhere to go. But in the late summer of 1946, there was no Belgian diplomatic representation in Hungary. The nearest consulate was in Vienna, but for entering Austria, I needed a Russian exit stamp in my passport. So having hired a smuggler to guide me through the border forest, I simply walked out of Hungary in full daylight on 18 September 1946 and, having received in Vienna my French and Belgian visas, I embarked on 30 September on a momentous journey, which lasted three days, that took me through the Russian and French zones of occupation in Austria and across devastated southern Germany, to

France. Leaving Strasbourg the following day, I reached Louvain on 2 October and I rang the doorbell of the community of the Fathers of Zion at 49 rue des Moutons, or Schaapenstraat in Flemish, as the bilingual numberplate indicated in the as yet linguistically undivided Belgium. It was in that old university town that I started my serious theological and biblical studies after four years of intellectual starvation in the Hungarian seminary.

First I followed a course of theology at the College of St Albert, run by French-speaking Belgian Jesuits, and continued three years later, having gained the licence or BA in theology, with a programme of ancient near-eastern history and philology at the Institut Orientaliste of the University, where I graduated in 1952. My first association with the Dead Sea Scrolls took place in Louvain in 1948 where I became an enthusiastic student of the Hebrew Bible.

Where did this enthusiasm spring from? One thing is certain: it cannot be credited to my family background. Neither my parents nor my other relations were practising Jews or knew any Hebrew or even Yiddish. My conscious memory preserves an anecdote about my awakening desire to learn Hebrew. The venue was my Hungarian-Romanian theological college in Nagyvarad and the date 1945. The seminary was situated in the largely unoccupied massive eighteenth-century episcopal palace where one day I entered a spacious room, previously the study of the director of the college, Geza Folmann, who was also the professor of biblical studies. He was by Hungarian standards an unusually well-trained man, having spent, shortly before the First World War, two years at the famous École Biblique (short for École Biblique et Archéologique Française) of the French Dominicans in Jerusalem. His sizeable library was filled with the large pink-covered tomes of the series Études Bibliques and he was also a subscriber to the École's influential periodical, the still flourishing *Revue Biblique*. In the room I chanced to enter, all these volumes were lying scattered on the floor amid general chaos. After the liberation of the city by the Red Army at the end of 1944, the bishop's palace served as living quarters for Russian soldiers who had no use for learned French books on advanced biblical studies. When they withdrew, they left their mess behind.

The director welcomed my offer to tidy up his office and thus I was given a chance to admire the books. They included Hebrew Bibles, and commentaries filled with Hebrew quotations. Out of intellectual curiosity or maybe atavism, I swore that I would make myself familiar with these fascinating and mysterious texts. Seven years later, on my first stay in the École Biblique in Arab Jerusalem, I met some of the teachers of my erstwhile professor. The world-famous Palestinian archaeologist L. H. Vincent and the great geographer of the Holy Land, F.-M. Abel, were still alive, but sadly neither of them remembered a former Hungarian pupil called Folmann, who never made a name for himself in the international club of biblical scholars.

To implement my vow of mastering Hebrew, I registered for a Hebrew course at the University of Budapest in the autumn semester of 1945, but had to interrupt my study when I was recalled to my provincial seminary. So I did my Hebraizing privately until finally I was given a real opportunity to delve into Hebrew on my arrival in Louvain. By the time I first had to face the Scrolls in 1948, I was competent in the language.

2. Biblical Studies in the 1940s

The course of study I was to embark on provides a good opportunity to sketch for the reader the state of biblical and post-biblical Jewish studies on the eve of the onset of the Qumran age. It is often claimed that the Dead Sea Scrolls have revolutionized our approach to the Hebrew Scriptures and to the literature of the age that witnessed the birth of the New Testament. Needless to say, my canvas will be schematic; these preliminary remarks are meant to serve only as a summary illustration of the state of play in Hebrew learning with a view to enabling the reader to grasp what was so extraordinary in the Dead Sea Scrolls.

For the general reader of the 1940s, the term 'Bible' designated the Holy Scriptures of Judaism and Christianity, divided in Christian parlance into Old Testament and New Testament. The Old Testament had a shorter and a longer version. The Palestinian Jewish Bible was held to consist of books written in Hebrew and Aramaic, while the Jews dispersed in the Greek-speaking countries of the ancient world translated this collection of thirty-nine books, and added to them the Apocrypha, that is, fifteen supplementary works either originally composed in, or later rendered into, Greek. The Christians further enlarged the Greek Bible they inherited from Hellenistic Judaism by twenty-seven books of the New Testament, also written in Greek. In the eyes of the non-specialist, these Holy Scriptures are the source, or one of the two sources, Church and Synagogue tradition being the other, of the Jewish and the Christian religions.

By contrast, those who adopt an academic approach

envisage the Bible as a group of ancient texts which, like all other ancient texts, must be read in their original languages and understood in their appropriate historical, cultural and literary contexts. To establish what later generations made of them is the business of the theologian or of the Bible scholar acting as a theologian. By necessity the critical study of ancient texts requires an investigation of the manuscripts which have preserved them and of the relevant literary parallels that are capable of shedding light on their meaning. It was taught in the 1940s that the purpose of textual criticism or comparative study of the manuscripts was the reconstruction of the *Urtext*, the authentic document composed by the original author, with the help of the variants attested in the surviving copies. Before Qumran, most of these variants were identified as scribal errors or as the result of a deliberate interference with the text by copyists.

When I first started serious Hebrew studies, the best critical text of the Bible was the third edition of *Biblia Hebraica*, published by the German scholar Rudolf Kittel in 1938, which contained a major innovation compared to its earlier versions. Instead of the text used in the first and second editions, based on the Bible printed in Venice in 1517, and relying on late medieval Hebrew manuscripts, Kittel's colleague, Paul Kahle, substituted the more reliable Leningrad Codex, dating to AD 1008. He would have preferred to use the Aleppo Codex (first half of the tenth century) rather than the manuscript from Leningrad, but the owners of the Aleppo manuscript were unwilling to allow their precious treasure to be photographed. The biblical text was accompanied by a critical apparatus containing the sporadic manuscript variants, mostly spelling differences, and some more meaningful discrepancies furnished by the Greek, Latin, Aramaic and Syriac translations of the Old Testament, all older than the Hebrew manuscripts, as well as some hypothetical improvements suggested by commentators, ancient and modern.

In parenthesis, for the study of the New Testament the standard edition we had in the 1940s was the twelfth edition (1937) of Eberhard and Erwin Nestle's *Novum Testamentum Graece*, before it was revised by Kurt Aland and others in 1981. The critically edited New Testament differed fundamentally from the scholarly version of the Hebrew Bible. The latter confronted the student with the uniform text of a given manuscript (the Leningrad Codex), whereas owing to the much larger quantity and diversity of the Greek variants, an eclectic text was made up by scholars with the help of readings borrowed from diverse manuscripts. It may cause a shock to the uninitiated to learn that the text arrived at by the learned authors of the most advanced critical edition of the New Testament does not correspond to any existing manuscript. Both the Greek text and the translations made from it are founded on a hypothetical reconstruction.

Of incomparable historical importance in themselves, but only indirectly relevant to the study of the Hebrew Bible, are the great nineteenth- and twentieth-century archaeological discoveries in Egypt, Mesopotamia and Syria. Scientific Egyptology started during Napoleon's campaign in the delta of the Nile in 1798 and reached its first climax with the decipherment of the hieroglyphs by Henri de Champollion in 1822. The Egyptological finds enlightened various aspects of the Old Testament, in particular Wisdom literature. Assyriology, the study of ancient Mesopotamian civilization, took off in the middle of the nineteenth century. The pioneers were bored European diplomats, the French Paul Émile de Botta who began to dig in Nineveh in 1842, and the Englishman, Austen Henry Layard, who soon joined de Botta and competed with him on the same site. Within thirty years the cuneiform or wedge-shaped script of Mesopotamia was decoded and opened up to students of the Hebrew Bible such treasures as the Babylonian myths of the Creation and of the Flood, prefiguring the parallel stories in the Book of Genesis, and various allusions to the conquest of Samaria and Judaea by Assyrian and Babylonian kings, clarifying episodes of biblical history. In 1929, French archaeologists tumbled on the ruins of the ancient city of Ugarit at Ras Shamra in Syria, which yielded a previously unknown alphabet written with cuneiform characters and revealed the language and literature of the Canaanites, the original inhabitants of Palestine, whose religious ideas and practices were the frequent target of criticism in the law and the prophets of the Old Testament.

A final area of knowledge that a prospective Scripture specialist was expected to master was extra-biblical Jewish religious literature in the inter-Testamental period (200 BCE– 100 CE) as it was then called, now more commonly referred to as the late Second Temple era. It was considered to be an indispensable tool for the study of the Old and New Testaments. Knowledge of these works called the Apocrypha (books included in the Bible of Diaspora Jews, but rejected by the Palestinian Jewish religious authorities) and the Pseudepigrapha (religious compositions which, although influential, have never entered the canon of either Palestinian or Hellenistic Jewry) was held to be essential, and was to play a major role in the treatment of the Dead Sea Scrolls.

In regard to the Apocrypha, transmitted in the codices

of the Greek Bible, a major breakthrough occurred in 1896 when two marvellously brave and enterprising Scottish lady travellers, the sisters Margaret Dunlop Gibson and Agnes Smith Lewis, discovered and acquired a gigantic collection of medieval Jewish texts in a *genizah* or manuscript depository attached to the Ben Ezra Synagogue of Fustat in Old Cairo. Among them figured remains of five copies, dating to the eleventh and twelfth century CE, of the Hebrew Wisdom of Jesus ben Sira, previously known from the Greek Bible as the Book of Sirach or Ecclesiasticus. Altogether the fragments represented two thirds of the original document translated into Greek by the author's grandson for the use of Hellenized Jews at the end of the second century BCE. They were first published in Cambridge in 1899 by Solomon Schechter and Charles Taylor under the title, *The Wisdom of Jesus ben Sira: Portions of the Book of Ecclesiasticus from Hebrew Manuscripts in the Cairo Genizah Collection*. On the eve of the Qumran discovery, two schools of thought were competing regarding the Ecclesiasticus from the Cairo Genizah. Important authorities held it to be the slightly distorted version of ben Sira's Hebrew original, whereas other scholars of repute believed that it was a medieval retranslation into Hebrew of the Greek Ecclesiasticus. New evidence was needed to settle the debate.

Of the Pseudepigrapha (or literary works spuriously attributed to Old Testament personalities), only a few titles were known in their entirety prior to the nineteenth century: the Fourth Book of the Maccabees and the Psalms of Solomon were preserved in some manuscripts of the Greek Bible and the Testaments of the Twelve Patriarchs was first published in Oxford in 1698 by J. E. Grabe and reissued by J. A. Fabricius in his noted Pseudepigraphic

Codex of the Old Testament (*Codex pseudepigraphus Veteris Testamenti*) in 1718. (Fabricius was the inventor of the term Pseudepigrapha.) Greek excerpts from the pseudepigraphic Book of Jubilees and Book of Enoch also survived in quotations by Church Fathers and Byzantine writers. But the major advances were made in the nineteenth century. They resulted from the discovery of ancient Ethiopian literature, rich in Pseudepigrapha. Robert Lawrence, Professor of Hebrew at Oxford, successively issued between 1818 and 1839 the Ethiopic version of the Ascension of Isaiah, the Fourth Book of Ezra and the Book of Enoch. In 1851, the renowned German Semitist, August Dillmann, published an improved version of the Ethiopic Enoch and added to it in 1859 the first edition of the Ethiopic translation of the Book of Jubilees. The Syriac Apocalypse of Baruch joined the collection in 1871 thanks to the Italian scholar, A. M. Ceriani. Textual information relative to the Greek Book of Enoch was further enriched with U. Bouriant's publication in 1892 of the Akhmim papyri and with the edition, in 1937, of the last chapters of the Greek Enoch from the Chester Beatty-Michigan papyri by Campbell Bonner. The Aramaic sayings of the wise Ahiqar, mentioned in the apocryphal Book of Tobit and known from numerous translations (Syriac, Arabic, Ethiopic, Armenian) unexpectedly showed up in the fifth-century BCE Aramaic papyri found at the beginning of the twentieth century at Elephantine in Egypt and published, in 1923, by Sir Arthur Cowley, Bodley's Librarian in Oxford. The Cairo Genizah further added fairly extensive Aramaic fragments of a Testament of Levi, possibly the source of the Greek version of the Testaments of the Twelve Patriarchs.

From the same Cairo source also emerged a curious

writing, attested in two medieval Hebrew manuscripts dating from the tenth to the twelfth century, that its editor, Solomon Schechter, called *Fragments of a Zadokite Work* when he published it in 1910. It also became known as the Damascus Document. Describing the doctrine and the laws of a Jewish sect, it caused a frisson in the scholarly world in the years immediately preceding the First World War, reminiscent, and not without good cause, of the excitement generated by the publication of the first Dead Sea Scrolls which contained several more than 2,000-year-old copies of the same work.

The new knowledge, accumulated between 1800 and 1900, was incorporated in the early twentieth century in two major fully annotated collections of the Pseudepigrapha edited by leading scholars with the help of the best specialists of the day. The first to appear in 1900 was *Die Apocryphen und Pseudepigraphen des Alten Testaments*, vols I–II, a German work under the editorship of Emil Kautzsch. It was followed in 1912–13 by R. H. Charles's *The Apocrypha and Pseudepigrapha of the Old Testament*. The latter, more thorough and up-to-date and still indispensable today in spite of its age, made use of the relevant Cairo Genizah material: the Hebrew ben Sira, the Aramaic Testament of Levi and the Hebrew Damascus Document.

Equipped with all these outstanding tools of research and, less commonly among non-Jewish students, with sufficient competence in rabbinic writings, Hebrew scholars were obliged to face up to the totally unbelievable discovery of the Dead Sea Scrolls. For prior to 1947 no such finds were expected. Indeed, they were declared to be impossible. In the light of a century of archaeological search, exploring every nook and cranny of the Holy Land from Dan to Beer Sheba, the excavators' spade had failed to turn up even a single ancient text written on skin or papyrus. Hence it was handed down from master to pupil as an axiom that no pre-Christian text recorded on perishable material could survive in the climatic conditions of Palestine. However, those who defined the axiom forgot that the area where the Dead Sea Scrolls were found lay 400 metres below sea level and that the climate of that part of the Judaean desert scarcely differed from that of Egypt where innumerable ancient papyrus documents survived.

The facts proved the axiom wrong.

Postscript: Biblical Studies in the Roman Catholic Church

In addition to the universally accepted rules governing biblical studies, Roman Catholic practitioners of scriptural or Scripture-related research were supposed to abide by the relevant directives of the Roman Catholic Church. (I remained a Catholic until the parting of the ways in 1957, when I left the church, the priesthood and France and settled in Britain, first in Newcastle then in Oxford, and slowly reverted to my Jewish roots if not to Jewish practice.)

The early years of the twentieth century were a period of gloom for Catholic exegetes. The war against 'critics' and 'modernists' was waged by the Vatican's 'watchdog', the Pontifical Biblical Commission, a body made up of cardinals and aided by expert consultants. The pontificate of Pope Pius X (1903–14, canonized in 1954) represented the darkest days of tyrannical Church interference with free inquiry. The dictates assumed to be scientifically sound and self-explanatory, issued by the Commission, strike an unbiased observer of today as hardly believable. The freedom to write and teach, in some way the livelihood of Catholic Bible professors, the majority of whom happened to be priests, depended on their blind acceptance of pre-modern positions considered by their non-Catholic colleagues as wholly untenable.

In the field of the Old Testament they had to accept that the five books of the Law (the Pentateuch) were written by Moses himself, because they are so cited in the Old and the New Testament, and to reject the multiple source theory of modern scholarship. They had to accept the biblical narrative of the creation as strict historical truth and any link with ancient Mesopotamian cosmogonies had to be denied. The whole book of Isaiah had to be ascribed to the eighth-century BCE prophet. Mention of a Second and Third Isaiah, responsible for chapters 40–66 and dating to the second half of the sixth century BCE, was taboo. Likewise in regard to the New Testament, the 'two-source' theory (the Gospel of Mark and a hypothetical other source called Q) was anathema and was not to be used to account for the similarities and discrepancies among the Synoptic Gospels of Matthew, Mark and Luke. As for the Fourth Gospel, it was firmly assigned to the apostle John and declared, contrary to the view of most critics, historically reliable.

The encyclical *Divino Afflante Spiritu*, issued by Pope Pius XII in 1943, allowed a chink to open up and a ray of light to shine through the dark clouds when it referred to 'literary genres' in Scripture (i.e. that everything was not to be taken strictly to the letter). Nevertheless Catholic teachers were still advised to proceed with extreme caution: if you wish to survive, beware of the Pontifical Biblical Commission!

In the subsequent years, chiefly under Paul VI and John Paul II, the Biblical Commission, the erstwhile savage Vatican guard dog, was tamed and reorganized in 1971, and the combination of cardinals and consultants was transformed into a board of twenty experts, though still under the chairmanship of the cardinal heading the Congregation for the Doctrine of the Faith (Cardinal Joseph Ratzinger until his elevation to the papal throne in 2005). Thanks to the presence of real specialists, the Commission became more enlightened and published liberal directives on *Bible and Christology* (1984) and on *The Jewish People and their Sacred Scriptures in the Christian Bible* (2002). Nevertheless, the recent book *Jesus of Nazareth* (2007) by Pope Benedict XVI, ex-president of the Biblical Commission, although repeatedly paying lip service to the historico-critical method of Bible interpretation, constitutes a volte-face and augurs ill for the future of Catholic scriptural exegesis. It would be interesting to know how many members of the Pontifical Biblical Commission in their heart of hearts agree with the Pope.

Only time will tell.

II

Epoch-making Discoveries and Early Blunders

The news of a sensational manuscript discovery in the Palestine of the British Mandate first burst on the unsuspecting world in the spring of 1948. Newspapers carried colourful headlines: the funniest I can remember announced in the leading Brussels daily, *La Libre Belgique*, the find of an 'eleventh-century BCE' biblical scroll on the coast of the 'Black Sea'. (The date should have been 100 BCE and the venue the shore of the Dead Sea.) The discovered material represented the Hebrew Bible and the literature of an ancient Jewish sect. Later in 1948 my professor of Hebrew showed me the photocopy and transcription of several lines of the Book of Isaiah which was claimed to date to the pre-Christian era, an assertion that was in breach of all the rules contained in the textbooks (see chapter I, pp. 16–17). Having thus tasted the sweet novelty of the Scrolls, with youthful recklessness I swore that I would devote myself to solving the mystery of what was called 'the greatest ever manuscript find in the field of biblical studies'. In retrospect, I can say that I have remained faithful to my vow: in a true sense, the Scrolls have become part of my life.

1. The Original Find and its Sequels

The story of the first Scrolls discovery is an amalgam of fairy tale, hesitant scholarship and heaps of erroneous judgements, perfectly understandable in a totally novel domain of research. In the opening scene of the fairy tale, three nomadic Palestinian Arabs of the Taamire tribe are looking for a stray goat on rocky cliffs not far from the Dead Sea. The date is uncertain: somewhere between the end of 1946 and the summer of 1947, probably in the spring of 1947. The youngest, by the name of Muhammed edh-Dhib (Muhammed the Wolf), was amusing himself by throwing stones. One of these fell into a small hole in the rock and was followed by the sound of the breaking of pottery. Muhammed climbed in and found several ancient manuscripts in a jar. Altogether seven scrolls were subsequently removed from the cave.

Act two of the drama revolves around the Bedouins' desire to make money and to this effect they approached the Bethlehem cobbler and antique dealer, Khalil Eskander Shahin, who was to gain international fame under the nickname of Kando, and entrusted him with the scrolls. Two prospective buyers were contacted through intermediaries. In the summer of 1947, Kando and his incompetent advisers, believing that the manuscripts were in Syriac (one of the dialects of Aramaic), offered some of them to the head of the Syrian monastery of St Mark in Jerusalem, Archbishop Mar Athanasius Yeshue Samuel. He apparently acquired four of them for 24 Palestinian dinars (just under $100).

Later in 1947, Eleazar Lipa Sukenik, the professor of archaeology at the Hebrew University of Jerusalem, was contacted through an Armenian acquaintance and invited to inspect some important manuscripts. Keeping his plan secret from his wife and disregarding the advice of his son, Yigael Yadin, then the Chief of Operations of the Jewish Defence Forces, Sukenik put his life in peril and visited the Arab sector of the city. A deal was struck on 29 November, on the day the United Nations decided to partition Palestine between Israel and Jordan. On that momentous date, Sukenik succeeded in purchasing three manuscripts: an incomplete Book of Isaiah, a Scroll of Hymns and the War Scroll. Having learned that further texts were held in the Syrian monastery, the lucky professor managed to borrow them for a few days, but his eventual bid was turned down. The Syrian monastery hoped for a larger sum of US dollars.

While the documents bought by Sukenik were in competent hands, the same could not be said of Mar Athanasius. He needed expert advice and in February 1948 the librarian of the monastery visited the American School of Oriental Research (ASOR) in Jerusalem and told a typical Levantine tale: he pretended that they had found in their library some ancient Hebrew manuscripts, about which the catalogue said nothing. The American scholar John C. Trever examined the four documents and promptly informed the archbishop about their supposed antiquity and importance: a complete Scroll of Isaiah, a commentary on the Book of Habakkuk, the Manual of Discipline, later called the Community Rule, and an unopened, hence unidentified, manuscript subsequently recognized as the Genesis Apocryphon. Trever was allowed to photograph the Scrolls and the archbishop authorized the American School to publish them in due course. In April 1948, both ASOR and Sukenik released the news of the discovery, which was broadcast worldwide by all the media. In the *Bulletin of ASOR*, leading American archaeologist and Orientalist Professor William Foxwell Albright called the Scrolls 'the greatest archaeological find of modern times' and his colleague, Professor W. E. Wright, writing in the *Biblical Archaeologist*, spoke in equally superlative terms of 'the most important discovery ever made in the field of Old Testament manuscripts'. Excitement was spreading like wildfire. My own lifelong involvement with Qumran studies goes back to that epoch. It was my first academic love affair.

With the war between Jews and Arabs threatening, in 1948 Mar Athanasius arranged for his treasure to be smuggled out of Jerusalem to Lebanon and later in January 1949 he took his Scrolls to the United States. Wishing to turn old inscribed leather into cash, but finding most libraries and museums too shy to buy them because archaeological finds were considered state property in most Middle Eastern countries, Mar Athanasius first sought publicity by allowing the Scrolls to be exhibited in various American museums, but at the end put this advertisement in the *Wall Street Journal*: 'For sale: biblical manuscripts dating back to at least 200 BC, an ideal gift to an educational or religious institution'. An anonymous buyer, secretly acting for the State of Israel, acquired the four Scrolls for $250,000, a quarter of the archbishop's original asking price, but still somewhat in excess of the sum of 24 Palestinian dinars Kando had been given to buy them from the Bedouin. So in 1954 all seven of the manuscripts and some fragments, removed from the cave by the Taamire goatherds, were reunited in Israeli Jerusalem, ultimately to be housed in the newly built Shrine of the Book. The seventh and as yet unopened Scroll, first designated as the Lamech document with the help of a detached fragment bearing the name of this antediluvian patriarch, was ultimately given the title of the Genesis Apocryphon, after Israeli technical experts had managed to unroll it.

2. Identifying the Manuscript Cave

Neither the Department of Antiquities of Jordan, nor the French École Biblique, the chief European archaeological institution in Arab Jerusalem, felt any urge to find out where the Scrolls came from. The initiative to do so came from a Belgian member of the United Nations Armistice Observer Corps, Captain Philip Lippens (whom I had the chance to meet and congratulate at the 1954 Journées Bibliques at Louvain). Bored by doing nothing, apparently he was looking for some excitement and persuaded Brigadier Norman Lash, a British senior officer of the Arab Legion of Jordan, to dispatch a small unit of soldiers in search of the mysterious cave out of which Muhammed edh-Dhib had lifted his seven Scrolls. They soon found the spot. Raised from their torpor by the news of the discovery of the cave, the head of the Jordanian Department of Antiquities, the Englishman Lankester Harding, and the director of the École Biblique, the French Dominican Roland de Vaux, examined the cave and removed from it remains of pottery and hundreds of manuscript fragments, some of them detached from the Scrolls acquired by Mar Athanasius and Professor Sukenik. On the way to the cave, de Vaux and Harding noticed the ruins known as Khirbet Qumran, but assuming these to be the remains of a fourth-century CE rural fortress and as such unrelated to the Scrolls, they paid no attention to

24

them. This was the first of a series of blunders. Khirbet Qumran, visited but never properly examined by earlier archaeologists, was to play a major role in the development of the Scrolls' saga. A second blunder soon followed. In their formal report to the French Académie des Inscriptions et Belles-Lettres on 8 April 1949, de Vaux and Harding unhesitatingly stated that the pottery found in the cave was Hellenistic, and that this proved that all the manuscripts predated the beginning of the first century BCE. In their judgement, the history witnessed by the Scrolls belonged to the Hellenistic era, which terminated in Palestine in 63 BCE with the Roman conquest of Jerusalem by Pompey the Great.

However, the unchallenged reign of the archaeologists did not stretch beyond the publication of the first texts. In 1950, the three American scholars, Millar Burrows, John C. Trever and William H. Brownlee published with admirable speed a facsimile edition and transcription of the complete Isaiah Scroll and the Habakkuk Commentary, followed in the spring of 1951 by the Manual of Discipline. The release of the ancient texts was not held back until their editors were ready to issue them, furnished with translation, commentary and notes. The self-denial and scholarly generosity of the American trio deserves full admiration. Sukenik, who had already produced two preliminary Hebrew publications in 1948 and 1950, entitled *Hidden Scrolls from the Judaean Desert* I and II, also moved fast, but first illness and then death in 1953 prevented him from seeing his manuscripts properly published. His edition of the second Isaiah Scroll, the Thanksgiving Hymns and the War of the Sons of Light against the Sons of Darkness appeared posthumously first in Hebrew in 1954 and then in English in 1955, equally without translation, commentary and notes. The best preserved sections of the Genesis Apocry-phon followed in 1956 thanks to Nahman Avigad and Yigael Yadin. They included a facsimile reproduction and transliteration with facing English and modern Hebrew translations. A marvellous example of speed and scholarly devotion was set by these pioneers that future Scrolls editors, apart from those of the fragments from Cave 1 issued in 1955, were unwilling or perhaps unable to emulate.

The two Isaiah Scrolls and the scriptural section of the Habakkuk Commentary presented the dazed Scripture scholars from all four corners of the earth with biblical texts which were a millennium older than the Leningrad Codex which they had been accustomed to use (see chapter I, p. 11). They contained real variant readings, different from the traditional wording of the Bible, which was a hitherto unimaginable phenomenon. In their turn, the Habakkuk Commentary and the Manual of Discipline (later renamed Community Rule) opened up previously undreamed-of vistas into the life and history of an ancient Jewish religious community nearly contemporaneous with Jesus and the beginnings of the Church. Incidentally, the Scrolls also enabled experts to compare the chronological verdict of the archaeologists with the contents of the manuscripts themselves. Indeed, a leading French orien-talist, André Dupont-Sommer of the Sorbonne, concluded against de Vaux's pottery-based Hellenistic dating of the Scrolls (late second or early first century BCE) that the Habakkuk Commentary's historical context extended into the Roman period, after 63 BCE. As a matter of fact, Dupont-Sommer was soon to launch the first Scrolls-based assault on the traditional explanation of the birth of the New Testament and Christianity. Others were to follow.

3. Ten More Caves Yield their Secrets

Cave 1 was just the start of the story. The Bedouin, roaming the desert and exploring the many holes in the cliffs both north and south of the original grotto of discovery, tumbled on further manuscript deposits: Cave 2, early in 1952, and Cave 6 later that year. They knew that de Vaux was a likely buyer of fragments and approached him one after another. During my four-week-long stay at the École Biblique in October 1952, I witnessed with my own eyes the way these oriental negotiations proceeded. The fragments were brought to the École in matchboxes. When the sellers realized that larger pieces of manuscript fetched a higher reward, they tried to stick them together with the edge of postage stamps, a method hardly more primitive than the use of Sellotape, of which some of the early western editors of de Vaux's team were guilty.

Hoping to beat the Arabs at their game, the École Biblique, the Palestine Archaeological Museum and the American School of Oriental Research of Jerusalem ganged together to launch a joint survey of the cliffs in the neighbourhood of Qumran. They were at it from 10 to 29 March 1952 but, lacking the natural instinct of the Bedouin, they scored only one hit with written material: out of Cave 3 they proudly lifted the famous Copper Scroll in addition to a small number of tiny fragments. The Copper Scroll survived in two rolled-up sections, but these were so badly oxidized that they could not be opened. In consequence, the script embossed on the inner side of the copper sheets was not revealed until 1955 when an expert metallurgist, Professor H. Wright Baker of Manchester, invented an instrument which enabled him to cut the two scrolls into twenty-three vertical slices. But even before the hidden contents could be deciphered, a perspicacious German scholar, Karl Georg Kuhn, managed to deduce from a few broken-off bits that this document dealt with hiding places of silver and gold. Not surprisingly in 1960, the Copper Scroll triggered off a treasure hunt conducted by John Allegro, the chief maverick of de Vaux's recruits. One of the London papers financed the expedition, which ended in a total fiasco.

The leaders of the search party paid no notice to cavities in the nearby marl terrace. They assumed, foolishly as it turned out, that these were due to erosion by rainwater and did not even bother to inspect them. 'In this we erred,' was de Vaux's marvellous understatement by which he swept under the carpet the implications of yet another colossal blunder. In reality, there were no less than six cavities in the marl terrace – Caves 4, 5, 7–10 – containing written material as well as pottery. On its own, Cave 4 yielded several tens of thousands of manuscript fragments, all of which were later picked up by the more businesslike Bedouin. Today, scholars believe that Cave 4 was either the library of a community or their manuscript storehouse in which the scrolls lay deposited on wooden shelves. The neighbouring Cave 7 was another curiosity in that it housed only Greek texts which were rare at Qumran. Unfortunately, most of the seventeen tiny papyrus fragments proved unidentifiable, but a few created a major storm when some twenty years later they were claimed by a Spanish Jesuit with the odd Irish name of José O'Callaghan and a few like-minded scholars to belong to the Gospel of Mark and other New Testament writings (see chapter IX, pp. 223–4).

The last significant scrolls' find happened at the

beginning of 1956 in Cave 11, about a mile north of the Qumran site. The Bedouin were once again lucky and put their hands on four scrolls and a good many assorted fragments. Among the manuscripts figured a substantial portion of the biblical Psalms, interspersed with non-biblical poems, some known, some unknown; part of the book of Leviticus written in the old Hebrew script; and sections of an Aramaic translation or Targum of the Book of Job. However, the crowning glory of them all was the Temple Scroll, measuring nearly 30 feet when unrolled, quite a bit longer than the big Isaiah Scroll from Cave 1, whose sixty-six chapters scarcely amount to 24 feet. The Temple Scroll, describing the architectural details and ceremonies of the Jerusalem sanctuary, was kept in Kando's house in Bethlehem in a Bata shoebox concealed under the floor until the beginning of June 1967 when in the course of the Six Day war Yigael Yadin prevailed on the Israeli army to find this elusive manuscript. Yadin reports that it was purchased for the State of Israel with the help of a cheque for $75,000 signed by Mr Leonard Wolfson, now Lord Wolfson.

All counted, the eleven Qumran caves yielded twelve scrolls: Isaiah A and B, the Commentary of Habakkuk, the Community Rule, the Genesis Apocryphon, the Hymns Scroll and the War Scroll came from Cave 1; the Copper Scroll from Cave 3; the Palaeo-Hebrew Leviticus, the Psalms Scroll, the Job Targum and the Temple Scroll from Cave 11. Add to these the many thousands of fragments, representing over 900 separate original works, with a quarter of them biblical, and 50 per cent belonging to the Apocrypha, the Pseudepigrapha and other known or unknown Jewish religious writings, while a special group, the final quarter of the total harvest, preserved the literature of a religious community, most likely the Essenes as I will try to show in chapter VIII.

Of the Apocrypha previously known from the Greek Bible, Qumran has revealed a Hebrew extract from the Wisdom of Jesus ben Sira (Ecclesiasticus) included in the Psalms Scroll from Cave 11. Largish fragments of seven columns of the same Hebrew ben Sira have also survived at Masada, predating the capture of the fortress by the Romans in 73/74 CE. Moreover, fragments of the Book of Tobit represent one Hebrew and three Aramaic manuscripts from Cave 4. Among the Pseudepigrapha, fragments of the Book of Jubilees, previously available in an incomplete Greek and a full Ethiopic translation, have been discovered in Hebrew in Qumran Caves 1, 2, 4 and 11, and Aramaic fragments of the Book of Enoch and the Testament of Levi come from Cave 4.

As far as languages are concerned, a handful of the texts are in Greek, about 20 per cent of the material is in Aramaic, and the rest, nearly four-fifths of the total, in Hebrew. They are mostly written on leather (specially prepared sheep or goat skin), some (14 per cent) on papyrus and a handful on potsherds to which we have to add two copper sheets. The scribes used vegetable ink kept in inkwells, three of which were found in a specific area of the building complex, and another at Ain Feshkha. All the manuscripts and fragments came from the caves. The only written documents yielded by the Qumran ruins themselves – two ostraca or inscribed potsherds – were accidentally discovered much later, in 1996, concealed in one of the boundary walls. Their significance is hotly argued about in scholarly circles (see chapter VII, pp. 169–170). Attempts to date the manuscripts have been made by means of palaeography (the study of ancient Hebrew handwriting) or through Carbon-14 tests. Palaeographical study of the Qumran scripts, in the absence of manuscripts contemporaneous with the scrolls or earlier than them, had to rely, in addition to the Nash papyrus, on inscriptions and ostraca. The result obtained placed the various specimens between *circa* 200 BCE and 70 CE. These findings were indirectly confirmed with the help of the leather and papyrus documents, many of them dated letters and contracts, found in caves in other areas of the Judaean desert and belonging to the first and second centuries CE (see Cross (1961), pp. 132–202). The first radiocarbon analysis was performed in 1951 on a piece of textile used for wrapping the Scrolls. The result arrived at was 33 CE (or 24 CE) plus or minus 200 years. Further, more advanced tests were made in the 1990s on tiny manuscript fragments, placing the bulk of the manuscripts to the last two centuries of the pre-Christian era and the rest to the first century CE, thus confirming the palaeographical dating (see Boniani et al. (1991) pp. 25–32; Jull et al. (1995), pp. 11–19).

4. The Excavations of the Ruins of Qumran (1951–6)

Having allowed nearly three years to elapse after his cursory glance at the ruins close to the first manuscript cave, and while scroll fragments found in other places (in the caves of Wadi Murabba'at, for example) began to be peddled by the Bedouin in Jerusalem, in November 1951 Roland de Vaux decided to investigate the site of Qumran itself.

Khirbet Qumran was visited by archaeologists several times during the previous 100 years. In 1851 the renowned French scholar Louis-Félicien Caignart de Saulcy suggested that Qumran was the site of the biblical Gomorrha (the Arabs pronounce the place name as Goomran). Charles Clermont-Ganneau, one of the greatest Palestinian archaeologists of the nineteenth century, surveyed the area in 1874; he declared de Saulcy's Gomorrha theory unsustainable and suggested after a brief inspection of the adjacent cemetery of some 1,000 graves that the bodies buried there were those of members of a pre-Islamic Arab tribe. Another cursory examination of the site followed in 1914 by the famous German Aramaist and Palestine scholar Gustaf Dalman. Judging from the architectural remains and from the aqueduct bringing water to the establishment, Dalman surmised that the ruins were those of a Roman fortress, a view repeated without further checking by Harding and de Vaux in 1949.

The first season of excavation at Qumran lasted from 24 November to 12 December 1951 and led to a complete reshuffling of de Vaux's ideas. After slightly over two weeks of digging (the results of which I could observe at my first visit to Qumran in October 1952), he concluded that the site was occupied both in the first century BCE and the first century CE, and was abandoned during the great Jewish rebellion against Rome between 66 and 70 CE. Among other things, Roman coins from the first century CE necessitated this redating.

Nearly a year before my actual visit to Qumran, I had the good fortune of being briefed about the new status quo by de Vaux's colleague, Dominique Barthélemy, who came to see me in Paris shortly before Christmas 1951. The detailed information I had received from him enabled me to reorient my doctoral thesis on the historical background of the Scrolls, taking into account de Vaux's latest unpublished finds.

Reporting the results of the first season of excavations at Qumran, Roland de Vaux was obliged to eat humble pie and admit his multiple *faux pas* before the assembled French scholarly elite at the session of 4 April 1952 of the Académie des Inscriptions et Belles-Lettres in Paris. '*Je me suis trompé* [I have erred] . . . *Je me suis trompé* . . . *Je me suis trompé* . . .', he confessed according to the minutes of the Académie. De Vaux made many valuable contributions to Qumran archaeology, but they were mixed with mistakes mainly attributable to haste.

By that time, Father de Vaux also subscribed to the theory that the ancient inhabitants of the Qumran ruins belonged to the Jewish sect of the Essenes described by the first century CE writers Philo, Pliny and Josephus, a view first mooted by E. L. Sukenik, and vigorously argued from 1950 onwards by A. Dupont-Sommer. The issue will be discussed in detail in chapter VIII (pp. 191–202).

Not counting the survey of the caves in the cliff, four more seasons of archaeological exploration followed the 1951 initial excavation of the Khirbet Qumran ruins, all directed by de Vaux: 9 February to 3 April 1953 (second season); 15 February to 15 April 1954 (third season); 2 February to 6 April 1955 (fourth season); 18 February to 28 March 1956 (fifth and final season). A further dig was conducted 2 kilometres further south at the farm associated with the Qumran establishment, at Ain Feshkha, from 25 January to 21 March 1958. Fifty years after the digs, and nearly four decades after de Vaux's death in 1971, the full publication of the archaeological report is still awaited.

For the sake of simplicity and clarity, the combined results of the excavations will be presented here in a single account. They are based on de Vaux's detailed preliminary reports, printed in the *Revue Biblique* between 1953 and

1959, and restated in *Archaeology and the Dead Sea Scrolls* (1973), the English revised edition of his Schweich Lectures delivered in French at the British Academy in London in 1959. Another French Dominican of the École Biblique, Jean-Baptiste Humbert, inherited de Vaux's archaeological legacy and is expected to issue his record in several volumes at some unspecified time in the future. So far only a large tome of photographs and de Vaux's diary notes appeared in print in 1994, followed by an English edition of the same, and a second volume on anthropology, physics and chemistry, both in 2003. The current state of the ongoing debate will be outlined in chapter VIII. Today, the Qumran archaeologists lag far behind the editors of the Dead Sea texts.

Roland de Vaux distinguished three main epochs in the occupation of the Qumran site. The earliest remains are walls dating back to biblical times, to the period of the monarchy of Judah in the eighth or seventh century BCE. A potsherd bearing a few letters of the archaic Hebrew alphabet and a stamped inscription on a jar-handle reading 'to the king' may be assigned to the sixth century BCE. The ashes which are connected with the broken pottery suggest that the settlement was burned down and destroyed during the campaign leading to the conquest of Jerusalem and Judaea by the Babylonians in 587 BCE.

The site lay abandoned for several centuries until the start of a fresh communal occupation. Its earliest stage, Period Ia in de Vaux's terminology, is attested by some rooms and various water installations (ditches and cisterns). Nothing reveals the date of Period Ia. However, the fact that the next stage began in the early first century BCE suggested to de Vaux that the modest reoccupation of the site happened in the closing decades of the second century BCE, during the rule of the Hasmonaean high priests John Hyrcanus I (135–104 BCE) and Judah Aristobulus I (104–103 BCE). Hyrcanus is represented by ten coins and Aristobulus by one in the Period Ia level. Eight Seleucid (Syrian Greek) coins were also retrieved on the site ranging from Antiochus III at the beginning of the second century BCE to Antiochus VII (138–129 BCE).

During Period Ib the settlement increased in size and complexity considerably. A two-storey tower was built to guard the entrance or serve as an observation post. An aqueduct secured water from Wadi Qumran, and an elaborate water storage system with numerous cisterns and pools, several of them with steps, as well as a tannery and a pottery workshop and two kilns, were constructed. A large but narrow room (22 metres long and 4.5 metres wide), with a low plastered bench running all around its walls, was recognized as a meeting hall and refectory in one. In a nearby room, more than 1,000 vessels were stacked or piled before an earthquake or some other violent occurrence smashed them to pieces. The archaeologists counted 708 bowls, 210 plates, 75 beakers, 38 dishes, 21 small jars and 11 jugs, the remains of the crockery of a communal pantry. There were no signs of individual habitation in the establishment. Where the members of the community slept is unclear. Part of the collapsed second floor may have served as living quarters and so also could neighbouring caves and possibly tents or huts which would have left no traces. Outside the buildings, animal bones (cow, goat and sheep) were deposited under shards or in pots. They represent remains of meals possibly hidden away from scavenging animals. The nature of these meals is the subject of controversy (ordinary communal meals, ritual meals, or less likely, sacrificial meals).

Period Ib is believed to have started under Alexander Jannaeus (103–76 BCE), whose reign is attested by 128 coins. One coin of Hyrcanus II (63–40 BCE) and six struck under Mattathias Antigonus (40–37 BCE) were also identified. Period Ib was brought to an end by an earthquake, probably the one mentioned by Flavius Josephus (*Jewish War* I:370–80; *Jewish Antiquities* XV:121–47) as having caused devastation in 31 BCE, the year of the battle of Actium in the Roman civil war between Mark Antony and Octavian, the future Augustus. The earthquake was also accompanied by a fire. According to de Vaux, the Qumran site was then abandoned until the end of the reign of Herod the Great in 4 BCE. He attributed the presence of ten (or 15) Herodian coins to Period II, but there are dissenting voices on this subject.

After twenty-seven years of abandonment, assuming that de Vaux's theory is accepted, the original group returned to the settlement. During this Period II, the place was cleaned up and repaired without being altered in any significant way. One of the modifications worth mentioning concerns the room designated by de Vaux as the *scriptorium* or writing workshop. It contained plaster tables, a mud-brick bench, two inkpots (one clay, one bronze) with a third one (also of clay) retrieved in a neighbouring room. One of them still contained residual dried ink. In de Vaux's opinion, this room served for the production of scrolls. Others, as will be shown, prefer different explanations (see chapter VIII).

A large amount of coins belong to Period II, starting with 16 coins of Herod's son Archaelaus (4 BCE–6 CE), 91 coins of the Roman prefects and procurators of Judaea (from 6 to 66 CE) and 78 coins of the Herodian Jewish king Agrippa I (41–4 CE). To these is to be added the hoard of 561 Tyrian silver drachms, the most recent of them dating to 9/8 BCE, found in a trench where the rubble cleared out of the rooms after the earthquake was put.

Ninety-four bronze coins, minted in years 2 and 3 of the first Jewish revolt against Rome (67–8 CE), mark the end of Period II. The destruction of the Qumran settlement resulted from a military attack. Arrowheads were found in the ruins and the roofs of the buildings were burned down. The usual date suggested is 68 CE. The twofold reason proposed is that Qumran yielded coins of the revolt up to the third year (68 CE) and we also know from Josephus that the Roman armies were in Jericho in the summer of that year. Vespasian himself visited the Dead Sea to check the claim that it is impossible to sink in its water. According to Josephus, Vespasian 'ordered certain persons who were unable to swim to be flung into the deep water with their hands tied behind them; with the result that all rose to the surface and floated, as if impelled upward by a current of air' (*Jewish War* IV:477).

The violent conquest of Qumran indicates that the people holding it in 68 CE resisted the Romans. If they were Essenes, they must have embraced the patriotic cause, as did John, the Essene mentioned by Josephus, who fought and died as a revolutionary general (*Jewish War* II:567; III:11, 9). However, it is also conceivable that bellicose resistance fighters from Masada took over Qumran after expelling its previous inhabitants and tried but failed to repel the Roman attack.

De Vaux's Period III corresponds to the occupation of the demolished settlement by Roman legionaries. There are signs of some clearing up and rebuilding. Father de Vaux surmised, without much evidence, that a small garrison remained at Qumran until the fall of Masada in 73/74 CE. Ten coins of the second Jewish rebellion, the Bar Kokhba war (132–5 CE), demonstrate renewed Jewish presence in Qumran in the early second century CE. The late Roman and Byzantine coins found in the ruins by the archaeologists are likely to have been lost by travellers who camped on the site.

The Qumran establishment had a nearby agricultural-industrial annex at Ain Feshkha, two kilometres to the south. As already noted, it was excavated in 1958. Pottery and coins suggest that it may have been started around the end of Period Ib at Qumran (before 31 BCE), flourished during Period II (first century CE), and terminated by the arrival of the Romans in 68 CE. Father de Vaux unearthed the remains of a main building (24 metres by 18 metres) surrounding an open courtyard to which were attached two enclosures, one industrial and the other a farm shed. The latter may have served for drying dates or reeds; the industrial quarter with water installations, using the local springs, housed a tannery in the opinion of de Vaux, but the absence of a deposit of animal hair militates against his hypothesis. Another theory floated was that the basins were used to keep fish. But were they large enough to make the exercise worthwhile?

The fishpool idea reminds me that in the course of my first visit to Qumran in October 1952, we went for a bath, one hardly can speak of a dip or a swim, in the Dead Sea at the point where a small stream takes the fresh water of the Feshkha springs to the Dead Sea. Just beyond the mouth of this stream, to my astonishment, I saw small fish venturing towards the extremely salty waters, but quickly changing direction and beating a retreat towards the more friendly environment of the stream. It reminded me of the famous Byzantine mosaic map of Madaba in Jordan, on the eastern side of the Dead Sea, which displays a happy fish swimming towards the sea at the mouth of the Jordan, but soon making a 180-degree turn with the smile turned into disgust on its face.

In short, de Vaux interpreted the Qumran ruins as the remains of a settlement of a Jewish religious group, identified as the Essenes. The large dining room, the numerous plates, pots and pans, and several stepped pools, constructed for ritual purification, confirmed, he thought, the communal character of the occupation of the site, and the discovery of several inkwells proved that substantial writing activity had taken place in one of the rooms. The scrolls and fragments found in the nearby caves were also believed to have been produced on the site. The explanation by de Vaux remained unquestioned for more than twenty years, but from the 1980s onwards revisionist interpretations began to emerge which will be discussed in chapter VIII.

5. The Qumran Cemetery

On the eastern side, beyond the perimeter wall of Qumran, lies a cemetery of approximately 1,200 individual graves, covered by stones, and oriented south (head)–north (feet). During the various campaigns, de Vaux's team opened forty-three of these in the main (or western) graveyard and in the various 'extensions'. In 1873, Clermont-Ganneau examined a few and H. Steckoll excavated others in the 1960s, but only de Vaux's record is available. With the exception of two tombs, with two skeletons in each, the excavated graves contained a single person. No valuables were retrieved. The gender of forty-one out of forty-three skeletons could be determined: thirty were male, seven women and four children. Apart from two, all the non-male bodies lay in the fringe cemeteries. Recently the physical anthropologist Joseph Zias has advanced the theory that most of the female and child skeletons can be explained as representing relatively recent Bedouin burials. If so, the distribution of the genders is even more disproportionate and puzzling.

As the sex or gender of the buried persons is of importance for the identification of the community resident in ancient Qumran, one may wonder why de Vaux was content with opening less than 5 per cent of the graves. The surprising answer I managed to elicit from Henri de Contenson, the French archaeologist who was in charge in the 1950s of the excavation of the Qumran cemetery, was this: We did not go on with it because it was too boring! A waste of time. No further work could take place in the cemetery as, since Qumran had come under Israeli control, violent objections to the 'desecration' of graves were voiced by ultra-orthodox Jews. When, in the course of the fiftieth anniversary celebrations of the discovery of the Scrolls, held in Jerusalem in 1997, I asked at an open meeting whether there was any chance of further excavations in the cemetery, a well-known Israeli archaeologist unenthusiastically remarked: 'Only if Qumran came under Palestinian or Jordanian rule.'

Postscript: Earlier manuscript discoveries in the Jericho area

The sensational news of the Qumran finds refreshed scholarly memories concerning similar occurrences in antiquity and the early Middle Ages in Palestine. The first of these, reported by the Church historian Eusebius, bishop of Caesarea (*c.* 260–340), occurred in the early third century CE. In his *Ecclesiastical History* (VI:16, 3) Eusebius relates that a manuscript of the Psalms was found 'at Jericho in a jar during the reign of Antoninus, the son of Severus', surnamed Caracalla (211–17 CE), and was used by the great Bible scholar Origen (*c.* 185–*c.* 254) when he was compiling his *Hexapla* or 'six-column' Hebrew–Greek edition of the Old Testament.

More exciting still is the story told by Timotheus I, Syrian Nestorian Patriarch of Seleucia (726–819 CE), in a letter written in *c.* 800 CE, addressed to Sergius, Metropolitan of Elam, about a recent important manuscript discovery. 'We have learned from trustworthy people that some books were found ten years ago (*c.* 790) in a small cave in the rocks near Jericho. The dog of an Arab hunter, pursuing some game, went into the cave and did not come out. The hunter entered the cave to look for it and found a chamber in the rock with many books in it. He went to Jerusalem and told his story to the Jews. They came out in large numbers and found books of the Old Testament written in Hebrew.'

The third possibly relevant source is Jacob al-Qirqisani of the medieval Jewish sect of the Karaites who, in his discussion of ancient Jewish religious parties, mentions in a work written in 937 CE the sect of the '*cave men*'

(*Maghariah*) who owed their name to the fact that their books were discovered in a cave (*maghar*). He places these 'cave men' between the Sadducees, or more likely the Zadokites, and the Christians. All three authors, Eusebius, Timotheus and Qirqisani, speak of manuscripts found in a cave and the first two also associate Jericho with the discoveries.

Of these three curious coincidences, the episode chronicled by Timotheus seems the most striking with the hunter's missing dog, like the modern Bedouin's stray goat, leading the respective owners to a manuscript deposit in a rock cavity in the Jericho area. Let us now recall in this connection the Cairo Genizah, the most notorious of the medieval Middle Eastern Jewish manuscript deposits. As has been explained in the previous chapter, three of the most significant manuscripts discovered in the Genizah were the Hebrew Ben Sira or Ecclesiasticus, the Aramaic Testament of Levi, and above all, the Damascus Document, which also bears the title of a Zadokite work. It is hard to resist the speculation that there was a link between the books acquired by Timotheus' Jewish contemporaries in Jerusalem and the manuscript collection hidden in the Qumran caves. The Qumran caves may have been visited in the age of Origen in the 210s, the days of Charlemagne (and Timotheus), *c.* 790, with some of the manuscripts ending up in the Cairo Genizah, and only finally by Muhammed edh-Dhib in 1947.

III

The École Biblique, Seedbed of Future Troubles

1. The Creation of the Official Editorial Team (1953–4)

Following the publication between 1950 and 1954 of the first six Scrolls from Cave 1 (the great Isaiah Scroll, the Habakkuk Commentary and the Community Rule, the incomplete Isaiah Scroll, the Scroll of Hymns and the War Scroll), and concurrently with the discoveries of the other ten caves and the archaeological excavations at Qumran, the period between 1950 and 1962 witnessed the start of Dead Sea Scrolls scholarship. This was a schizophrenic era, displaying signs of high promise and admirable enthusiasm on the one hand, but also foreshadowing the many troubles which were to follow. The large majority of those involved first perceived only the rosy side of the future; it took some years to realize the enormity of the task and to foresee the upheavals that lay ahead.

Since the first scroll discovery was unique and completely unparalleled, procedural rules had to be devised for the publication of the thousands of fragments. No institution stood formally behind the venture and in the absence of a supervisory body (neither the Jordanian Department of Antiquities, nor the Rockefeller Museum in Jerusalem, or the French School of Bible and Archaeology could act as such), influential individuals used their authority to lay down the law. On the Israeli side, Eleazar Sukenik, the Hebrew University's professor of archaeology, had been director of the Museum of Jewish Antiquities since 1938, and locally he had unchallenged authority. His son Yigael, who had adopted his underground codename Yadin, inherited his father's chair and influence. The two of them, with the archaeologist and epigraphist Nahman Avigad, completed (or as far as the Genesis Apocryphon was concerned, initiated) in record time the basic edition of the second Isaiah Scroll, the Hodayot or Thanksgiving Hymns and the War Scroll. In the circumstances, their contribution was truly outstanding.

On the Jordanian side, the situation was less satisfactory. Gerald Lankester Harding, the English director of the Department of Antiquities, appointed during the Mandate in 1936 and holding his post for twenty years, was a Near-Eastern archaeologist, but not a Hebrew expert. When called upon to act after the Arab Legion had identified the first scroll cave in 1949, he invited the Frenchman Father Roland de Vaux, who was both a biblical scholar and an archaeologist, to collaborate with him. Owing to the difference in qualifications, it was quite natural that de Vaux soon outshone Harding and took on himself the supreme leadership in Scrolls matters in Arab Jerusalem. He enjoyed great authority, which derived from his directorship of the prestigious École Biblique, an internationally famous establishment, arguably the world's leading institution in Palestinian archaeology and biblical studies. It was a kind of academic sanctuary in the eyes of Catholic Scripture interpreters, but viewed in the past, during the tyrannical days of the Pontifical Biblical Commission, with a degree of suspicion by the retrograde Church authorities in Rome.

The School, which was to become the main centre of research on the scroll fragments in Arab Jerusalem, was founded in 1890 by the brilliant French Dominican scholar, Father Marie-Joseph Lagrange (1855–1938), who also launched the quarterly *Revue Biblique* in 1892. Originally known as the École Pratique d'Étude Biblique, indicating that the scriptural realia (archaeology, geography and history) were in the forefront of its teaching programme, it was renamed the École Biblique et Archéologique Française after its elevation in 1920 to the status of a national institute of higher education by the French Académie des Inscriptions et Belles-Lettres. In the absence of an appropriate school run by the Jordanian state and of comparable learned establishments financed by western countries in Jerusalem, the École was the obvious choice for the planning and organization of Qumran research. The Jerusalem branch of the American Schools of Oriental Research (since 1970, the W. F. Albright Institute of Oriental Research) had no permanent academic personnel at the time and was staffed by a small number of professors, who held their positions for a year only.

After the exploration of Cave 1 and the collection of the hundreds of manuscript fragments left there by Muhammed edh-Dhib and his companions, de Vaux took it upon himself to find and commission editors. No one among the experienced teachers of the École Biblique was thought to be suitable for the job or was willing to undertake it. Fortunately de Vaux recruited two young Hebraists who, without previous experience, were prepared to make their apprenticeship on the Scrolls, and he charged them with the study and edition of the fragments retrieved in Cave 1. One of these was the young French Dominican Dominique Barthélemy (born in 1921), a student of the

École between 1949 and 1951. The other was a philological and epigraphic genius, the even younger Polish priest, Józef Tadeusz Milik (born in 1922), a student of biblical and oriental languages and cultures in Rome, who had come to de Vaux's notice as the author of several impressive articles on the Scrolls in Latin, Italian and English, published in 1950 and 1951. The two formed an ideal pair and having devoted an almost excessive amount of zeal and loving care even to the most insignificant bits of manuscript, they completed their almost Herculean task in practically no time. When I visited the École in October 1952 with the permission of de Vaux – who was charm and kindness personified while I was his guest – I was invited by Barthélemy and Milik to acquaint myself with their unpublished material, which was to form volume I of the series *Discoveries in the Judaean Desert*. To all intents and purposes their text was ready for Oxford University Press by the end of 1952 and OUP seems to have needed more time to typeset, print and bind the volume (published in 1955) than Barthélemy and Milik had required for researching and writing it. This was a brilliant beginning and the two novice scholars earned full marks. Their lucky boss, chief editor de Vaux, could enjoy the reflected glory.

While Barthélemy and Milik were labouring on the Cave 1 fragments, the Bedouin, as we know from the previous chapter, were not inactive either and by 1952 they had sniffed out further manuscript deposits in several caves in the Qumran region and a little further afield. These fresh finds, culminating in the giant cache in Cave 4, created a situation never faced before in the field of Hebrew manuscript research. De Vaux was confronted with a double problem: how to recruit manpower and how to raise money to finance the project. The limited funds the Jordanian Department of Antiquities was able to grant de Vaux to conduct his oriental bargaining with the Bedouin had run out long before all the fragments on offer could be acquired. The going rate for fragments was apparently $2.80 per square centimetre. To refill de Vaux's coffers, a dual stratagem was devised. Institutions in Europe and North America were approached for financial support, coupled with a tentative promise that some time in the future they would receive a certain quantity of textual pieces after they had been published. Contributions were obtained from McGill University of Montreal, the Vatican Library, the universities of Heidelberg, Oxford and Manchester, McCormick Theological Seminary, Chicago, and All Souls Church, New York. As a further incentive, some of the academic institutions were invited straightaway to suggest the names of gifted young scholars for appointment to the editorial team. This was the idea behind the creation of the notorious 'international and interconfessional' body of editors. The centre of research being in Arab Jerusalem, Israeli scholars were excluded and non-Israeli Jewish Hebraists unwelcome. (My visit in 1952 preceded the creation of the team and in any case I still counted as a Christian until 1957.) The plan to distribute some of the fragments to foreign libraries or universities was soon countermanded by the Jordanian government, which declared the Dead Sea Scrolls national patrimony, and volumes III–V of *DJD* (1962–8) appeared under the title, *Discoveries in the Judaean Desert of Jordan.*

The new editors were appointed by de Vaux in 1953–4. The two tried and tested scholars, Dominique Barthélemy and Joseph Milik, had already earned their stripes. Milik became the pillar of the project, but for reasons known only to himself, Barthélemy declined the invitation. He thereafter devoted himself to the study of a Greek translation of the Twelve Minor Prophets discovered in a different area of the Judaean desert (Nahal Hever), and published an outstanding study of the Greek versions of the Bible under the title of *Les devanciers d'Aquila* in 1963. Subsequently he turned his back on Qumran studies as such and spent the next forty years of his life in research on biblical textual criticism in the framework of the United Bible Societies' Hebrew and Old Testament Bible Project, until his death in 2002.

Two established scholars then joined de Vaux's team: Monsignor Patrick Skehan, professor of Scripture at the Catholic University of America, and the Abbé Jean Starcky, a well-known French Orientalist from the Centre National de la Recherche Scientifique (CNRS) of Paris, an expert in Aramaic dialects. The other five were at the start of their careers: the French Abbé Maurice Baillet, also of the CNRS, the American Frank Moore Cross, of McCormick Theological Seminary, Chicago (later professor at Harvard University), the German Claus-Hunno Hunzinger from the University of Göttingen, and two from Britain, John Allegro of Manchester University and the Benjamin of the group, John Strugnell, in his early twenties, freshly graduated from Oxford in 1954 (and later employed at Chicago University, Duke University, and finally at Harvard). Most of the editors were gifted or highly gifted, but they formed an odd bunch. Without counting de Vaux, there were four Catholic priests – Starcky, Skehan, Baillet and Milik (the latter subsequently left the priesthood); one Presbyterian (Cross) and one Lutheran (Hunzinger, who later resigned and his lot was inherited by Baillet); one Methodist (Allegro, who turned agnostic); and one Anglican (Strugnell, who became a convert to Roman

Catholicism). Two of them were, or soon turned into, alcoholics. Even without the wisdom of hindsight it would have been easy to foresee troubles looming on the horizon.

But at the beginning all was joy, sweetness and enthusiasm. Learned periodicals were filled with studies and preliminary editions of fascinating Dead Sea texts. Scholars watching the events from the sidelines did not yet feel excluded as fresh revelations were promptly put at their disposal piecemeal. The editors, or at least some of them, were still very conscious of their duty towards their fellow researchers and the interested public. I heard Milik deliver a report at an international Old Testament congress in Strasbourg in 1956, whose concluding paragraph is worth quoting as it revealed the spirit that animated the team, or at least Milik himself, in the early years.

The point that will particularly interest you is that of the delays in publishing. The interval separating volume II [of *DJD*] from volume I [published the year before in 1955] may seem long. It is due to the large amount of work, partly material, that the discoveries of 1952 (Caves 2–10) have imposed on us. In any case, once volume II is published, the remainder will follow at the speed of *one or several volumes per annum*. (my italics)

(*Volume du Congrès, 1956, Vetus Testamentum, Supplément IV*, 1957, p. 26)

In the 1950s the world still trusted the editorial team. The large amount of work alluded to by Milik concerned the thousands of fragments amassed in the 'scrollery' of the Rockefeller Museum in Jerusalem which were eagerly studied. Bits belonging to the same piece of skin, showing the same colour and bearing the same handwriting, were set apart and painstakingly pieced together. The world's greatest jigsaw puzzle was progressively assembled. Texts were identified, catalogued and given a preliminary translation. Words in their contexts were copied on to index cards and index cards arranged alphabetically in boxes. Under the moral and academic leadership of Milik, the future was envisaged with rosy optimism. But everything was not as smooth and promising as the insiders imagined.

From the very beginning de Vaux, hovering above and watching his underlings with a hawk's eyes, adopted a proprietorial attitude towards the Scrolls. Matters relating to them were to be kept under a bushel until the editor-in-chief and his team had agreed to release them. I had personal experience of this change in attitude. The charm and friendliness Father de Vaux had shown me while I was at the École vanished. The copy of my book, *Les manuscrits du désert de Juda*, published in December 1953, in which I thanked him for his kind hospitality and help, was coolly received. In his reply of 31 January 1954, de Vaux reproached me – after glancing at, but before reading the volume – with making public 'without authority', some of the 'friendly information' (*renseignements amicaux*) I had received during my one-month stay at the École.

In de Vaux's mind, all the Qumran manuscripts were to be kept secret until their definitive publication in *Discoveries in the Judaean Desert*, however long the editorial work might take. The unpublished scrolls were in his and his collaborators' safekeeping, and were not to be made available for study to outsiders. Already by 1954, when I was reprimanded by de Vaux, a 'closed shop' had been set up for Scrolls editors. However, my 'indiscretion' was insignificant compared with the first serious trespass. It occurred within the team itself, engineered by John Allegro when he acted as intermediary in arranging the opening of the

Copper Scroll at the Manchester College of Science and Technology. After divulging bits of this Scroll, which did not belong to his lot, in a BBC broadcast in 1956, he succeeded, without de Vaux's agreement or even knowledge, to obtain permission to publish the whole document from the Jordanian Director of Antiquities, Dr Awni Dajani. His edition of *The Treasure of the Copper Scroll* appeared in 1960, two years before de Vaux's appointee, J. T. Milik, brought out the official (and much better) edition in volume III of *Discoveries in the Judaean Desert*. As for Allegro's treasure hunt to retrieve the hidden gold and silver, predictably he returned from it empty-handed (see chapter II, p. 28).

The one positive outcome of the Allegro adventure was the relatively prompt publication of the contents of the so-called minor caves (Caves 2–3, 5–10), including the Copper Scroll from Cave 3, by Milik and Baillet in 1962. In the absence of Allegro's provocative intervention the volume might have been delayed considerably longer. Thus the first period of modest editorial activity came to an end, nine years after the birth of de Vaux's brainchild, the international and interconfessional editorial team. The heart of the matter – the mass of the fragments collected from Cave 4 – was not even touched until 1968 when Allegro's slim and far from perfect *DJD V* appeared. We had then to wait until long after de Vaux's death in 1971 before genuine progress was actually made, beginning in the 1990s.

2. The Initial Phase of Scrolls Scholarship and Early Controversies

The enthusiastic announcement of 'the most sensational Hebrew manuscript discovery of all time' was not immediately endorsed by the whole scholarly community. Two kinds of objection were raised by academics prior to the archaeological investigation of the Qumran caves and ruins: some doubted the authenticity of the manuscripts, chief among them Professor Solomon Zeitlin of Dropsie College, Philadelphia, while others queried their antiquity in the wake of the famous Oxford Semitist, Professor G. R. Driver.

At the start, a number of established scholars remained on the fence as they recalled the ill-famed fake Deuteronomy Scroll of Shapira. It consisted of fifteen leather strips with archaic Hebrew characters, recalling the script of the inscription of Mesha, king of Moab (eighth century BCE), discovered at Diban in Transjordan in 1868. With his Deuteronomy manuscript, William Moses Shapira, a Jerusalem antiquity dealer, nearly managed to fool the authorities of the British Museum in 1883. He pretended that the strips (probably cut off from the margins of an old synagogue roll of the Bible) were 2,500 years old. The fraud was denounced by the French archaeologist Charles Clermont-Ganneau, who happened, also, to be one of the first modern visitors in 1873 to Khirbet Qumran (see chapter II, p. 32). When found out, Shapira committed suicide. Thereafter the leather strips disappeared so that they could not be checked in the light of the Dead Sea Scrolls. But the story explains the initial nervousness of established Hebraists. They did not want to become the laughing stock of academia.

In the wake of the first Qumran find, Professor Solomon Zeitlin, a well-known rabbinic expert and editor of the influential *Jewish Quarterly Review*, filled the pages of successive issues of his periodical with a series of articles aimed at denouncing and discrediting the discovery. He rejected the view that the texts belonged to antiquity at all and suggested instead that they were recent forgeries planted in the cave by crooks with a view to deceiving, and extracting money from, credulous collectors. The titles of the articles reveal Zeitlin's thought: 'Scholarship and the Hoax of the recent Discoveries', 'The Fiction of the recent Discoveries near the Dead Sea', 'The Propaganda of the Hebrew Scrolls and the Falsification of History', etc., all published between 1949 and 1955. The renowned British Semitic scholar, Professor G. R. (later Sir Godfrey) Driver, without going as far as Zeitlin and calling the Scrolls a fraud, arrived at the conclusion in 1951 that the biblical text and some of the grammatical peculiarities contained in them pointed to a date of around AD 500. He later recanted, became one of the founding fathers of the Zealot theory, and dated the Scrolls to the first century CE. Others, apparently including the great Palestinian archaeologist of the École Biblique, the Dominican Father L. H. Vincent, when told about the complete Isaiah manuscript in 1948, thought that it was medieval.

Among the established authorities, who, at the risk of their reputation, favoured the authenticity and antiquity of the manuscripts discovered in 1947, we find, in addition to their publishers, E. L. Sukenik and M. Burrows, W. F. Albright, the famous American archaeologist; Paul Kahle, the editor of the critical text of the Hebrew Bible, and H. H. Rowley, an influential British Old Testament expert from Manchester; the well-known French Orientalist André Dupont-Sommer, professor at the Sorbonne; and Otto Eissfeldt, a leading Old Testament scholar from Halle in Germany and author of the standard introduction to the Hebrew Bible. The hesitancy of the large majority of the great and the good gave a chance to brave and enterprising young scholars to win their spurs: among them (in alphabetical order) were J. M. Allegro (who in 1970 compromised his academic reputation; see pp. 61–2), D. Barthélemy, F. M. Cross, J. T. Milik, G. Vermes and Y. Yadin (a relatively late starter at the age of thirty-five, on his retirement from the office of Chief of Staff of the Israel Defence Forces). We all began to make our contribution to Qumran studies in the 1950s.

From 1951, serious research into the Dead Sea Scrolls was on its way, and by 1956, the year of the preliminary publication of the last of the seven manuscripts from Cave 1 (the Genesis Apocryphon), following the edition of the fragments collected from that cave in 1955, a substantial literature became available in all the major languages, addressed both to the academic and the intelligent non-specialist readership, first in the form of articles in newspapers and periodicals, but soon also as books. The prompt development of Scrolls studies was due to a fortunate accident: with the exception of the Temple Scroll found in Cave 11 and published in 1977, all the major manuscripts came from Cave 1 and were the first to be discovered and their contents were the first to appear. If, instead of the big Scrolls, the early editors had been obliged to struggle with the thousands of jumbled fragments, no general understanding of Qumran literature would have been possible for many, many years. One must also bear in mind that, as far as history and doctrine were concerned, the Scrolls from Cave 1 were not the only documents to provide source material for the reconstitution of the Qumran community and its cultural and religious message. It was realized almost from day one that the two manuscripts of the Damascus Document preserved in the Cairo Genizah were somehow related to Qumran (see chapter I, pp. 15–16). Moreover, as soon as the fragments from Cave 4, and also from 5 and 6, were identified, it was realized that they also included remains of the Damascus Document.

In three areas there was fast and substantial progress in Qumran research, leading at a remarkably early stage to extensive agreement on various points among researchers and thus promptly developing what can be described as mainstream or consensus opinion (a dirty word for the dissenting minority). These three areas were the Scrolls' contribution to biblical study; the identity of the Qumran sect or community; and the historical context of the sectarian writings.

(1) At the start, the two Isaiah manuscripts and the bibical text in the Habakkuk Commentary from Cave 1 constituted the basis of the evaluation of the Scrolls for scriptural research. Amusingly, though the diverse opinions voiced by scholars pointed ultimately to the same conclusion, namely that the Isaiah Scrolls were in substantial agreement with the traditional (or Masoretic) text of the Old Testament, they were expressed in seemingly opposite fashion, like one man calling a cup half full when it is half empty for another. Likewise, for one school of thought, the Qumran biblical manuscripts were substantially identical with and confirmed the Masoretic Old Testament,

whereas for the other they displayed significant differences in their meaningful variant readings. It was especially after the preliminary study of the biblical fragments from Cave 4 that the true contribution of the Scrolls came to light. As a result, an entirely new phase of biblical textual criticism began, which would have been inconceivable before the Qumran discoveries. This will be discussed in chapters VI and IX.

(2) The next point on which there was soon general agreement was the identification of the community or sect described in the non-biblical Scrolls (Community Rule, Thanksgiving Hymns, War Scroll) and in the Damascus Document. There has never been unanimity on this question, but since the earliest years of Scrolls research there was substantial support for the theory that the Qumran sectaries were identical with or in some serious way linked to the ancient Jewish sect of the Essenes about whom three first-century CE writers, the Jewish Philo and Josephus and the Roman Pliny the Elder, had left fairly detailed accounts. Sukenik, in his preliminary publication, proposed this identification in 1948 and Dupont-Sommer argued it in greater detail from 1950 onwards. Further disparate voices could be heard in favour of the Pharisees, the Sadducees, the Zealots and even the early Christians, but these formed a minority compared with the holders of the Essene thesis whose champions comprised in the early days, in addition to Sukenik and Dupont-Sommer, Roland de Vaux and all the members of the editorial team, Y. Yadin, and others, including myself.

(3) The reconstruction of the history of the Qumran sect was based on the Damascus Document, the Habakkuk Commentary and other works of Bible interpretation found in the caves, in particular the Nahum Commentary,

the Commentary on Psalm 37, and fragments of a historical calendar.

In chronological order, the first theory (championed by H. H. Rowley) found the period of the conflict between the Syrian Greek king Antiochus IV Epiphanes (175–164 BCE) and the Jewish nationalist rebels led by the Maccabees the most appropriate setting for the clash of the founder of the community, the Teacher of Righteousness and his opponent, nicknamed the Wicked Priest.

The next hypothesis focused on the Maccabee high priests Jonathan and/or Simon as the Wicked Priest, more than on the anonymous Teacher of Righteousness (G. Vermes, J. T. Milik, F. M. Cross, R. de Vaux).

Further down the chronological ladder stands the hypothesis centred on the Hasmonean Jewish priest-king Alexander Jannaeus (103–76 BCE) in conflict with the Pharisees (M. Delcor, J. M. Allegro).

Next in order comes the thesis built on the identification of an allusion in the Habakkuk Commentary to the conquest of Jerusalem by Pompey in 63 BCE (A. Dupont-Sommer).

Following a totally different line of reasoning, the idea was advanced that the Qumran sect was the early Jewish-Christian community of the Ebonites (J. L. Teicher).

The last slot is the period of the first rebellion of the Jews against Rome (66–70 CE), with the Jewish revolutionary party of the Zealots-Sicarii being identified as the Qumran community (C. Roth, G. R. Driver).

An assessment of the serious hypotheses will follow in chapters VIII and IX.

Postscript: Qumran and the Riddle of Christian Origins

The question of the significance of the Scrolls in the interpretation of the origins of Christianity had already arisen at the very beginnings of Qumran research and has gone on haunting the scene over the years. This was to be expected. The near-eastern archaeological and literary discoveries of the past century and a half have always produced scholars who saw in the new finds the long-awaited key capable of opening up the mystery of Jesus and the birth of the Church. We observe this phenomenon in the nineteenth and early twentieth centuries apropos the Assyro-Babylonian texts which mention the dying and rising nature god Tammuz, the Oriental and Graeco-Roman mystery cults, and the worship of the Persian saviour deity, Mithras. Predictably, in the mid-twentieth century it was the turn of the Dead Sea Scrolls.

André Dupont-Sommer, professor at the Sorbonne in Paris and John Marco Allegro, assistant lecturer at the University of Manchester, were the first to try to argue the case. Others such as Barbara Thiering and Robert Eisenman followed (see chapter VIII, pp. 190–91). Thus the ground was prepared for rumour-mongering that the Scrolls could reveal secrets about Jesus and the early days of Christianity that the Church, first and foremost the Vatican, would prefer at all price to keep locked away.

A clear hint at what he believed to be a major break-through was given in the concluding paragraph of Dupont-Sommer's initial communication on the Habakkuk Commentary as early as the session of the Académie des Inscriptions in Paris on 26 May 1950.

Renan has characterized . . . Essenism as a 'foretaste of Christianity' and Christianity as 'an Essenism that has largely succeeded' . . . Today, thanks to the new texts, connections spring up from every side between the Jewish New Covenant, sealed in the blood of the Teacher of Righteousness in 63 BC and the Christian New Covenant, sealed in the blood of the Galilean Master around AD 30. Unforeseen lights are shed on the history of the Christian origins – one of the major problems of history – from where will no doubt come also the answers to many questions.

(Observations sur le Commentaire d'Habacuc découvert près de la Mer Morte, Paris, Adrien-Maisonneuve, 1950, p. 29)

A few months later, Dupont-Sommer further developed his revolutionary ideas, presenting Jesus and Christianity as deeply influenced by, indeed modelled on, the Dead Sea sect and its Teacher of Righteousness.

Everything in the Jewish New Covenant [the Qumran sect] announces and prepares the Christian New Covenant. (Jesus) . . . appears, from many points of view, as an astonishing reincarnation of the Teacher of Righteousness . . . Like him, he will be the supreme Judge at the end of time . . . Like him, he was condemned to death and executed. Like him, he rose to heaven . . . Like him, he inflicted judgement on Jerusalem . . . All these similarities . . . constitute an almost hallucinating whole . . . Wherever the similarities demand or suggest the idea of borrowing, the borrowing was made by Christianity. On the other hand, however, the appearance of faith in Jesus . . . is hardly explicable without the real, historical activity of a new Prophet, a new Messiah . . .

(Aperçus préliminaires sur les manuscrits de la Mer Morte, Paris, Adrien-Maisonneuve, 1950, pp. 121–2).

With French panache, Dupont-Sommer put the agnostic cat among the Catholic pigeons of de Vaux and his team. But in the Jerusalem 'scrollery' the professor of the Sorbonne found a pair of attentive ears – those of the former Methodist but by then fellow agnostic Scrolls editor, John Allegro, who was ready to shock the Christian world with what they both believed to be a bombshell concealed in the Dead Sea Scrolls.

In January 1956 Allegro gave three fifteen-minute radio talks on the BBC Northern Home Service. The first two were lively and informative, but the third contained dynamite, or so Allegro believed. The Assistant Lecturer of Manchester, being an insider of the editorial team, was better informed than Sorbonne professor Dupont-Sommer, and was able to disclose in his talks what he had read or imagined he had read in the Nahum Commentary and the Commentary on Psalm 37 from Cave 4 (both texts belonged to his lot) and in the Copper Scroll (which did not). He deduced from his reading that the Teacher of Righteousness, the founder of the Dead Sea sect, was captured by the 'Wicked Priest', the high priest Alexander Jannaeus, and was given by him into the hands of his Gentile troops to be crucified. After the executioners had departed, the disciples of the Teacher took down the broken body of their leader and guarded it, awaiting the imminent coming of the Day of Judgement. On that day they believed that the risen Teacher of Righteousness would usher his followers towards the new Jerusalem.

Although the audience of the broadcast was confined to people from northern England, its sensational content was picked up by the press, not only the British but also the world media, including the *New York Times*. For the ordinary newspaper reader, Allegro's hints signified that

Jesus and Christianity were second-hand imitations of the person and destiny of the Essene Teacher of Righteousness. Not surprisingly, there was an outcry and the only persons capable of checking Allegro's claims – de Vaux and the other members of the editorial team – hastened to issue a firm denial in the correspondence columns of the London *Times* on 16 March 1956.

In view of the broad repercussions of his [Allegro's] statements, and the fact that the materials on which they are based are not yet available to the public, we, his colleagues, feel obliged to make the following statement ... We find no crucifixion of the 'teacher', no deposition from the cross, and no 'broken body of their Master' to be stood guard over until Judgement Day ... It is our conviction that either he has misread the texts or he has built up a chain of conjectures which the materials do not support.

The letter was signed by de Vaux, Milik, Skehan, Starcky and Strugnell. The fact that the first four out of the five were Catholic priests played a significant part in the later development of the controversy. In his reply to *The Times* on 20 March, Allegro admitted that his surmises about the crucifixion and resurrection of the Teacher of Righteousness were not literally stated in the Scrolls, but resulted from inference. He maintained, however, that these inferences were well founded and wholly legitimate. For scholarly readers, this was a backing down, but for many of the non-specialists and for sensation-seeking journalists this was just the start of a brave young lion's fight against the conventional and mostly clerical fuddy-duddies. In consequence, and notwithstanding Allegro's subsequent 'academic suicide' with the publication in 1970 of *The Sacred*

Mushroom and the Cross, an odd book in which he attributed the origin of religion, Judaism and Christianity included, to the influence of *ammanita muscaria*, a hallucinogenic fungus, the seeds of the gossip were sown regarding a Catholic conspiracy about the Scrolls that has relentlessly continued until the present day.

IV

Somnolence – Politics – Scandal

Intense activity marked the opening years of the 1960s on the publications front. In 1961 volume II of the *DJD* series appeared, but it had nothing to do with the Dead Sea Scrolls. It was devoted to the documents discovered by the Bedouin in 1951–2 in caves situated in Wadi Murabba'at some eleven miles south of Qumran Cave 1. They yielded some biblical fragments and religious objects – phylacteries (small boxes with a biblical text inside) and mezuzot (cases to be attached to doorposts, containing biblical texts) – but the material was chiefly non-literary: contracts and legal documents of various kinds in Hebrew and Aramaic, dating to the second half of the first and the early decades of the second century CE, and letters written during the second Jewish rebellion against Rome (132–5 CE), including missives sent by the leader, Simeon bar Kosiba (Bar Kokhba) to local commanders. The remainder of the find consisted of Greek economic and legal texts, including one in shorthand, as well as a few badly damaged Latin papyri and a small number of Hebrew, Aramaic, Greek and Latin ostraca or inscribed potsherds. The Semitic texts, some of them written in a previously un-known cursive script, were magisterially edited by J. T. Milik and the Greek and Latin fragments were published by the Dominican Pierre Benoit. If proof was needed, this more than 300-page-long quarto-sized volume demonstrated that, when they were so minded, members of the editorial team were capable of working not only well but also fast.

Other manuscript discoveries followed in caves lying on the Israeli side of the pre-1967 borders, partly due to the Bedouin and partly to a search performed by Israeli archaeologists under the leadership of Yigael Yadin. The documents retrieved were similar to those found in Wadi Murabba'at, comprising legal documents and Bar Kokhba letters. They were edited in *DJD*, VIII (E. Tov, 1990) and XXVII (H. Cotton, 1997). Further Greek papyri have been published in *The Documents from the Bar Kokhba Period in the Cave of Letters* (1989) by N. Lewis. The remainder of the finds is still awaiting authoritative publication, although a good deal of them are available in preliminary editions by Yigael Yadin, Jonas C. Greenfield and others.

In 1962 appeared *DJD*, volume III, disposing of the largely insignificant fragments of the minor caves (Caves 2–3 and 5–10), edited by M. Baillet, and the peculiar and significant Copper Scroll, of which Milik produced a brilliant, though far from decisive, pioneering decipherment and study, overshadowing the amateurish effort, mentioned earlier, of J. M. Allegro (see chapter III, p. 51). Another speedy publication is owed to Professor James A. Sanders who, without being a member of the official editorial team, was commissioned by the American Schools of Oriental Research, owners of the publication right, to edit the Psalms Scroll found in Cave 11 (*DJD*, IV, 1965). But with *DJD*, III, the editorial activity of de Vaux & Co. ground to a halt. The thousands of fragments of Cave 4, except the relatively small lot allocated to John Allegro, who issued them in *DJD*, V, in 1968, were still kept close to their chests by the insiders, and remained inaccessible to the not-so-privileged outside world. After publishing preliminary studies of the most important texts in his section, Allegro, with the assistance of his Manchester colleague, Arnold Anderson, quickly knocked together a slender volume by September 1966. Originally it was meant to form part of a larger collection of texts, but since the editor of the Cave 4 biblical texts, Patrick Skehan, was in no way ready with his material, de Vaux decided to give the green light to Allegro, who proceeded on his own. Owing to the habitual dilatoriness of Oxford University Press, volume V of *DJD* appeared as *Discoveries in the Judaean Desert of **Jordan*** in 1968, a year after the Qumran area had come under Israeli administration as a result of the Six Day War of June 1967.

While in the 1950s members of the editorial team had spent substantial periods of their time in Jerusalem, working on the fragments in the Rockefeller Museum's 'scrollery', by the 1960s they all left for other havens, university posts which provided them with regular salaries. J. T. Milik moved first to Beirut, then to Rome, where he left the Catholic priesthood and married, and finally settled at the CNRS in Paris. Jean Starcky and Maurice Baillet also returned to France and to the CNRS, and Claus Hunno Hunzinger to Germany. In 1971 Hunzinger resigned and his assignment was passed on to Baillet. Patrick Skehan reverted to his old chair in the Catholic University of America, and F. M. Cross took up the prestigious chair of Semitic languages at Harvard, where John Strugnell, too, joined him after two prior spells in Chicago and at Duke University in Durham, North Carolina. None of the three contributed, or were anywhere near contributing, to *DJD* until twenty or thirty years later and with the assistance of other scholars. However, Cross, and especially Strugnell, excelled as supervisors of Harvard graduate students to whom they 'sublet' Scrolls entrusted to them for publication. In fact, between 1968 and 1992, when the first Cave 4-related *DJD* volume published under the editorship of Emanuel Tov appeared, only a smallish collection by Milik of excerpts of biblical nature (*DJD*, VI, 1977) and Baillet's weighty volume of non-biblical writings (*DJD*, VII, 1982) saw the light of day. The latter was put on paper, in Baillet's own unexplained curious French wording, '*avec des souffrances, et parfois avec des larmes*' ('amid sufferings and sometimes amid tears'). This was indeed a period of somnolence, aggravated by the impact of the political changes in the Middle East.

Although Roland de Vaux maintained a regular exchange of offprints with the Israeli Yigael Yadin (in the absence of postal connections between the two halves of divided Jerusalem in the 1950s, I volunteered to act as their letterbox in Paris), he, like most of the old staff at the École Biblique (except Father Roger Tournay) and the majority of the editorial team (except Frank Cross), were decidedly pro-Arab and anti-Israeli. For instance, in some of his correspondence Strugnell refused to call the city by its Hebrew name 'Jerusalem', and dated his letters from El Quds (The Holy City), the Arab substitute for Jerusalem. For the anti-Israelis of the École, the Jewish victory in the Six Day War was a profound blow. Despite the gentlemanly reassurance given by the Israeli Department of Antiquities that they would not interfere with the running of the editorial work (a generous but foolish move as it turned out), de Vaux found it impossible to tolerate the change in the ultimate controlling authority. During the last four years of his life (from 1967 to 1971), editorial activity came to a standstill.

With de Vaux's death at the age of sixty-eight, a new chief editor had to be found, and the members of the editorial team, already active (or mostly inactive) from a distance, made the choice of another professor of the École, who, like de Vaux, was a French Dominican, Father Pierre Benoit. The Israeli archaeological establishment sheepishly approved his appointment in 1972. Not being a Hebraist, but a New Testament scholar, Benoit was hardly the right leader from the academic point of view. Lacking the firmness and diplomatic skill required by the office, he was not the man likely to put an end to the editorial sleepiness, which was more and more beginning to resemble a coma.

A fresh shake-up was needed. Having left France, the priesthood and Catholicism in 1957, and in charge of Jewish studies in Oxford since 1965, I felt it was my turn to make a move. Since the Israelis were unwilling to intervene, was there any other institution, connected with the project and endowed with enough muscle, that might be able to exert pressure on Benoit and his underlings? Oxford University Press, the publishers of the *DJD* series, seemed to me just what the doctor ordered. The 400-year-old OUP was, after Her Majesty's Stationery Office, the largest publishing establishment in Britain, and its director, C. H. Roberts, bearing the modest, old-fashioned title of '*Secretary* to the Delegates', was a powerful man not only by virtue of his office, but also as one of the world's most famous Greek papyrologists. He was not just a colleague, but also an ally. A few weeks earlier, in the correspondence columns of the London *Times* (7 April 1972), he supported with his unique authority my attack on the Spanish Jesuit

José O'Callaghan's theory that tiny Greek papyrus fragments found in Qumran Cave 7 represented the Gospel of Mark and other New Testament texts among the Dead Sea Scrolls.

At our meeting on 15 May 1972, Colin Roberts had needed only a few words before he expressed his agreement with my premise that a great responsibility towards the scholarly community lay on the Press's shoulders, and declared himself prepared to act in the name of OUP. In the presence of his senior colleague in charge of *DJD* matters, we decided that the new editor-in-chief Benoit would be required to present the Press with a firm undertaking and impose a detailed and binding timetable on his procrastinating editorial team.

If the affairs of the editor-in-chief were in chaos, so were also – as I was to discover – those of OUP. It turned out that they did not have any list of the names, let alone of the addresses, of the members of the editorial team, so could not communicate with them. When I supplied both names and addresses, the senior OUP official contacted the defaulting editors, but only the Anglo-American contingent was prepared to answer. Milik, Starcky and Baillet simply turned a deaf ear to the request. By contrast, Strugnell, Cross and Skehan, as befitted 'Anglo-Saxon' gentlemen, promptly replied and forecast a rosy future, firmly assuring Benoit and OUP that their finished typescripts would be delivered at various precise dates between 1973 and 1976. Skehan, however, attached conditions to the delivery of his material. He would not allow his name to appear in the volume if it visibly entailed any association with an Israeli institution such as the Shrine of the Book or the Department of Antiquities. Should a link of this sort prove unavoidable, his contribution could be published as long as it remained anonymous. Circumstances prevented his determination from being tested. In 1980 Patrick Skehan died without his editorial task – embarked on a quarter of a century earlier – being anywhere near to completion, since *DJD*, IX, on which his name featured, did not appear until 1992.

To revert to 1972, the date of the signed undertakings, the years passed – 1973, 1974, 1975, 1976 – and none of the promised manuscripts materialized and reached Oxford University Press. The solemn commitments turned out to be empty words. After a delay of five years, I uttered a prophecy of doom in the opening address of my Margaret Harries Lectures at Dundee University, which was to form the first chapter of *The Dead Sea Scrolls: Qumran in Perspective*, published later in the same year of 1977:

On this thirtieth anniversary of their coming to light the world is entitled to ask [the editors of the Qumran Scrolls] ... what they intend to do about this lamentable state of affairs. For unless drastic measures are taken at once, the greatest and most valuable of all Hebrew and Aramaic manuscript discoveries is likely to become *the academic scandal par excellence of the twentieth century.* (pp. 23–4)

This outcry was noted and regularly repeated in the press, but without receiving serious acknowledgement from Benoit and his troops. But their time was running out. Public protest was reactivated by John Allegro, already in disgrace among academics after the *Sacred Mushroom*, but still having access to the letters' columns of *The Times* (17 April 1982), where he expressed 'doubts of the scholarly integrity' of the editorial team. Benoit endeavoured to answer publicly not only the accusation of mischievous critics (meaning Allegro), but also the concern of 'honest scholars' in a note appended to a book review in the *Revue Biblique* (1983, pp. 99–100).

Besides malicious and dishonest criticisms, I perceive in the scholarly world, among decent people who do not suspect anything sinister, astonishment and regret provoked by the slowness of the large 'definitive' volumes of *DJD*, a slowness by which I am the first to be upset. I wish to give a clear explanation and offer a ray of hope.

He blamed the disruption of the 'good continuation' of the *DJD* series on the political events that disturbed the Middle East. First, the Jordanian government nationalized the Rockefeller Museum, then, following the Six Day War, the Scrolls came under the authority of 'another government'. Fortunately the editors were granted freedom to get on with their work and they were doing so, but slower than one would have wished. Benoit was thick-skinned enough to place part of the blame for procrastination on OUP! The apology ended on an optimistic note: 'One cannot promise miracles, but every effort will be deployed to advance the publication as fast as possible.'

This blow of hot air was Benoit's swansong. Next year, in 1984, he divested himself of the editorial mantle, which subsequently fell on the shoulders of John Strugnell. In 1987 the eighty-one-year-old Pierre Benoit died, having produced only a slim *DJD* volume by Milik and a fat one by Baillet in twelve years of stewardship.

Dissatisfaction grew and the atmosphere turned explosive. More than thirty years after its creation, the editorial team had a mere three volumes of Cave 4 material to their credit. The still unpublished Cave 4 texts were to fill twenty-three further volumes. My prophecy regarding the academic scandal of the century came to fulfilment. The time for action had arrived.

V

The Battle over the Scrolls and its Aftermath

After decades of procrastination, the highly privileged editorial team exhausted the patience of the scholarly world and the interested, but increasingly suspicious and impatient public. After Pierre Benoit had inherited the editorial office from the omnipotent Roland de Vaux, the *New York Times* (9 August 1972) devoted one of its leaders to the Dead Sea Scrolls, and firmly admonished the newly appointed editor-in-chief to get on with the job to avoid 'public outrage'. With no sign of a change of heart in the editorial camp and no noticeable progress in the rate of publication, general dissatisfaction grew and approached boiling point. As was signalled in the previous chapter, resignations and 'natural wastage' progressively reduced the size of the notorious 'international and inter-confessional' editorial team.

1. Growing Frustration

Roland de Vaux had died in 1971 without even beginning to write his archaeological report. Monsignor Patrick Skehan followed him in 1980, with his bunch of biblical manuscripts nowhere near to going to the printers. Eugene Ulrich of the University of Notre Dame became his heir.

The German Claus Hunno Hunzinger withdrew, and the fragments of the War Scroll acquired a new editor, Maurice Baillet. The ailing Benoit resigned in 1984 and died in 1987. In 1988, the French Orientalist Jean Starcky died with his large collection of Aramaic Qumran fragments left completely unedited. It was passed on to Émile Puech, another French Catholic priest, employed by the CNRS. John Allegro, treated as the black sheep of the team, whose chief merit was that he had put together a shabby edition of *DJD*, V, in 1968, quit or rather was squeezed out of the select company of the chosen.

Those who theoretically continued were J. T. Milik, whose last volume appeared in 1977, and two Harvard professors, Frank Moore Cross and John Strugnell. As far as *DJD* was concerned, these two were unproductive ever since joining the team in 1953 and 1954, respectively. Strugnell's largest contribution to Qumran was an over 100-page-long book review, rightfully demolishing his colleague Allegro's *DJD*, V. It was only after recruiting collaborators that two volumes bearing the name of Strugnell and one that of Cross were belatedly published. Strugnell was assisted respectively by Elisha Qimron and D. J. Harrington for completing *DJD*, X, in 1994 and XXXIV in 1999, and Cross's edition of *DJD*, XVII, the Samuel fragments of Cave 4 entrusted to him more than fifty years earlier, was published in association with D. Parry in 2005. The last three volumes of the series (*DJD*, XXXII, by Eugene Ulrich and Peter Flint, XXXVII, by Émile Puech, and XL by Eileen Schuller and Carol Newsom) are dated 2008 and 2009.

The scholars who were steadily increasing in number and were either directly involved with Qumran or working in fields closely or remotely associated with the Scrolls were becoming more and more restless. Their research was hindered by their inability to consult the unpublished Qumran texts. Even worse, since no catalogue of the discovered Dead Sea documents was released, researchers did not even know whether Jerusalem did or did not hold texts which might be of interest to them. (The first full list of the contents of Caves 4 and 11, compiled by Emanuel Tov, was published by him, at my invitation as editor, in the *Journal of Jewish Studies*, in the spring issue of 1992 (volume 43, pp. 101–36).) The privilege conferred on the members of the group by their invitation to the editorial team was not put to good use. Requests for information were not refused; quite often they were simply met by a stone wall of silence and remained unanswered. There may have been exceptions of which I am not aware, but if there were they only proved the rule.

The resentfulness of the 'have-nots', the vast majority, was exacerbated by the two unproductive Harvard professors' nonchalant and snail-pace practice of editing by proxy. They passed on the texts entrusted to them to their graduate students, and a series of doctoral dissertations – some of them excellent – slowly trickled in while the rest of the learned and learning world was kept at a safe distance from the promised land of the unpublished Scrolls.

Hearing the groans of scholars, the press, too, pricked up its ears. The propriety was queried, even the legality, of the 'closed shop' policy introduced by de Vaux and maintained by his successors, Benoit and Strugnell. Moreover, investigative journalists began to wonder whether something sinister was going on behind the smokescreen of non-publication. Following earlier accusations levelled by Allegro against the Catholic conspiracy of de Vaux and his associates, and ignoring the fact that F. M. Cross was a Protestant, they began to circulate the rumour that the absence of editorial activity resulted from an order issued by the Vatican. It was murmured that some Qumran texts contained matters highly damaging to Christianity and consequently de Vaux was ordered by his Roman task-masters to keep them secret at all cost. To put an end to the growing speculations and, if possible, reawaken the lethargic editorial process, an opportunity arose in Britain to bring this whole scandalous business into the open. Mark Geller, director of the Institute of Jewish Studies at University College London, received in 1986 a substantial sum of money to organize an international conference on an academic subject connected with Judaism that would be of interest to the general public as well as to scholars. He came to Oxford to consult the renowned Roman historian Fergus Millar and myself and we agreed that a symposium on the present state of Dead Sea Scrolls research would be an appropriate topic, especially as the year of the Symposium, 1987, would mark the fortieth anniversary of the discovery of the first Qumran Scrolls. Bringing together all the official editors and subjecting them to the moral pressure of public scrutiny might force them to put their cards on the table and come up with an acceptable plan of action. The logjam might thus be unblocked . . . provided that the editors accepted the invitation and attended the conference.

Almost all came, led by Strugnell, since 1984 editor-in-chief designate after the resignation of Benoit. (Editor-in-chief designate means that, having been elected three years earlier by his colleagues on the editorial team, his appointment was still under consideration and thus unconfirmed by Israel's Department of Antiquities.) Only Milik stayed away: he did not decline the invitation; according to his time-honoured habit, he just refrained from answering. Despite the coincidence of the opening of the Symposium with the British general election on 11 June 1987, the London press devoted much attention to the event and followed it with keen interest. The week before the meeting, on 6 June 1987, *The Times* called for action in the knowledge that many scholars from outside the closed circle of the editors were raring to do the job. The outcome of the conference was to a large extent predictable. There were superficial apologies from the tardy editors and optimistic, but vague, predictions were made regarding the completion of the publication. Strugnell promised a detailed schedule. All that scholars and the world were expected to do was to trust it and him.

But Strugnell was faced with an unexpected proposal which was moved in the opening address and repeated at a public meeting held in the British Museum. As the organizer of the Symposium most directly involved with Qumran, it fell to me to welcome the participants and, carefully navigating between Scylla and Charybdis, I put forward what I thought was a fair middle course of action, catering for the conflicting interests of the editors, on the one hand, and the rest of the scholarly world on the other. The editors should have all the time they needed to complete their onerous work of detailed, punctilious transcription, commentary and annotation, but in the interest of the public good, they should in turn release *at once* the photographs of the unpublished texts so that anyone interested and academically qualified might have access to them for their research. The members of the editorial team had enjoyed many years of monopoly over the rest of the world. If, despite this, newcomers were to beat them in the race, they should blame only themselves. These words were received in dead silence in editorial quarters. However, when I repeated the proposal at a large public meeting – in front of the microphones of the BBC – it was met with an emphatic 'No' from editor-in-chief-to-be Strugnell. In his view, photographs without the editors' detailed explanations would be useless, misleading and would result in bad scholarship, implying that only members of the official group had received the divine charisma to enable them to read and understand the documents. Besides, he wondered, impertinently, about all the fuss. Another mammoth collection of ancient documents, the Greek papyrus fragments from Oxyrhynchus in Egypt, relating to the New Testament and early Christianity, although discovered at the end of the nineteenth century, was still far from being fully edited. Compared with Oxyrhynchus, the publication of the Qumran manuscripts was proceeding rapidly! The protesters' complaints were hysterical.

On the face of it, then, the British effort to breathe life into the editorial process proved useless. Nevertheless it had the indirect effect of increasing public awareness of the 'academic scandal of the century'. I also made a private approach to the Israeli minister of education, who was ultimately in charge of the Scrolls, and advised him not to confirm Strugnell's appointment as editor-in-chief unless he gave free access to the photographs of the unpublished Scroll fragments without delay. This initiative also petered out. Receipt of the communication was never acknowledged and its contents were somehow leaked to Strugnell and his colleagues. However, according to a well-informed Jerusalem source, the letter was noted and had its effect three years later when Strugnell's six years of inefficient editorship were brought to an inglorious end.

Meanwhile, the pretence that all was well continued with the blessing of the Israel Antiquities Authority (IAA), whose leaders, after years of hesitation, rubber-stamped Strugnell's appointment. The depleted editorial team was enlarged by including several former Harvard doctoral students who had been working on the edition of various Cave 4 texts. There was even a major innovation: Israeli Qumran experts Elisha Qimron and Emanuel Tov, the first Jews to be involved with the Cave 4 material, were added to the team of editors. Yet Strugnell's days as Scrolls' boss were numbered. The international media, alerted in the wake of the London Symposium, were after his blood. In 1989, a columnist of *Scientific American* accused him of impeding the research of other scholars; and the editor of *Biblical Archaeology Review* (*BAR*), Hershel Shanks, declared open season on Strugnell. A series of articles appeared and Strugnell was given the right of reply. He treated his critics as people of no significance: they were in his words 'a bunch of fleas who are in the business of annoying us'. *BAR* retorted with a caricature picturing the fleas and quoting their 'bites', starting with my by then proverbial 'academic scandal of the twentieth century'. Under the pressure of this kind of 'persecution', on top of his drink problem, John Strugnell broke down. Interviewed by a reporter from *Ha'aretz*, the leading Tel Aviv daily (on 9 November 1990), he completed the process of self-destruction by declaring Judaism a 'horrible religion' which should have disappeared long ago. He later denied that he was an anti-Semite and attributed his outburst to one of his manic-depressive fits. Nevertheless, this unfortunate act was too much even for his colleagues on the editorial team and he was forced to resign. In December 1990, the IAA, suddenly opting for diplomatic tact, relieved him of his editorship on health grounds, and appointed as his successor the Israeli Emanuel Tov, professor of biblical studies at the Hebrew University of Jerusalem early in 1991. After nearly four decades, a new age was dawning, but all was not yet sunshine and blue sky.

2. An Israeli Editor-in-Chief

Tov started his editorship with two masterstrokes. Whether by persuasion or arm-twisting, he first prevailed upon Joseph Milik, who by then had been editorially largely inactive in the Qumran field for a dozen years, to relinquish the huge pile of unpublished manuscripts given to him by de Vaux almost forty years earlier. This was a sad occasion as Milik was incontestably by far the best decipherer and editor of Qumran texts and the most productive of all the members of the editorial team. But by 1991, pushing seventy, affected by earlier alcoholism and other health problems, he was no longer his genial self of the 1950s. He reacted badly to this act of 'ingratitude', but alas the move was necessary. He was, however, generous enough to help younger scholars who inherited his unfinished lot. Turning his back on the Scrolls, and devoting himself instead to Nabataean epigraphy and Polish philology, he died in Paris in January 2006, aged eighty-three years.

Tov's second brilliant move was to increase tenfold the size of the original editorial team, raising it to over sixty – Jews and non-Jews, Israelis and people from all the various continents. I was one of them and had the privilege of being allowed to choose the texts (the Cave 4 fragments of the Community Rule) I wanted to edit. I invited my former student, Professor Philip Alexander of Manchester, to join me and our volume, *DJD*, XXVI duly appeared in 1998 and we contributed also to *DJD*, XXXVI in 2000.

However, there was one thing Emanuel Tov would not or maybe could not do. He did not abolish the closed shop system invented by de Vaux, and inexplicably adopted by the IAA. Nevertheless, this nefarious policy was already doomed. Unwittingly its upholders themselves undermined it in the wake of the 1973 Arab–Israeli war. It was then decided in Jerusalem that as an insurance policy for the protection of the Scrolls in the event of another armed conflict, photographic archives would be deposited in the United States and Britain. Three such safe havens were selected: Hebrew Union College in Cincinnati, Ohio, the Ancient Manuscript Center in Claremont, California, and the Oxford Centre for Hebrew and Jewish Studies at Yarnton, outside Oxford. The condition laid down by the IAA was that photographs of unpublished texts must not be shown to anyone apart from the official editors or persons formally authorized by the editor-in-chief. As an illustration, a notice affixed to the door of the Oxford Centre's 'Qumran Room', containing a filing cabinet filled with photos of unpublished Dead Sea documents, proclaimed that no one could gain access to them without the written permission of Professor John Strugnell. Protests to the president of the Oxford Centre (David Paterson) were of no avail as he himself, unknown to the Board of Governors, had signed an agreement with the IAA.

More or less simultaneously with the handing over of the photographic collections came the production of a handwritten catalogue or concordance of all the words appearing in the non-biblical Qumran texts. The listing of each word within its context on index cards goes back to the late 1950s. It was only in 1988, however, that John

Strugnell decided to publish privately twenty-five photo-copied exemplars of this index to be made available only to official Scrolls editors. Unauthorized copies of the con-cordance circulated widely all over the place. In Oxford there were at least three of them, one belonging to me. Unforeseen by the IAA and the editorial team, these photographic archives and the concordance sounded the death knell to the policy of secrecy. Plans to lift the embargo on general access to the Scroll images were con-ceived in at least two of the three centres with photo-graphic archives, one of which was successful.

A petition by graduate students of Hebrew Union Col-lege to be allowed to consult the archive was given short shrift by the College authorities. On a higher level, two governors of the Oxford Centre for Hebrew and Jewish Studies (Martin Goodman and myself) submitted at the end of August 1991 a proposal to the board to rescind the agreement with the IAA on the grounds that it was against freedom of research and, in case the Israeli authorities refused to negotiate, to unilaterally grant bona fide scholars access to all the photographs, published or unpublished. That there was little chance to persuade the IAA to change their mind was obvious from a letter written by General Amir Drori, director of the IAA, to the president of the Oxford Centre: 'Your request to grant Professor Vermes permission to study unpublished Qumran material de-posited in your photo collection contradicts our recent agreement which guarantees that such material is merely safeguarded in your institution. Please reaffirm our pro-vision that this material is strictly beyond the reach of scholars save those who were allotted material personally by us.'

A meeting of the board of the Oxford Centre was called

for the beginning of October 1991 and promised to be stormy as the president opposed the idea and the governors were divided. Meanwhile, to my regret, the initiative was overtaken by events in the United States. In 1991 Ben Zion Wacholder, professor of Talmud at Hebrew Union College, Cincinnati, obtained permission from John Strugnell to photocopy the concordance for the HUC library. A graduate student of the College, Martin Abegg, by now an internationally renowned Qumran scholar and the compiler of the two-volume standard concordance of the Scrolls, explained to Wacholder that with computer help he would be able to reconstruct whole texts from the word list. The professor at once proposed that they should proceed to publish them. Though worried, needlessly as it turned out, that the venture might compromise his academic future, Abegg agreed and with the help of Hershel Shanks and the Biblical Archaeology Society of Washington, DC a slim volume entitled *A Preliminary Edition of the Unpublished Dead Sea Scrolls* appeared on 4 September 1991. Next day, the *New York Times* trumpeted, 'Computer hacker bootlegs version of Dead Sea Scrolls'. Piracy, screamed some of the official editors – one of them (É. Puech) referred to it as plagiarism even in 2006 – and they threatened to sue authors and publishers, though nothing happened immediately.

Here I am obliged to introduce another personal detail. On 20 September, I received a telephone call from the archaeology correspondent of the London *Times*, Professor Norman Hammond, and was informed of the imminent release by the Huntington Library of Pasadena, California, of a full photo archive of the Dead Sea Scrolls. He asked me for a comment. Next morning *The Times*, beating the American media by twenty-four hours, announced the lifting of the embargo on the Dead Sea Scrolls and quoted my enthusiastic endorsement of it.

One might have thought the Huntington Library was the last place to pull off such a coup. It specialized in Shakespeare, Renaissance literature and English and American history. Its involvement with the Scrolls was purely accidental and is connected with the nearby Claremont Ancient Manuscript Center, and its patroness, Mrs Elizabeth Hay Bechtel. Wishing to obtain photographs of all the Dead Sea Scrolls for her Claremont Library, Mrs Bechtel, accompanied by the Huntington's chief photographer, paid a visit to the IAA in Jerusalem and, as it can happen only to multi-millionairesses, she returned to California not with one, but with two copies of the photo archive of the Scrolls. One of them went to the Claremont Center under the usual proviso of keeping the unpublished material locked away, but Betty Bechtel treated the other set as her personal property. Soon afterwards, she clashed with the directors of Claremont and unwisely they removed her from the board.

Understandably piqued, she decided to deposit her Dead Sea Scrolls pictures at a rival institution, the much more prestigious Huntington Library, and subsequently donated them to it together with funds to construct an air-conditioned vault for the photographic negatives. This happened in the early 1980s and the legal deed of gift, of which I have a copy, and in which Mrs Bechtel asserted her right of ownership and inserted no clause concerning an embargo on any part of the collection, dates to April 1982. Nothing was heard about the Huntington Scrolls during the following eight years, but they were accidentally 'rediscovered' in 1990 by the newly appointed director of the library, Dr William A. Moffett. During a visit to the librarians' office, Moffett noticed the air-conditioned vault and learned to his amazement that it concealed hot property, the photographic duplicates of the Scrolls which in 1990 had been the talk of the town in the international media. Wrongly deducing from articles he had read in the British press in the summer of 1991 that the Oxford Centre for Hebrew and Jewish Studies was ready to open to the public its Qumran photos, Moffett, with the blessing of the Huntington board, decided to beat Oxford to it. A press conference was originally scheduled for 16 October to coincide with an American TV special on the Scrolls, but fearing that he might miss the boat, Moffett advanced the news release to 22 September 1991, announcing that any authorized reader of the Huntington would have access to all the photos of the Dead Sea Scrolls! Although the full front-page article in the *New York Times* had been scooped by the London *Times* twenty-four hours earlier, it was still an epoch-making news story.

3. Outbreak of Revolution

The mother of all Scrolls rows broke out next day. The IAA and members of the original editorial team, whose forty-year-long privilege was on the point of being shattered, were talking of theft and threatened with legal proceedings, but within three days came a volte-face. No doubt advised by their lawyers that they had no leg to stand on vis-à-vis the Huntington, and that the question of the legal ownership of the Scrolls was political dynamite, the Israeli archaeological leadership was advised to climb down. On 25 September it made a complete U-turn and issued a statement: 'The Israel Antiquities Authority agrees in principle to facilitate free access to the photographs of the Scrolls.' They invited all the institutions with photographic archives to meet the IAA and the official editorial team the following December to discuss how to proceed in the new circumstances, and how to protect, if not all the old procrastinators, then at least the work of scholars recruited in recent years. They were clinging to a broken reed and sought some extra time to lick their wounds.

Moffett, encouraged by many and after consulting me on the telephone, declared his unwillingness to attend the Jerusalem gathering without a prior 'unequivocal surrender' by the Israeli opposition. Realizing the hopelessness of their case and pressed by the education committee of the Israeli parliament, the IAA and the editors caved in and on 27 October 1991 all the restrictions were lifted. The Qumran revolution, fighting for research freedom, triumphed. Even before the official lifting of the embargo, I decided to make the unpublished Cave 4 fragments of the Community Rule allocated to me the subject of open weekly seminars at the Oriental Institute of Oxford. Not only local Hebraists flocked to it, but also a number of colleagues and research students from Cambridge and London, as well as columnists of London newspapers.

The doom-laden forecast by the official editors, who predicted a flood of errors and 'bad scholarship' arising from uncontrolled access to the Scrolls, of course did not materialize. There were no more silly ideas floated after 1991 than there had been before. On the contrary, free access to the unpublished fragments breathed new life into the scholarship and Qumran specialists were in constant demand by newspapers for fresh reports, proving that the subject continued to be of great interest all over the world.

Soon, the four institutions – HUC, Claremont, Oxford and the Huntington – ceased to be the only, somewhat cumbersome, pathways to the Scrolls. One month after the IAA's change of policy, in November 1991, the Biblical Archaeology Society published in two volumes *A Facsimile Edition of the Dead Sea Scrolls*, a complete set of photographs, edited by two Californian professors, Robert H. Eisenman and James M. Robinson. In 1992, with the approval of the IAA, Emanuel Tov, the new editor-in-chief, issued a microfiche edition of the whole Qumran material. Finally, in 1997, entering the computer age, a digitized version of all the manuscript images of the Dead Sea Scrolls was brought out on three CDs by Oxford University Press in association with the Dutch firm, Brill Academic Publishers of Leiden. So today, scholars capable of deciphering these images can pursue their Qumran research in the comfort of their own studies at any time, day or night.

How has the new situation affected the publication of the Scrolls, first and foremost, the large bulk of fragments from Cave 4? Let us look at the facts. Before the watershed year of 1991, only three volumes of the *DJD* series devoted to Cave 4 had appeared – in 1968, 1977 and 1982. From 1992 to 2005 twenty-three further volumes saw the light of day, the rest following in 2008 and 2009. The change in publication rate was due to the highly efficient and per-suasive stewardship of the editor-in-chief, Emanuel Tov, and to the awareness of the editors that unless they hurried, someone else might publish their texts first. Removal of the monopolistic status seriously improved the speed of production. Besides, as I have noted, the images are already available in photograph, microfiche or CD-ROM form. Moreover, a two-volume study edition, published in 1997–8 by F. García Martínez and E. J. C. Tigchelaar, includes the Hebrew transcription and English translation of all the texts.

The armistice that followed the war over the Scrolls brought together combatants from both camps. Collaboration has restarted and there have been only rare signs of surviving animosity. A large international conference and the exhibition of a rich collection of Qumran Scrolls and artefacts were organized by the IAA in 1993 at the Library of Congress in Washington, DC, at which I, a constant former critic of the policy adopted by the original editorial team, was invited to deliver the keynote address. Four years later, in 1997, the monumental Golden Jubilee Congress, convened in Jerusalem, attended by everybody who was somebody in Scrolls research and concluded with a magnificent open air dinner at Qumran, brought together the previously warring factions in peaceful scholarly communion in a place where the thermometer showed 40 degrees Celsius at midnight. In true Israeli fashion, the specially composed music was broadcast so loud that it threatened to wake up the dead sectaries in the nearby cemetery.

The only occasion on which old resentments resurfaced was during the lawsuit initiated by Elisha Qimron of the University of Beer Sheba (Strugnell's late recruit to the official team) and supported by the Israeli archaeological establishment, against the editor of *Biblical Archaeology Review*, Hershel Shanks, considered in Jerusalem to be the chief culprit for the IAA's loss of face. Shanks, in his preface to the photographic edition of the Qumran fragments by Robert Eisenman and James Robinson, reprinted Qimron's reconstructed text of a Qumran document (MMT, short for *Miqsat Ma'ase ha-Torah* or 'Some Observances of the Law'), but without acknowledging Qimron's contribution to it. Qimron would have been totally justified in demanding that this omission be put right. Instead he sued Shanks for damages amounting to $250,000 and was awarded less than one fifth of this sum ($43,000) by the Jerusalem district court and subsequently by the Israeli supreme court. A modern author's entitlement to copyright in an ancient text has become a legal test case and has been the subject of a conference in 1999 at the University of Edinburgh, followed by a printed version of the papers, *On Scrolls, Artefacts and Intellectual Property* (2001), edited by Timothy H. Lim and others.

The copyright formula attached to *DJD*, X, edited by Qimron and John Strugnell (with further contributions from J. Sussman and A. Yardeni), is quite unusual. Instead of assigning the copyright, as did all the previous volumes, to Oxford University Press, this volume omits the mention of the co-editor and other contributors and singles out Qimron as the owner of the copyright in combination with the IAA: '© Elisha Qimron 1994, without derogating from any right vested in the Israel Antiquities Authority with regard to the Scrolls' fragments, photographs, and any other material which is in the possession of the Authority, and which the Authority has permitted Qimron to use for the purposes of the Work, and its inclusion therein.'

This provides a splendid caveat for copyright lawyers in future.

The release of the hitherto unpublished Qumran material has placed the whole contents of the eleven caves at the disposal of the confraternity of scholars and all interested persons. As far as the scriptural books are concerned, English readers can avail themselves of *The Dead Sea Scrolls Bible*, translated with commentary by Martin Abegg, Jr.,

Peter Flint and Eugene Ulrich (1999). The volume comprises all the scriptural texts from Qumran as well as those Apocrypha (Ben Sira and Tobit) and Pseudepigrapha (Jubilees, 1 Enoch and apocryphal Psalms) that the authors think belonged to the Qumran Bible. There are three English translations of the non-biblical documents. My 1962 volume, *The Dead Sea Scrolls in English*, became in 2004 *The Complete Dead Sea Scrolls in English* in the Penguin Classics series. Textual quotations in the present volume are borrowed from this translation. F. García Martínez and E. J. C. Tigchelaar issued in 1997–8 a two-volume Hebrew/Aramaic study edition, *The Dead Sea Scrolls*, with facing English rendering. Finally, Michael Wise, Martin Abegg and Edward Cook produced *The Dead Sea Scrolls: A New Translation* in 1996 and revised it in 2005. My translation is intended to be literary; the other two strive to remain as close as possible to the Semitic original.

After sixty years of discovery and study, the text of the Dead Sea Scrolls and the enormous scholarly and general literature generated by them stare at us at long last from the bookshelves. All that remains for us to find out is what they actually mean.

Postscript: The Nonsensical Theory of a Vatican Conspiracy

After John Allegro's earlier insinuations of a Church conspiracy, two 'investigative' writers, Michael Baigent and Richard Leigh, came up with the answer to the dilemma in a book melodramatically entitled *The Dead Sea Scrolls Deception*, published in London in May 1991. They believed they had found the key to the Vatican conspiracy in the institution of the Pontifical Biblical Commission (on the Commission, see chapter I). Misrepresenting it as a latter-day Inquisition steeped in secrecy, and noting that Father Roland de Vaux had become a consultant of the Commission, the two authors drew the conclusion that the editor-in-chief from 1955 until his death in 1971 was under obligation to ensure (a) that the Scrolls are dated so early (second and first century BCE) that they are chronologically neatly distanced from the New Testament; and (b) that no manuscript that might threaten Catholic doctrine was released. This explains the years of inactivity of the editorial team under de Vaux and under his successors.

Yet the theory is without any foundation. The dating of the historical context into which the Scrolls are placed by mainstream scholarship had been worked out by historians who were not controlled by the Catholic Church (Sukenik, Dupont-Sommer, Vermes, Yadin). Members of de Vaux's editorial team later adopted their views. As for stopping the publication to keep religiously compromising texts away from public gaze, it does not make sense. All the manuscripts from Caves 1–3 and 5–10 appeared between 1950 and 1962 and the longest Qumran document, the Temple Scroll, was published by the Israeli Yigael Yadin in Hebrew in 1977 and in English in 1983. So the presumed secrets must have lain among the thousands of fragments found in Cave 4. But de Vaux was not a decipherer of texts. If something explosive had been discovered in them, it would have been done by members of the team, several of whom (Allegro, Cross and Hunzinger) had never been, and Milik ceased to be, under the control of the Vatican. It is inconceivable that they would have remained silent just to please de Vaux or honour his memory.

Besides, in October 1991, a bare five months after the

appearance of the notorious *Dead Sea Scrolls Deception*, all restrictions had been lifted and, despite the keenest search by the entire scholarly world for hidden explosives, no one came up with anything that might shake the foundations of Christianity, Judaism or any religion. The one claim advanced by Robert Eisenman and Michael Wise that among the unpublished Cave 4 fragments there was a reference to a 'slain Messiah' turned out to be the result of a misinterpretation. The Messiah was not slain; he did the slaying.

This would leave only one further possibility to account for the conspiracy theory. Roland de Vaux, on his own, unnoticed by the members of the editorial team, selected and destroyed materials held by him to be inimical to Christianity. Only ignoramuses could imagine such a scenario. Without the full cooperation of his colleagues, he would not have been able to find and decipher those dangerous fragments. A more sensible explanation for the delays must be found.

In fact, to those familiar with the Qumran editorial problems and with the editors who were put in charge, the mystery of their procrastination was not a mystery at all: it resulted from the combination of three defects. The edition of the Qumran texts was a complex operation which required good organization and strategy – and de Vaux's plan was inadequate. The original team assembled by him was too small for the enormous task and was not kept under strict control. When progress proved slow and unsatisfactory, the editor-in-chief did not enlarge his staff. Some of the untried editors did not possess the publishing expertise that was expected of them, and should have resigned or been dismissed. Finally, in the absence of a strong hand overseeing the project, obstinacy was allowed to prevail among inefficient editors. They were determined to resist outside pressure; instead of asking for help from a multitude of willing hands, their attitude was 'Keep off our patch!'

The truth is that the delays in publishing were due not to machinations and conspiracy from Church authorities, but to very ordinary human failings on the part of Roland de Vaux and his over-privileged, obstinate and unco-operative 'international and interconfessional' team of editors.

Part Two

VI

What is New in the Non-Sectarian Dead Sea Scrolls?

The rehearsing of the heated debates about the Dead Sea Scrolls, written in Hebrew, Aramaic and Greek and retrieved from eleven Qumran caves, has never ceased to be fascinating, but exhilaration was occasionally mixed with anger and despondency. These negative reactions were provoked by human weaknesses. The ideal course of action inspired by scholarly zeal was often interfered with by obstinacy, jealousy and plain selfishness. Viewed from the perspective of six decades of study within the multicoloured background of the ancient world, how do the Qumran texts appear today and what have we learned from them? I will try to provide an answer under three headings:

1. What has Qumran taught us about ancient Hebrew and Aramaic manuscripts?

2. Have we discovered anything new about works previously known in Jewish literature?

3. What kind of novelty have the hitherto unknown Dead Sea Scrolls, which contain no sectarian ideas, revealed to the interested public?

The contribution of the manuscripts which mirror the particular preoccupations of the authors representing the Qumran sect will be examined in chapter VII.

1. Qumran and Ancient Hebrew and Aramaic Manuscripts

The most amazing novelty of the Dead Sea Scrolls consists in their sheer existence. Ancient Jewish leather and papyrus manuscripts, dating to the period preceding the destruction of the Temple of Jerusalem in 70 CE, or more precisely to the epoch between the last quarter of the second century BCE and 68 CE, the presumed capture of Qumran by the Roman army, is to all intents and purposes unparalleled, or almost unparalleled. Before 1947 we had only a small Hebrew papyrus fragment from that age, the Nash papyrus, variously dated from the second century BCE to the first century CE, which contained brief extracts from the Bible, including the Ten Commandments. By contrast, Qumran has yielded a variety of over 900 original compositions, most of them written on leather, about 14 per cent (131 texts) on papyrus, and a handful on broken pottery known as ostraca. Of course, we had some idea from rabbinic writings of a later age, especially from the post-Talmudic tractate *Soferim* (Scribes), about how manuscripts, above all biblical manuscripts, had to be produced, but it was at Qumran that scrolls originating from the era preceding the destruction of the Temple of Jerusalem came to light for the first time and disclosed how in reality the scribes of antiquity practised their profession.

The technical term describing the process of manuscript-making is 'codicology', but in the Qumran context the word, though regularly used, is strictly a misnomer. Codicology refers to the production of codices or books, consisting of leaves of leather or papyrus sown together into a volume. But in the Dead Sea manuscripts the texts are inscribed only on one side of the sheets and they are then rolled up. They are scrolls, not books.

What kind of writing material did the scribes use? Most of the manuscripts were penned on sheep or goat skin specially prepared by craftsmen. According to Roland de Vaux, both at Qumran and at the nearby Ain Feshkha there was a tannery which, among other things, could produce leather suitable for manuscripts (see chapter II, pp. 35, 38). Once prepared and smoothed down, the skin was cut to varying sizes. The scribe, having chosen the correct number of sheets, appropriate for the length of the work he was to copy, first proceeded to line them horizontally for the writing of the text – the letters hanging from and not written on the lines – and vertically at both ends of the columns, thus determining their width. On average, a Qumran sheet carried five columns of text. The scribes used vegetable ink which was kept in inkpots. Some of these were made of baked clay, others of bronze. The latter could affect the chemical composition of the ink, which in time could damage the leather, as was the case with several columns of the document known as the Genesis Apocryphon from Cave 1.

When a work, written on several sheets of leather, was completed, the scribe or some other craftsman stitched them together to form a scroll. To ensure that the sheets would be sown together in the correct order, the scribe discretely numbered them, using the successive letters of the Hebrew alphabet at one of the top corners. Some of these marks have survived. Also, to safeguard the text on the opening sheet of a scroll, the scribe left a broad unwritten margin at the beginning to protect the first column of writing from obliteration by repeated finger-marks. Finally, to indicate the identity of the document contained in a rolled-up scroll, the title was written on the outside, as a few surviving examples demonstrate.

Codicological features have been used by scholars in the interpretation of the contents of manuscripts. The Aramaic Genesis Apocryphon, just mentioned, lost both its beginning and its end. As it now stands, the early biblical story starts with the birth of Noah and the narrative breaks off soon after the beginning of the section dealing with Abraham. It had been supposed that not a great amount was missing from the opening of the document until a hawk-eyed young Anglo-Israeli scholar, Matthew Moshe Morgenstern, noticed the Hebrew letter *pe*, which is the seventeenth letter of the alphabet, at the top of column 5 of the surviving manuscript. The next sheet carried the eighteenth and the following one the nineteenth letter. These observations led Morgenstern to the conclusion that no less than sixteen sheets were missing from the beginning, leaving ample space for a detailed retelling of the accounts of the creation of the world, Adam and Eve, Cain and Abel, Enoch, etc.

On one occasion, a codicological feature also helped me to explain a peculiarity distinguishing one of the ten Cave 4 manuscripts of the important Community Rule (4Q258) from the complete scroll of this document found in Cave 1 (1QS). The latter is made up of an introductory section describing the ritual of the entry into the covenant (columns 1–4), the main body of the rules (columns 5–10), and a final hymn (columns 10–11). By contrast, the Cave 4 manuscript in question (4QSd or 4Q258) begins directly with the rule section, corresponding to column 5 of the Cave 1 Scroll, but it is preceded by a wide blank margin which suggests that this was the start of the manuscript. This peculiarity, combined with characteristic linguistic details, appears to imply that this version of the Community Rule represents an earlier – possibly the earliest – version of the writing and that its placement between the introductory liturgy and the poetic conclusion of the Cave 1 manuscript represents the augmented final edition of the text.

2. Qumran and Previously Known Jewish Literature

Thanks to the Qumran discoveries, three classes of ancient Jewish literature, the Bible or Palestinian Jewish Holy Scriptures, the Apocrypha or books added to the Hebrew Bible in Greek-speaking Jewish circles, and the Pseudepigrapha, or influential Jewish religious writings written in Hebrew or Aramaic that failed to enter the Palestinian or the Hellenistic Bible, can now be seen in a totally fresh light. Our survey will first consider the list or canon of the Jewish scriptural books and afterwards the text of the official or canonical Hebrew Bible.

(a) The canon of the Scriptures

What constitutes the Bible is nowhere strictly defined in the ancient literary sources of Judaism. It was the privilege of the successive religious authorities (Sadducee chief priests, Pharisee leaders and rabbis) to determine the list of books. It was later called the 'canon', using Christian terminology from the Greek word meaning 'rule', which in various places, circles and ages formed the authoritative sources of the Jewish religion. Traditionally the canon is divided into two or three sections. We encounter in several of our sources, including the New Testament, the twofold designation referring to Scripture as the Law and the Prophets, but at the end the rabbis settled for the threefold *TeNaK*, the abbreviation or acronym of *T*orah, *N*eviim, *K*etuvim, or Law–Prophets–Writings. About the end of the second century BCE, the grandson of Jesus ben Sira, author of the Book of Ecclesiasticus, translating into Greek his grandfather's work, speaks in his foreword of 'the Law, the Prophets and *the other books*', while Jesus of Nazareth is quoted in the Gospel of Luke as alluding to 'the Law, the Prophets and the Psalms' (Luke 24:24), the Psalter being the first work in the third section of the Hebrew canon, the *Ketuvim* or the Writings. One of the Dead Sea Scrolls, 'Some Observances of the Law' (*MMT = Miqsat Ma'ase ha-Torah*), also attests a formulation similar to St Luke, namely 'the Law and the Prophets and David'. However, none of the surviving Qumran documents or any other Jewish writing of the period defines the content of the canon by actually enumerating the titles of all the sacred books. Owing to this absence of a list and to the fact that even in the early second century CE questions were raised in rabbinic circles about the canonicity of the Song of Solomon (too erotic for the liking of some rabbis) and Ecclesiastes (because of the apparent doubts expressed in it regarding God), more than one Qumran scholar maintains that no proper canon of the Old Testament existed until some time after the destruction of the Temple in 70 CE.

Such academic scepticism, arising from the lack of positive evidence of an official canon, fails to pay sufficient attention to a statement of the most reliable witness of first century CE Judaism, the generally well-informed historian Flavius Josephus, who himself belonged to the upper class of the Jerusalem priesthood. On one occasion he expressly declared that among the Jews only *twenty-two* books enjoyed confidence, implying that only they were held to be authoritative or canonical, and no other writing was worthy of equal trust (see *Against Apion* I:38). Without citing individual titles, Josephus lists the five books of Moses, thirteen books of the Prophets and four books of hymns and wisdom (I:38–40). According to St Jerome (*c.* 342–420), who lived for many years in Palestine and was well versed in rabbinic traditions, the figure twenty-two was commonly accepted by Jews – and not only by Josephus – as representing the number of books in the biblical canon. In his Prologue to the Books of Samuel, Jerome presents the Jewish account of the books of the Old Testament as follows: (1–5) Law of Moses, (6) Joshua, (7) Judges + Ruth, (8) 1–2 Samuel, (9) 1–2 Kings, (10) Isaiah, (11) Jeremiah + Lamentations, (12) Ezekiel, (13) Twelve Minor Prophets, (14) Job, (15) Psalms, (16) Proverbs, (17) Ecclesiastes, (18) Song of Solomon, (19) Daniel, (20) 1–2 Chronicles, (21) Ezra + Nehemiah, (22) Esther.

So assuming that the traditional Palestinian Hebrew canon of the Bible was already in existence in the first century CE, or maybe even in the first century BCE, – the last composition to slip into the canon was the finally edited Book of Daniel around 160 BCE – what can one learn from the Dead Sea scriptural documents regarding the state of the Bible in the age of Jesus?

The first obvious conclusion one may draw is that the Dead Sea scriptural manuscripts do not represent a Samaritan collection since the Samaritan Bible consisted only of the Law of Moses. (The Samaritans were the inhabitants of the central region of the Holy Land between Judaea in the south and Galilee in the north, who cut themselves off from the Judaean Jews after their return from the Babylonian exile in the sixth century BCE.)

Next, since the eleven caves have proved the presence of all the books of the Bible except Esther either in scroll form or as fragments, it may be deduced that these books commanded at Qumran the same respect as in the rest of Palestinian Jewry. In other words, there was no difference between the Qumran Bible and the Hebrew Bible of the Palestinian Jewish population at large. Whether the absence of Esther is significant – it is missing also from the canon of the Greek Old Testament of Bishop Melito of Sardis (who died in 180 CE) – or merely accidental, is impossible to decide. From the fact that Cave 4 yielded remains of a writing akin to Esther, a kind of Aramaic proto-Esther (4Q550), published by J. T. Milik, we may infer that the Book of Esther was not deliberately excluded from the Qumran canon.

There are Scrolls experts, for instance the compilers of *The Dead Sea Scrolls Bible* (Martin Abegg, Peter Flint and Eugene Ulrich), who presume that at Qumran the Scriptures included works considered non-canonical in mainstream Judaism. As has already been stated (see chapter V, pp. 88–9), they suggest that Ecclesiasticus and Tobit from among the Apocrypha, the Books of Jubilees and Enoch from the Pseudepigrapha and some apocryphal psalms included in the Psalms Scroll from Cave 11, had attained canonical status among the Qumran people. The hypothesis is not unthinkable, but it is in no way compelling either. After all, the Letter of Jude (verses 15–16) in the New Testament quotes a prophecy of Enoch without necessarily implying that for universal Christianity the Book of Enoch counted as Holy Scripture just as it did for the Ethiopian Church where it was held to be canonical.

The number of copies in which a biblical book is extant among the Dead Sea Scrolls is considered significant by many scholars and probably rightly so. Among the 215 biblical manuscripts found in the Qumran caves, the books best attested are the Psalms (37 copies), followed by Deuteronomy (30) and Isaiah (21). It is worth noting that these are the works that are the most often cited in the New Testament too: the Psalms 68 times, Isaiah 63 times and Deuteronomy 39 times. This can hardly be due to pure coincidence.

(b) The biblical text

One may recall from chapter I that the chief characteristic of the traditional or Masoretic Bible (Masorah = tradition) was textual uniformity. The strictly controlled medieval manuscripts produced by careful scribes displayed practically no meaningful variants. The only discrepancies, apart from very occasional scribal errors, related to systems of spelling. The Dead Sea scriptural manuscripts, on the other hand, present a more heterogeneous picture. According to the classification of Emanuel Tov, one of the greatest experts of the text of the Hebrew Bible and the editor-in-chief of the Scrolls, the scriptural manuscripts from Qumran fall into five categories. Of these, the largest, representing 60 per cent of the total, is designated as proto-Masoretic, being very similar to the text handed down by later Jewish tradition. Another 20 per cent attest the technical idiosyncrasies, peculiar orthography and grammar of the Qumran scribes (for instance the use of archaic Hebrew letters for the writing of divine names and the copious occurrence of certain consonants to indicate vowels, for example Y (*yod*) and W (*waw*) to suggest the vowels *i* and *o* or *u*. There is a smaller group, amounting to 5 per cent of the total, reminiscent of significant variants found in the Samaritan Bible and in the old Greek or Septuagint version of the Hebrew Scriptures. Finally, a not-insubstantial number of manuscripts (15 per cent) are classified as non-aligned because they sometimes agree with the Masoretic text, sometimes with the Samaritan or the Septuagint, and on other occasions depart from all of them. Tov's arguments, set out in two major books, *Textual Criticism of the Hebrew Bible* (1992) and *Scribal Practices and Approaches reflected in the Texts found in the Judean Desert* (2004), though questioned by some, are solidly argued and largely persuasive.

Non-specialist readers may find these remarks some-what baffling, but a few illustrative examples will help to understand the nature and importance of the Qumran contribution to the textual study of the Bible. Before the Dead Sea discoveries, some of the discrepancies in the Samaritan Torah were identified as changes due to doctri-nal differences (e.g. the replacement of Jerusalem and Mount Zion by Samaria and Mount Gerizim, the site of the Samaritan Temple). Also, variant readings in the Greek Bible were often attributed to the Greek translator's de-liberate or unintentional interference with the original Hebrew text. As has been noted in chapter I (p. 11), before 1947, Bible experts still believed in the recoverability of the *Urtext* (the original author's original text), the recon-struction of which – with the help of the surviving copies and ancient translations – constituted the textual critic's ultimate aim and dream.

Now let us look at the Qumran evidence, first with a view to the Samaritan Law of Moses. In Exodus 10:5, both the traditional Hebrew Masoretic text (MT) and the Greek

Septuagint (LXX) offer a succinct statement regarding the plague of locusts:

And they (the locusts) shall eat every tree of yours which grows in the field.
(MT, LXX)

By contrast, the Samaritan version has a longer account which we find also in a Hebrew fragment of Exodus from Qumran Cave 4. (The details supplementary to the traditional Hebrew are printed in italics.)

[And they (the locusts) shall eat ev]ery *grass of the land and every* [*fruit of* the tree of yours which grows in the field.]
(4Q12, Sam)

Clearly the expansion has no doctrinal import. Hence the Cave 4 variant may, and probably should, be interpreted as an alternative reading of Exodus current among Jews before the parting of the ways with the Samaritans in the sixth century BCE. This reading was then adopted by the Samaritans but it continued to be copied, as the Qumran fragment indicates, by Palestinian Jews as well.

Moving now to the relationship between the Masoretic Hebrew text and the ancient Greek translation, at 2 Samuel 8:7 the Septuagint displays a considerably expanded version compared to the Hebrew text. The latter reads:

And David took the shields of gold which were carried by the servants of Hadadezer and brought them to Jerusalem.
(MT)

Against this stands the Greek text which adds the name of the land over which Hadadezer ruled, together with further details lifted from 1 Kings 14:25–6. (The supplements are printed in italics.)

And David took *the golden ornaments* which were *on* the servants of Adraazar, *king of Souba*, and brought them to Jerusalem. *And Sousakim, king of Egypt, took them when he went up to Jerusalem in the days of Roboam son of Solomon.*

(LXX)

The Hebrew fragment from Cave 4 attests a similar long account of the events including the Sousakim=Shoshak episode.

[And] David [t]ook th[e shields of gold which were on the servants of Hadadezer and brought them to Jerusa]l[em. *After-wards Shoshak, king of Egypt took*] them also [*when*] *he went up to Jer*[*usalem*] *in the days of Rehoboam son of Solo*[*mon.*]

(4Q51, 82–3)

We may conclude that this reading represents a Hebrew text current in Palestine which happened to be used by the Septuagint translator. Consequently, the divergence between the Masoretic text and the Septuagint must not be assigned to the action of the translator, but echoes a pre-existent Hebrew wording. It also suggests that in the Qumran age Hebrew texts corresponding to the Samaritan and the ancient Greek versions jointly circulated, thus buttressing the theory that the proto-Masoretic, Samaritan and Septuagint-type of Hebrew text forms happily co-existed before rabbinic censorship eliminated the last two around 100 CE.

The last sub-group, the non-aligned variety, exhibits features from diverse text forms, without wholly agreeing with any one of them. The Song of Moses in Deuteronomy 32:43 supplies a good example. The traditional Hebrew is noteworthy for its brevity.

> Rejoice, O nations, with his people;
> for he avenges the blood of his servants,
> and takes vengeance on his adversaries.
>
> (MT)

The Septuagint has an extended version in which the expressions 'sons of God' and 'angels of God' alternate as synonyms.

> *Rejoice, O heavens, with him*
> *and let all the angels of God worship him.*
> Rejoice, O nations with his people
> *and let all the sons of God declare him mighty.*
> For he shall avenge the blood of his *sons*,
> and shall take revenge on, *and pay justice to*, his enemies
> *and shall reward them that hate him.*
>
> (LXX)

The medium-length Qumran version constitutes a kind of halfway station between the long Septuagint and the short Masoretic text and uses the phrase 'gods' (*elohim*) in lieu of 'angels' or 'sons' of God.

> Rejoice, *O heavens*, with him
> and *all you 'gods'*, worship him.
> For he shall avenge the blood of his *sons*
> and shall take revenge *on* his enemies
> *and shall reward them that hate him.*
>
> (4Q44, fr. 5ii)

As has been observed, the traditional Masoretic text is usually the shortest whereas the Samaritan, the Septuagint and some of the Qumran versions are more verbose. However, it is impossible to decide whether the shorter text is an abridged version or the longer one an expansion. The axiom *lectio brevior est potior* (the shorter reading is stronger) is the brainchild of eighteenth- and nineteenth-century German textual critics closeted in their studies far distant from the reality of the ancient world.

The distinctive mark of the biblical texts found in the Qumran library is their elasticity. Before the establishment of the authoritative wording of the Hebrew Scriptures, as a result of the Pharisaic-rabbinic reorganization of Judaism in the decades following the destruction of the Temple in 70 CE, textual pluriformity reigned. The choice of the text and its interpretation were left in the hands of the local representatives of doctrinal authority. We even have evidence that a Qumran Bible commentator was aware of the existence of variants and was ready to employ them in his exposition of a biblical passage. In Habakkuk 2:16, 'Drink and *show your foreskin!*' (*he'arel* from the root *'RL*), the traditional Hebrew uses the image of a drunkard, who like Noah, discards his clothes and allows his foreskin to be seen. The Septuagint, in turn, translates a slightly differently structured Hebrew verb, *hera'el* (from the root *R'L*, made up of the same consonants as the forgoing verb *'RL* but placed in different order) which means 'to stagger', and gives, 'Drink and *stagger!*' The author of the Qumran Habakkuk Commentary, applying the prophecy to the 'Wicked Priest', the priestly enemy of the Dead Sea Community, skilfully plays with both ideas: 'For he did not circumcise *the foreskin* (*'RLH* from *'RL* as the traditional Hebrew) of his heart and *walked in the ways of drunkenness*', i.e. staggered as in the LXX (Commentary of Habakkuk 11:13–14). By contrast, the biblical manuscripts dating to the early second century, yielded by the caves of Murabba'at, attest only the traditional (proto-Masoretic) form of the scriptural text.

The causes of the textual elasticity of the Qumran Bible are manifold. On a superficial level they may be seen as the result of efforts of modernization of spelling and grammar, the search for stylistic variation and harmonization, but above all, in Professor Shemaryahu Talmon's words, they are due to 'insufficiently controlled copying'. Put positively, the Qumran scribes arrogated to themselves the right to creative freedom and considered it their duty to improve the work they were propagating. Such relative liberty could go hand in hand with the conviction that all they were doing was to transmit faithfully the *true meaning* of Scripture. As is often the case, Flavius Josephus has the last word on the matter. In his *Jewish Antiquities* I:17, he maintains that he has reproduced the details of the biblical record without adding anything to it, or removing from it, when in fact he has been doing the exact opposite while intending to transmit what in his view Scripture actually meant. Allowing us to perceive the situation that preceded the enforced unification of the biblical text is one of the chief innovations of the Dead Sea Scrolls. It is a major, indeed unique, contribution to an improved understanding of the history of the Bible.

(c) The Apocrypha

Of the fifteen books of the Bible of Hellenistic Jewry which are additional to the Palestinian Hebrew canon, only two are presumed to have been originally composed in

Greek (Wisdom of Solomon and 2 Maccabees), while the rest are translations into Greek from Hebrew or Aramaic. None of these were known in their Semitic original until the discovery of the Hebrew Ecclesiasticus in the Cairo Genizah in 1896. Even there, as has been noted in chapter I (p. 14), scholarly opinion was divided between those who held that the Hebrew was that of the author, Jesus ben Sira, a priest from Jerusalem who flourished at the beginning of the second century BCE, and those who thought it was a medieval retranslation into Hebrew from the Greek of the Septuagint. How did Qumran affect the complex of the Apocrypha?

Compared to the Scrolls' impact on the study of the Bible, their influence on the Apocrypha has been more limited. The only two titles belonging to this class, yielded by Qumran in a Semitic form, are Ecclesiasticus and Tobit. The first of these is the Hebrew Ben Sira, of which in addition to small insignificant fragments from Qumran Cave 2 (2Q18), belonging to Ecclesiasticus chapter 6, the Psalms Scroll from Cave 11 has preserved eleven verses of a poem in Hebrew, starting with Ecclesiasticus 51:13. This manuscript, dated to the first half of the first century CE, and the incomplete scroll found at Masada, necessarily in existence before the fall of the fortress in 73/74 CE, both substantially identical with the Hebrew Ecclesiasticus of the Cairo Genizah, prove that the Genizah text is definitely not a medieval retranslation into Hebrew of the Greek Jesus Sirach. Moreover, the Cave 11 passage is demonstrably closer to the original than the corresponding section in the Genizah manuscript. The Qumran version of Ecclesiasticus 51 presents an alphabetical acrostic poem, that is one in which each line correctly begins with the successive letters of the Hebrew alphabet, line 1 starting with *alef* or A, line 2 with *bet* or B, whereas in the Genizah manuscript the sequence of the opening letters has been jumbled.

The twenty-six leather fragments of the Masada Ecclesiasticus, dated by the editor, Yigael Yadin, to the early or mid-first century BCE, furnish badly damaged portions of chapters 1 to 7 and reasonably well-preserved columns corresponding to chapters 39 to 44 and thus allow a somewhat better grasp of the original work of Ben Sira than the medieval documents or even his grandson's Greek translation, written half a century after the original composition, before the death of Ptolemy VII Euergetes in 116 BCE.

The Book of Tobit is the other apocryphal work for which Qumran has yielded important fresh information; but even at the level of the Greek translation Tobit's text fluctuates. There is a long and a short version of which the long, attested in the fourth century CE Codex Sinaiticus and in the Old Latin translation (third century), is considered the more authentic. The Qumran evidence, copied in the first century BCE or at the turn of the era, and attested by five fragmentary scrolls, is equally fluctuating. Four manuscripts are in Aramaic and one in Hebrew. The Aramaic appears to be the original. All of them represent a Semitic text from which the reasonably free longer Greek version was made. For instance, in Tobit 1:22 the Aramaic text reads: 'He was the son of my brother, of my father's house and of my family' as against the Greek: 'He was the son of my brother and of my kindred'. In Tobit 2:11 the Aramaic has 'On the festival of Weeks' and the Greek, 'On the feast of Pentecost which is the sacred festival of the seven weeks'. Finally, compare the Aramaic Tobit 14:2, 'He was fifty-eight years old when he lost his sight and afterwards he lived fifty-four years' to the Greek 'He was sixty-two years old when he was maimed in his eyes' (Sinaiticus) or 'He was fifty-eight years old when he lost his sight and after eight years he regained it' (Codex Vaticanus).

Bearing in mind that the Apocrypha are treated as Scripture in the most ancient branches of Christianity (Roman Catholic and Eastern Orthodox Churches), perhaps the most significant feature disclosed by the Qumran Scrolls in their regard is the fact that neither the Semitic texts nor the Greek translations display the same level of unification as do the canonical books of the Hebrew Bible.

(d) The Pseudepigrapha

The Pseudepigrapha, a loosely defined collection of important Jewish religious writings, presumed to have been composed between the third century BCE and 100 CE, form the last literary class after the canonical and apocryphal Scriptures. In 1913, the rigorously selective R. H. Charles included only sixteen works in his collection, dating between 200 BCE–100 CE (plus the Damascus Document which now sails under the Qumran flag), whereas the more elastic James H. Charlesworth extended the chronological catchment area from the second century BCE to 900 CE and increased the selection to twenty-eight documents in the two volumes of *The Old Testament Pseudepigrapha* (1983–5). Originally composed in Hebrew or Aramaic, and some like 4 Maccabees and the Sibylline Oracles in Greek, they have been transmitted by Christians either in the original Greek or in Latin, Syriac and Ethiopic etc. translations. Some of them were highly influential and the Book of Enoch even reached canonical status in the Abyssinian Church. Two or possibly three of the Pseudepigrapha surfaced in their original Semitic language in the Qumran caves. Jubilees and Enoch are both well attested, but smaller remains of the Testaments of the Twelve Patriarchs (Levi, Judah, Joseph and Naphtali) also survive. The Book of Jubilees, which was preserved among the Pseudepigrapha partly in a Greek and fully in an Ethiopic version, is attested in eighteen Hebrew manuscripts from Qumran Caves 1–4 and 11. The text was not yet unified and interesting variations can be detected. Eleven copies of the Book of Enoch were retrieved in Cave 4, to which should be added nine manuscripts, found in Caves 1, 2, 4 and 6, of a composition akin to Enoch, called the Book of the Giants. The language is Aramaic and the two works have survived in more than 130 fragments of various shapes and sizes. It should be recalled that the compilers of *The Dead Sea Scrolls Bible*, M. Abegg, P. Flint and E. Ulrich, suggest that Jubilees and Enoch were part of Scripture at Qumran, but this is not generally agreed.

Of the five books of the Ethiopic Enoch, only four are reflected in the Aramaic fragments; missing is the second section, known as the Parables, which frequently uses the expression 'Son of Man', familiar also from the Gospels. In his pioneering work, *The Aramaic Books of Enoch* (1976), J. T. Milik advanced the theory that in the original composition of Enoch, the Book of Giants, mentioned earlier, occupied the place of the Book of the Parables. The latter should probably be dated to the final quarter of the first century AD. This was not the view of Milik, but he was almost certainly mistaken when he declared it a Christian work composed in Greek in 270 CE or later. In fact, none of the surviving Greek manuscripts or citations comprises this part, that is to say chapters 37–72 of the Ethiopic book. The Aramaic fragments of the Testament of Levi

(4Q537, 540–41, as well as those extant in the Cairo Genizah), of the Testament of Judah (4Q538) and of the Testament of Joseph (4Q549) and the Hebrew relics of the Testament of Naphtali (4Q215) may either be the sources of the Greek Testaments of the Twelve Patriarchs or works related to them.

In brief, without fundamentally affecting their significance, the Hebrew and Aramaic fragments among the Dead Sea Scrolls afford for some of the Pseudepigrapha a fresh vantage point and a deeper and more nuanced understanding. With them a new chapter begins in the study of this important category of Jewish literature too.

3. The Hitherto Unknown Mainstream Jewish Literature

The eleven Qumran caves have yielded, in addition to the previously known Pseudepigrapha, a considerable number of further religious compositions produced by Jews in the latter part of the Old Testament era before the first war against Rome in 66–70 CE. A good many of these are definitely of sectarian character, that is, deriving from a community that had cut itself off from the body of Palestinian Jewry. They will be surveyed in chapter VII. But apart from these, we find in the Qumran collection a large number of works which show no particular sectarian features and are likely to have originated in mainstream Judaism. Of course, some of them may have been written within the community without displaying any of its particular ideas or customs, and others may have been adopted by the sect for its own use. Nevertheless, they should be kept separate from the sectarian literature proper and classified as supplements to the general Jewish Pseud-epigrapha.

The best-preserved specimens in the latter category are the non-canonical Psalms, some of them interspersed among the biblical poems in the Psalms Scroll from Cave 11. One of these Hebrew compositions corresponds to Psalm 151, an additional poem preserved in the Greek Bible, and four others have been known since the eighteenth century in Syriac translation. Thanks to Qumran, they can now be read in their original Hebrew wording. Here is a sample of this previously unknown religious poetry, entitled a Hymn to the Creator (11Q5, 26), which is scarcely dis-tinguishable from the poems included in the Psalter:

The Lord is great and holy,
The most holy for generation after generation.
Majesty goes before him,
And after him the abundance of many waters.
Loving kindness and truth are about his face;
Truth and judgement and righteousness are the pedestal of
    his throne.
He divides light from obscurity;
He establishes the dawn by the knowledge of his heart.
When all his angels saw it they sang,
For he showed them that which they had not known.
He crowns the mountains with fruit, with good fruit for all
    the living.
Blessed be the master of the earth with his power,
Who establishes the world with his wisdom.
By his understanding he stretched out the heaven,
And brought forth wind from his stores.
He made lightnings for his rain,
And raised mist from the end of the earth.

Wisdom compositions are a further class of literature exhibiting no sectarian features. Among them figures a sapiential poem known as the 'Beatitudes', dated to the first century BCE, which is partly reminiscent of the Beatitudes of Jesus from Matthew 5:3–11, although it differs from the Gospel by adding to each virtue an antithetic parallel.

> Blessed are those who hold to her (Wisdom's) precepts
> and do not hold to the ways of iniquity.
> Blessed are those who rejoice in her,
> and do not burst forth in ways of folly.
> Blessed are those who seek her with pure hands,
> and do not pursue her with a treacherous heart.
> Blessed is the man who has attained Wisdom,
> and walks in the Law of the Most High.
>
> (4Q525, fr. 2)

A third quite substantial group of writings consists of biblically inspired apocryphal books, most of them badly preserved, but sufficiently clear for indicating the literary type. They are sometimes designated as 'parabiblical'. The following extract from the Moses Apocryphon from Cave 4 will give a foretaste of the genre. The quoted passage describes how someone claiming to be a prophet is to be treated. If he exhorts the people to return to God, he is a genuine prophet and must be followed, but one who preaches defection from Judaism must be put to death as a false prophet. However, if his tribe comes to his defence and claims that he is a preacher of truth, the matter must be brought before the high priest for judgement.

[You will do all that] your God has commanded you from the mouth of the prophet. You will keep [all] these [pre]cepts and you will return to the Lord your God with all [your heart and al]l your soul. And your God will desist from the wrath of his great anger [to save you] from your misery. And the prophet who will arise and speak defection in your midst, turning you away from your God, shall be put to death. But if the tribe from which he originates stands up (for him) and says, 'Let him not be put to death, for he is righteous; he is a [trus]tworthy prophet', you, your elders and your judges will come with that tribe [t]o the place which your God will choose within one of your tribes (to appear) before [the] anointed priest on whose head the oil of anointing has been poured.

(4Q375, fr. 1)

The overall conclusion of the survey is clear. Thanks to the Dead Sea Scrolls, the literary legacy of Judaism of the so-called inter-Testamental or late Second Temple era (200 BCE–100 CE) has become much richer and more nuanced, and in certain respects, such as the status of the biblical text, quite different from what pre-1947 scholarship held it to be. In short, even without the consideration of the sectarian writings, which constitute the main novelty of the Scrolls, the claim that Qumran has revolutionized our understanding of the religious culture of Judaism in the age of Jesus must be accepted as proven.

VII

The Novelty of the Sectarian Scrolls

In the Qumran library, next to the Bible, the Apocrypha and the Pseudepigrapha, we find another impressive pile of manuscripts in which members of a particular Jewish group record their special customs, laws, scriptural interpretation and beliefs. Since they considered themselves distinct from the rest of their Jewish contemporaries and refused to mix with them, they can be correctly designated as the initiates of a sect. From the moment of the discovery of the first Dead Sea Scrolls, scholars hastened to put a name to this separatist community and identified them as the Essenes, a religious group known from classical Jewish and Roman sources written in Greek and Latin. This allowed the interpreters of the newly discovered scrolls to take into account the rich additional information regarding the Essene sect, handed down by Philo of Alexandria (*c.* 20 BCE–*c.* 50 CE), Flavius Josephus (37–*c.* 100 CE) and Pliny the Elder (23/24–79 CE). In dealing with the scrolls, I will resist the temptation to employ straightaway evidence extraneous to Qumran, and try instead to understand the Community of the Scrolls with the help of its own writings and leave to chapter VIII the presentation of the ongoing debate between the proponents and the opponents of the Essene theory.

The sectarian documents found in the Qumran caves

fall into four main categories. To begin with, we have various rules of the Community and the exposition of Jewish religious law as practised by its members. These rules are followed by compositions describing the worship and prayers characteristic of the sectaries, performed in conformity with their distinctive calendar, and by collections of hymns and psalms which, together with the rules, reveal their religious ideas and demonstrate their piety. The third literary class contains the material that may be used for the reconstruction of the history of the Dead Sea community. These can be found in the Exhortation section of the Damascus Document and in works belonging to the peculiar kind of Bible interpretation known as *pesher* (plural, *pesharim*) produced by the sectaries. To these we may add the exposition of scriptural citations included in the rules. Sapiential literature is the fourth main category dispensing information with regard to the wisdom seekers' attitude towards God and man. Various otherwise unrelated Qumran miscellanea will be listed in the Appendix to this chapter.

A. THE RULES

The rules themselves are neither transparent nor uniform and require some legal, social and historical elucidation. They have enough in common to show that the groups that used them were interlinked, yet the differences are such that one is obliged to inquire into the nature of the connection between them, namely, whether they represented legal development in distinct branches of the same single movement or in separate institutions which in some way were related to one another.

In addition to the discrete fragmentary texts found in Cave 4 relative to Sabbath observance, compensation for injuries, forbidden marriages and ritual uncleanness (4Q181, 251, 264A, 274–7, 284A), the Qumran library has yielded six major documents dealing fully or partly with the essentials pertaining to the organization of a community, and to the way of life and moral principles followed by its members. One of the six, the Temple Scroll from Cave 11, dating to the first half of the second century BCE, may have been produced before the birth of the Qumran sect. If so, its original version was later adopted by the sect and in part adapted to its particular requirements in the final decades of the second or at the beginning of the first century BCE. Some of the legal practices listed in the Temple Scroll, e.g. the ban on royal polygamy (57:16–18), on marriage between uncle and niece (66:15–17), and on married sectaries having sexual intercourse in 'the city of the sanctuary' in Jerusalem (45:11–12), are closely paralleled in another Qumran rule, the Damascus Document (4:20–25:11; 12:1–2).

1. The Statutes of the Damascus Document (CD (Cairo Damascus Document), 4Q265, 5Q12, 6Q15)

The Damascus Document, the rule first found in the Cairo Genizah at the end of the nineteenth century and later on at Qumran, is unquestionably a sectarian composition. It was originally revealed by the two medieval Cairo manuscripts dating to the tenth and the twelfth centuries (see chapter I, pp. 15–16), and from eleven fragmentary texts from Qumran Caves 4, 5 and 6, which also contain additional regulations about skin disease, sexual conduct within marriage and the community's Feast of the Renewal of the Covenant. The Damascus Document consists of an Exhortation with sectarian historical, doctrinal and exegetical content, and a list of Statutes referring to the structure and discipline of a separatist religious society. The historical and social context of the Exhortation places the Damascus Document before the other rules, except possibly MMT *Miqsat Ma'ase ha-Torah* or Some Observances of the Law (see pp. 140–41). It definitely envisages a married community of Jews that presumably preceded and produced the unmarried sect depicted in the Community Rule. Also the historical framework of the Damascus Document belongs to the Hellenistic age where Seleucid rulers (kings of Yavan or Greece) are the foreign enemies of the Jews, whereas other rules, the War Scroll, the Book of War (4Q285) and the commentaries on Habakkuk and Nahum identify the final foe as the Kittim (Romans), whose conquest of Judaea in 63 BCE marked the end of the Hellenistic age in Palestine. Their dominion culminated in the destruction of Jerusalem in 70 CE. Consequently, the date of composition of the Damascus Document can safely be placed to the final decades of the Hellenistic age in Palestine, probably somewhere close to 100 BCE.

The Exhortation of the Damascus Document (CD A 1–8, B 1–2, supplemented by fragments from Caves 4, 5 and 6), comprises a sermon addressed by a teacher of the Community to his 'sons'. It sketches the origins and early years of the movement, which will be discussed in the context of the history of the sect (see pp. 203–6), and also contains moral admonitions. The title 'Damascus' derives from the phrase 'the new covenant (made) in the land of Damascus' which appears seven times in the Cairo manuscript and once in a Cave 4 fragment. Like many similar phrases employed in the biblical commentaries from Qumran to designate persons, places and events associated with sectarian history, the land of Damascus is not to be taken literally. In the opinion of many scholars it probably alludes to Qumran.

The legal material relating to the 'Damascus' Community is included in the Statutes (CD 9–16 and numerous Cave 4 fragments). These Statutes legislate for the premessianic age, indicated by a passage which speaks of the future coming of two Messiahs, the Messiah of Aaron and the Messiah of Israel. They also hand out moral and ritual rules and define the governance of the 'Damascus' Community. The beginning and the end of the Statutes are missing from the Cairo manuscripts, but can partly be restored from the Cave 4 material. Pages 15 and 16 are misplaced in the Genizah text and in the light of the Qumran fragments should be brought forward before page 9.

The Community is envisaged in the Statutes as a miniature biblical Israel, divided into priests and laity, and more specifically into priests, Levites, Israelites and proselytes. The term 'proselytes' probably designates figuratively Jewish applicants for membership of the sect before their formal admission, and literally Gentile slaves after they had converted to Judaism. In further imitation of the biblical Jewish nation, the Community is symbolically subdivided into twelve tribes and into camps of thousands, hundreds and fifties, down to the minimum group of ten.

The 'Damascus' sect was led by priests, belonging to the tribe of Levi, and more specifically to the family of Aaron. They claimed association with the family of Zadok, the high priest under king Solomon, whose clan supplied the chief priests down to the early second century BCE. Even the smallest unit, a camp of ten men, was to be headed by a priestly Overseer or Guardian, a man aged between thirty and sixty years, who had to be an expert in the Book of Meditation (probably the Law of Moses) and learned in sectarian jurisprudence. 'The Guardian of all the camps' was the title of the superior general who must have been between thirty and fifty years of age, versed in 'all the secrets' and familiar with all the languages. The Guardian's duties included the instruction, examination, rejection or acceptance, ranking and pastoral care of candidates and members. It is possible that in the selection of suitable candidates, he employed the arcane science of astronomical physiognomy, the study of the physical appearance of individuals. Three 'horoscopes', contained in 4Q186 and 561, which might have served such a purpose, have survived, each depicting a person made up of a mixture of nine parts of light and darkness. Shortness, fatness and irregular or ugly features were associated with wickedness, and tallness, a slim body and a pleasant appearance with virtue.

Admission of new candidates and dismissal, accompanied by a curse, of defaulting members took place in a yearly ceremony 'in the third month' (the month of Sivan) of the Jewish year, no doubt at the Feast of Weeks or Pentecost celebrated on the fifteenth day of the month. The priestly Guardian regulated the activities of the members of his unit, including business deals, and advised them in matters of marriage and divorce too. Another of his tasks was to disqualify priests with speech defects, those who could not express themselves clearly and distinctly, to determine the dues members had to pay to the priests, and to diagnose contagious skin diseases ('leprosy') which required the segregation of the sick and their eventual readmission after cure. As the latter right was a privilege explicitly reserved for priests in the Bible, a curious stratagem was devised for the case when only a simple-minded (i.e. mentally handicapped) priest was available. A learned Levite among the members of the camp had to guide him through the ritual and tell him what he had to do, but, as ordained by the Bible, only a priest was allowed to perform this ceremony.

Next to the Guardians, the sect had also ten Judges, elected for a specified time, four from among the priests and Levites, and six lay Israelites. In addition to administering justice, they also handled, together with 'the Guardian', no doubt 'the Guardian of all the camps', the communal funds destined for the support of the poor and the orphans as well as for the redemption of war prisoners.

The sectarian judicial system was run on the basis of biblical law adapted to the Community's needs. The members were prohibited under pain of death from handing over a Jew to a Gentile court if he was charged with a capital case. The Statutes envisage death sentences pronounced by the Judges of the Community. Biblical law requires two or three witnesses in a case carrying a death penalty, but the Damascus Document foresees the possibility of judging a capital crime committed before a single witness. It obliges the witness to bring the culprit before the Guardian and to rebuke him in his presence. The matter was then recorded by the Guardian on a register. Should the crafty criminal commit the same offence twice more before a single witness, the repeated transgressions would be treated by the Guardian and the Community court as a single crime attested by three witnesses.

There were two kinds of new members awaiting

initiation: the children of the sectaries who were born and brought up within the Community and adult Jewish outsiders. The former gained full membership at the age of twenty (assuming that the legislation laid down in the Messianic Rule applied also in historical times in the 'Damascus' Community). Grown-up Jews, who had notified the Guardian of their desire to join, were enrolled after one year of study, during which period all the secret teachings of the sect, including its particular solar calendar, modelled on the important pseudepigraphic Book of Jubilees, were revealed to them. No one mentally or bodily disabled could be admitted to full membership of the Community.

The 'Damascus' sect consisted of married Jewish couples and their offspring. Among the leaders, explicit reference is made to persons of both sexes, called 'the Fathers' and 'the Mothers', though democratic equality was not part of the system. According to a Cave 4 text (4Q270, fr. 7), murmuring against 'the Fathers' entailed irrevocable expulsion from the sect, but an offender against 'the Mothers' could get away with a punishment for a mere ten days! An interesting detail relating to marital sex is recorded in the same fragment. A husband sleeping with his wife 'against the rules' was declared a fornicator and dismissed from the community (see more on this in chapter VIII, p. 184). Three further restrictions relating to marriage legislation are mentioned in the Exhortation. Sectarian matrimony was to be monogamous, whereas biblical Judaism permitted polygamy. Marriage between an uncle and his niece was prohibited and sex between husband and wife was forbidden in Jerusalem (or at least in the area designated as 'the city of the Sanctuary' according to the wording of both the Damascus Document and the Temple Scroll), no doubt during the presence of sect members in the Holy City at the three pilgrim festivals of the year (Passover, Feast of Weeks and Feast of Tabernacles).

The Statutes' version of biblical laws concerned with purification and Sabbath observance is generally more rigorous than the practice of the Jews of that age. For instance, on the Sabbath the sectaries were forbidden to assist a domestic animal in labour, nor were they allowed to pull it out from a cistern or a hole as ordinary Jewish farmers did according to the words attributed to Jesus in the New Testament (Matt. 12:11; Luke 14:5). No rope or ladder could be used in the rescue of a man who had fallen into water. Commerce with non-Jews was restricted, but not altogether prohibited (see chapter VIII, pp. 183–4).

In sum, the 'Damascus' Community was a free association of Jewish families, governed by the priests, Sons of Zadok, and embracing a more stringent version of the Mosaic law which, together with their sectarian practices, set them apart from the main body of Palestinian Jewry. Nevertheless the extra dose of asceticism that lasting celibacy implies appears nowhere explicitly in the Statutes, although it has been tentatively suggested that the group practising 'perfect holiness', distinct from those who 'marry and beget children', refers to a separate unmarried branch of the sect (see CD 7:4–8).

2. The Rule of the Congregation or Messianic Rule (1QSa)

Fifty-two fragments found in Cave 1 have been meticulously assembled by Dominique Barthélemy and Joseph Milik to form two almost complete columns of text. They once belonged to the manuscript of the Community Rule (*Serekh ha-Yahad* or 1QS) and came from the pen of the same scribe. The date of the document, known as the Rule of the Congregation or Messianic Rule (*Serekh ha-'Edah* or 1QSa), falls most probably to the middle of the first century BCE. The text briefly sets out the purpose and the regulations of a community that is either the same as the one described in the Damascus Document or is very similar to it. The principal difference between them is that whereas the 'Damascus' Statutes relate to the pre-messianic age, in the Rule of the Congregation the two Messiahs – the Priest and the Messiah of Israel – are already present and the eschatological war is looming on the horizon. The Rule of the Congregation is linked to the Damascus Document on the one hand through its reference to the 'Book of Meditation' (probably the Pentateuch) and to the Sons of Zadok, the priests. On the other hand, it is related to the Community Rule in its description of the sectarian meal and to the War Scroll in its sketch of the military organization of the sect in the final eschatological age.

The epoch envisaged is described as 'the last days', when a large crowd of the congregation of Israel was expected to join the Community of the Sons of Zadok. They are all to participate in a ceremony of entry into the Covenant and hear the exposition of the sect's laws and statutes. Like the Community of the Damascus Document, the Rule of the Congregation is also for a married group, as wives and children – as well as their education – are expressly mentioned in it.

The text offers an unparalleled insight into the life of the members. We learn that from early childhood they were instructed in the Book of Meditation and from the age of ten years in the communal statutes. On having reached the age of majority at twenty, they were enrolled in the Community, and the young men were allowed to marry and also to act as witnesses in court proceedings. At the age of twenty-five, they qualified for lower offices, and at thirty for higher offices in the Community and could become chiefs of units, judges and tribal officers under the supervision of the Zadokite priests and their intermediaries, the Levites, who acted as administrative officers. It was the Levites' duty to summon the congregation, no doubt with their trumpets, as we learn from the War Scroll, for court sessions, communal council and when war was to break out.

The council of the Community, presided over by Zadokite priests, consisted of the sages, the judges, the chiefs of the tribes, and the chiefs of lower divisions (thousands, hundreds, etc.). Only unblemished and ritually clean persons could attend and play a role in the council because 'the angels of holiness were with their assembly', the Community being the terrestrial division of the heavenly army.

The council in the messianic age was to be led by the Priest Messiah, followed by his brethren, the priests. Next proceeded in a parallel procession the Messiah of Israel with his lay officials, each in the order of his rank. The council meeting is associated with a messianic meal which was to be blessed by the Priest Messiah. According to the Rule of the Congregation, the daily meal of the sect, depicted in the Community Rule (see p. 148), was an anticipation of the messianic ritual at the end of time.

3. The Community Rule or *Serekh ha-Yahad*
(1QS, 4Q255–64, 280, 286–7, 502, 5Q11, 13)

The Community Rule, originally called the Manual of Discipline, is arguably the most important and interesting source of legislation concerning the organization of the sect. It is dated by its script and its content to *circa* 100 BCE. Its vantage point is pre-messianic as its Community, like the 'Damascus' sect, was still awaiting the arrival of an ultimate prophet and the Messiahs of Aaron and Israel (1QS 9:11). It has reached us in a complete scroll whose final column is left half empty, indicating the end of the document. Moreover, fragments, some of them substantial, of fourteen further manuscripts were yielded by Caves 4, 5 and 6, several of them representing a somewhat different version of the rule.

The complete scroll consists of three parts. The first section (columns 1–4) describes the ceremony of the entry into the Covenant, entailing a communal baptism ritual and an instruction on the two spirits of light and darkness whose impact on individuals determined the spiritual history of humanity. The second part (columns 5–9) includes the statutes relating to the life and governance of the Community and directives addressed to the Master or *maskil*, and the third (columns 9–11) consists of the hymn sung by the Master.

The Community Rule lays down a stricter and more detailed set of regulations than either the Damascus Document or the Rule of the Congregation. Compared to them, its principal peculiarity is the total absence of reference to women. From this is deduced that the members of the group were male celibates. In a mixed-gender association characterized by normal and lasting husband–wife relations, legislation relating to female uncleanness resulting from menstruation or childbirth, as well as to marriage, the education of children, and divorce, would have been a necessity. Silence here speaks loud and clear and indicates that these matters were not applicable to the Community described in this particular rule book which legislated for unmarried male members, pointing to the Essenes (see chapter VIII, pp. 191–202) and anticipated Christian monasticism launched a few hundred years later.

Just like the 'Damascus' sect (see p. 122), that of the Community Rule is envisaged as a miniature Israel, divided into priests, Levites and laity, and the latter subdivided into twelve tribes, and smaller units down to tens, but no proselytes are mentioned. The supreme council is made up of three priests and twelve men, referred to also as 'fifteen men' (4Q265, fr. 7 ii), no doubt corresponding to the leaders of the three Levitical clans and the twelve tribal chiefs of Israel. The representatives of the priestly directorate are designated either as Sons of Aaron or, more restrictively, as Sons of Zadok (see pp. 122–3). In one of the Cave 4 manuscripts (4Q258), which may reflect the original form of the Community Rule, we encounter a democratic social structure with the congregation, literally 'the many', being the supreme authority in matters of doctrine, justice and property. The complete final document (1QS) identifies the main governing body with the high-priestly Sons of Zadok, suggesting an oligarchic Zadokite takeover of the original body at an early stage of the history of the sect.

On the individual level, as in the Damascus Document (see p. 122), the government of the whole congregation and its constitutive parts was in the hands of a priest, called the Guardian, who was assisted by a Bursar. The former presided over the meetings, instructed the members and accepted, rejected and trained new candidates. The Bursar administered the funds and the property of the sect and provided for the needs of the individual members, who lived in religious communism.

The initiation of newcomers was much more complex than in the married 'Damascus' sect. The Jewish male volunteers ('every man, born of Israel, who freely pledges himself') were scrutinized by the Guardian and were made to swear, in the course of a ceremony, to return to the Law of Moses and observe every single precept of it according to the interpretation of the Sons of Zadok, the priestly leaders of the sect. An indeterminate period of instruction ensued, followed by a public examination in the presence of the whole Community. The successful candidates underwent further training during which they were forbidden to touch the pure (solid) food of the community for one year. They had to hand over their property to the Bursar, who administered it without, however, merging it with communal property for another twelve months. In the course of this second year of training, the 'novices', a convenient term borrowed from Christian monastic terminology, could come into contact with the pure food, but were still kept away from the pure drink of the Community as liquids were considered more susceptible to ritual impurity than solid food. After the third and final examination at the end of the second year of the 'noviciate', those who successfully passed the test became full members and renounced all right to control their belongings, agreeing to their absorption into communal property. Moreover, the freshly initiated were ranked according to their spiritual achievement, a ranking reviewed annually during the Feast of the Renewal of the Covenant, no doubt identical with the ceremony occurring 'in the third month' (the Feast of Weeks) mentioned in a Cave 4 manuscript of the Damascus Document.

The new members embraced the Community's strict discipline regarding the Mosaic Law and the sectarian regulations. Apart from celibacy and obedience to superiors, they had to keep away from the outside world, both Jewish and Gentile, as it was considered irreligious and unclean. They were in particular forbidden to mix the pure property of the community with the 'wealth of wickedness'. To prove that they were separated from outsiders, the members had to abstain from making donations to them. Any exchange of goods had to be accompanied by payment of money. They were also forbidden to communicate the secret teachings of the sect to non-members.

A severe penal code controlled the conduct of the sectaries. In addition to the deliberate breach of any precept of the biblical law, four specific transgressions carried the penalty of permanent expulsion from the community: the utterance, even an inadvertent utterance, of the divine name (the tetragram YHWH); the slandering of the Community; the murmuring against communal authority (this is identical with the murmuring against 'the Fathers' in the Damascus Document, see p. 125); and deserting the community after ten years of membership. The latter misconduct carried with it a prohibition for members to maintain any contact with the traitor on pain of expulsion. Other serious transgressions included withdrawal from the sect due to discouragement over the severity of the rules (a repentant member was punished by exclusion for two years during which he had to undergo a complete retraining), lying about property (punished by exclusion from touching the pure meal for one year and by the reduction of his food to one quarter of the full ration), angry words addressed to a priest or disrespect towards a senior member (exclusion for one year) and slandering a companion (prohibition for one year of touching the pure meal). Other offences were punished for six months, three months, two months, one month, down to the minimum penalty of ten days (for interrupting a senior colleague during a meeting or gesticulating with the left hand).

The Rule of the Community contains no precise directives concerning the members' work. All we know is that they had to hand over their salaries to the Bursar, who would spend the money on the Community. As for their occupations, the sectaries may have been employed by outsiders and from the archaeological data we may surmise that at Qumran they practised agriculture and various industries (pottery, tannery) and some of them were also professional scribes manufacturing books, not only for the Community, but also possibly in part for sale.

The daily routine included at least one communal meal, presided over and blessed by the leading priest. There was also a vigil of prayer, study and discussion occupying one third (four hours) of each night. One member, no doubt the priestly leader, was to be continuously engaged in the study of the Torah. Moreover, the Community imagined itself in the pre-messianic age as the spiritual replacement of the Jewish Temple. Qumran was their sanctuary and prayer and holy life were the substitutes for the sacrifices and free-will offerings performed by the priests in Jerusalem.

Three further documents have a less direct significance for the description of the Qumran sect or sects: the War Scroll is an eschatological legislation for the final battle between good and evil; the Temple Scroll is a rewritten Torah, apparently addressed to all Israel, but appropriated and revised by the Qumranites; and Some Observances of the Law (MMT) conveys an appeal of the early leaders of the Qumran sect to the priestly head of the Jerusalem Temple to adopt the Community's interpretation of a selection of biblical laws. They will all be presented in turn.

4. The War Scroll (1QM, 1Q33, 4Q471, 491–7)

The rules of the War Scroll concern not the present but the future age, laying down in advance the scenario and the imaginary regulations concerning eschatological behaviour for the members of the community during the final stages of the conflict between the sons of light and the sons of darkness. The War Scroll has been preserved in a large, but damaged manuscript of nineteen columns from Cave 1, and in further fragmentary manuscripts from Cave 4. On the basis of palaeography and contents the writing is dated to the last decades of the first century BCE or the beginning of the Christian era. Since the Kittim, the final enemy, are led by a king, they must apply to the Romans after 27 BCE when Augustus became Princeps or Emperor.

The War Scroll is a composite work. Columns 1 and 15 to 19 offer an imaginary historical sketch of the reconquest of Jerusalem and the Holy Land by the host of the Sons of Light from the Sons of Darkness (Jewish and Gentile), and the defeat of the armies of the ultimate foe, the Kittim. Between columns 1 and 15 is inserted a series of equally fictive regulations relating to the reorganization of the worship in the Temple of Jerusalem by the priests of the Community, the schedule of the forty-year-long war against the non-Jewish world, the sequence and precise length of the battle against each nation being determined in advance. This single feature suffices to prove that we are faced with an imaginary warfare. There also follow regulations concerning the trumpets, standards, weapons, and the strategy and tactics of the infantry and cavalry. The details of the descriptions remind the reader of the Roman army and its style of strategy and tactics. The age of the combatants and the duties of the priests and Levites, who were to direct the battle with their trumpet signals, the addresses delivered by the chief priest to the soldiers, the battle liturgy and the ceremony of thanksgiving after the final victory over the Kittim complete the document. While some of the accounts and prayers are outstandingly beautiful, the composition as such reflects only the ideas of the sect about the end of time and cannot be used for the reconstruction of the organization and way of life of the Community. To consider the document as a handbook for actual warfare is childishly naive.

Akin to the War Scroll is the set of fragments known as *The Book of War* (4Q285) which, without setting out battle rules, foresees the fight culminating in the defeat of the king of the Kittim by the sea. It was wrongly made notorious by Robert Eisenman and Michael Wise for its supposed reference to a murdered Jesus-like messianic figure. Accurately understood and translated, the text speaks of a 'slaying' or bellicose, and not a 'slain', Messiah.

5. The Temple Scroll (11Q 19–21, 4Q365a, 4Q524)

The Temple Scroll is the longest of all the Qumran manuscripts. It stretches to over twenty-eight feet when unrolled and contains sixty-seven columns of text. Beginning with the Covenant between God and Israel, it is presented as a record of divine legislation relative to the Temple and its sacrifices, together with the purity requirements for Jerusalem and the cities of Israel (columns 2–51). The last quarter of the manuscript is made up of miscellaneous laws concerning judges, idolatry, oaths, apostasy, priests, Levites, the Jewish king who must have only one wife, witnesses, war, crimes against the state punishable by crucifixion, and incest (columns 51–66). The top few lines of column 67 are missing but the rest of the column is blank, indicating that the document ended there.

While the Bible formulates the Torah as a revelation given by God, which the mediator Moses was to receive and transmit to the Jews, the Temple Scroll appears as a direct divine communication to Israel. Consequently it is believed to possess greater holiness and authority because of its direct divine origin, as can be seen in the following parallel quotations in the first of which the speaker is Moses and in the second, God himself.

And the priests, the sons of Levi shall come forward, for *YHWH your God* has chosen them to minister to *Him* and to bless *Him in the name of YHWH*.

(Deut. 21:5)

And the priests, the sons of Levi, shall come forward, for *I* have chosen them to minister to *Me* and to bless *My name*.

(11QTemple 63:3)

Some of the laws of the Temple Scroll differ from their biblical sources by combining two or more scriptural precepts and generally rendering the rules more severe. Take the case of the *seducer* of a non-engaged virgin. Exodus 22:16 obliges him to marry her after paying her father an unspecified sum of bride money. On the other hand, the *rapist* of a non-engaged virgin must give her father fifty shekels of silver, marry her without retaining the right to any subsequent divorce according to the biblical law of Deuteronomy 22:28–9. In the Temple Scroll, where the two scriptural commandments are conflated, the seducer's treatment is made more severe, but applies only if no legal impediment prevents him from marrying the girl:

When a man seduces a virgin who is not betrothed, but is suitable for him according to the rule, and lies with her, he who has lain with her shall give the girl's father fifty pieces of silver and she shall be his wife. Because he has dishonoured her, he may not divorce her all his days.

(11QTemple 66:8–11)

Similarly, Deuteronomy 21:10–14, the case of a woman captured in war, is given a facelift in the Temple Scroll. According to the Bible, her captor must grant the woman a month's respite before getting her into his bed and thus making her his wife. He is forbidden thereafter to sell her as a slave. The Qumran document adds a ritual proviso, however: the woman continues to be held ritually unclean for a long period (seven years) and is not permitted to cook for her husband or partake in sacrificial meals.

When you go to war against your enemies ... and you capture some of them, if you see among the captives a pretty woman and desire her, you may take her to be your wife. You shall bring her to your house, you shall shave her head, and cut her nails. You shall discard the clothes of her captivity and she shall dwell in your house, and bewail her father and mother for a full month. Afterwards you may go to her, consummate the marriage with her and she will be your wife. *But she shall not touch whatever is pure for you for seven years, neither shall she eat of the sacrifice of peace offering until seven years have elapsed.*

(11QTemple 63:10–15)

As has been remarked, several laws of the Temple Scroll are paralleled in other Qumran writings. The liturgical calendar of feasts, dealt with in columns 43–4, is based on the solar year of 364 days adopted by the Dead Sea sect, as well as the Book of Jubilees and the first Book of Enoch. More specifically, the feast of oil mentioned in the Temple Scroll (21:12) also figures in the sectarian liturgical calendar prefixed to Some Observances of the Law or MMT (4Q394 5:5).

The law which, contrary to the Bible, forbids the Israelite king to have several wives simultaneously (Temple Scroll 57:16–18), is used in the Damascus Document (CD 5:1–2) as an argument for the monogamous marriage of any Jew. Deuteronomy 18:18 is understood by the compiler of the Temple Scroll to declare that not even the king is permitted to 'multiply wives to himself'. The Damascus Document's descriptive condemnation of marriage between an uncle and his niece (CD 5:7–11) is given in a legal formulation in the Temple Scroll:

A man shall not take the daughter of his brother or the daughter of his sister for this is abominable.

(11QTemple 66:15–17)

Furthermore, the ruling of the Temple Scroll (45:11–12), which prohibits a man to enter any part of the city of the Sanctuary for three days after he has had sexual intercourse with his wife, underlies a statute set out in the Damascus Document:

No man shall lie with a woman in the city of the Sanctuary to defile the city of the Sanctuary with their uncleanness.

(CD 12:1–2)

Finally the crucifixion by a Jewish ruler of his captured Jewish opponents, guilty of allying themselves to an invading Greek king, referred to in the Nahum Commentary (4Q169; see pp. 163–4), seems to be in line with the law recorded in the Temple Scroll:

If a man slanders his people and delivers his people to a foreign nation and does evil to his people, you shall hang him on a tree and he shall die.

(11QTemple 64:7–8)

If the Temple Scroll predates the sect, these correspondences indicate that the Qumran community was influenced by it. If, on the other hand, the Temple Scroll is a Qumran composition, the quoted sectarian practices may be understood as directly dictated by the Temple Scroll. In the latter hypothesis, the Temple Scroll partly reflects sectarian legal practice, but as far as the Temple and the cult performed in it are concerned, the legislation is for future use when the Sanctuary will be administered by the Qumran priests, as appears in column 2 of the Scroll of the War of the Sons of Light against the Sons of Darkness.

6. Some Observances of the Law (4Q394–99)

Six badly preserved manuscripts from Cave 4, bearing the title of 'Some Observances of the Law' (*Miqsat Ma'ase ha-Torah*, abbreviated as MMT) reveal elements of a legal controversy. Addressed to the leader of the Jewish nation – no doubt the high priest of the Temple of Jerusalem – it seeks to persuade him to accept the Qumran understanding of some twenty biblically based laws whose mistaken interpretation, championed by a third religious party, has been adopted by the high priest. It is assumed that the recommended explanation of these precepts corresponds to the teaching of the founding fathers of the Qumran sect, and its rejection by the Temple authorities was the reason for their breakaway from the Jerusalem priesthood. If this general exegesis of the document, proposed by its editors, John Strugnell and Elisha Qimron, is correct, MMT would represent the original kernel of distinctive sectarian law. To be precise, the editors think that MMT is a letter sent by the Teacher of Righteousness, founder of the Qumran sect, to the ruling high priest, who later acquired the title of Wicked Priest. However, the epistolary character of the writing is questionable, because it lacks the standard introductory and concluding formulae of a letter. It is safer to call it a polemical legal tractate.

The main points of the controversy relate to the solar calendar, prefixed to one of the manuscripts, and to matters pertaining to ritual purity: prohibition from accepting Temple offerings from non-Jews, rules governing the slaughter of sacrificial animals, performance of the ritual of the 'red heifer' (Numbers 19:2–10), exclusion of the physically handicapped (deaf, blind and lepers), purity of liquids, simultaneous slaughtering of a mother animal with her young, a ban on dogs in Jerusalem (to prevent the desecration of remains of sacrificial meat attached to bones), rules governing marriage and intermarriage (e.g. no priest was allowed to marry a woman born in a non-priestly family), etc. Some of the laws recall the practice attributed to Sadducees in rabbinic literature, but since Sadducee means Zadokite, the title given to the sectarian priesthood, this should not be surprising. The original Community was firmly bound to ritual observance and was definitely a non-celibate institution.

If this judgement is correct, MMT reveals the interpretation of parts of the traditional priestly legislation inherited by the sect's founders rather than a legislation freshly devised for the newly established Community. The document will be significant for the study of the historical origins of the Qumran sect as set out in biblical commentaries (see chapter VIII, p. 209).

To conclude this section, the various Qumran regulations indicate that the Community Rule dealt with a male celibate association that followed a regime of common ownership of goods under the leadership of the Sons of Zadok, the priests. The 'Damascus' sectaries, by contrast, were property-owning married Jews, also governed by Zadokite priests. They both expected in the not too distant future the coming of the kingdom of God at the end of an eschatological war, ushered in by two promised Messiahs and, according to the Community Rule, by an eschatological Prophet.

Were the two organizations – the married Community of the Damascus Document and of the Rule of the Congregation and the unmarried male ascetics of the Community Rule – separate institutions or two distinct branches of a single sect?

The strong organizational similarities, the entry of the new members at the Feast of the Renewal of the Covenant and the role of the chief Guardian seem to favour the view that we are facing a sole movement with two divisions whose members jointly celebrated the great Feast of the Renewal of the Covenant. In this case, the most likely hypothesis is that at some stage the married branch of the sect produced and nurtured the ascetics of the Community Rule rather than the converse development which envisages the creation by the more severe group of a looser, married and property-owning sister branch – a 'third order' to borrow the terminology of the later Christian religious organizations.

B. PRAYER, WORSHIP AND BELIEF

The second category of manuscripts, disclosing essential aspects of sectarian religious life, deal with the formal and personal piety and belief of the members. The official liturgical worship entails ceremonies and the recitation of prescribed blessings at fixed dates and times for the understanding of which the compulsory calendar, recorded in various manuscripts (4Q317–30, 334, 337, 394), plays an important part. Most of the psalms and hymns of the sect are formulated in the first person singular; hence they are meant for individual use and express personal beliefs and piety. Whereas the rules have been preserved in easily distinguishable legal documents, the evidence relating to sectarian liturgy and prayers may be found either in distinct scrolls like the Hodayot or Thanksgiving hymns (1QH, 4Q427–32), the Songs of the Holocaust of the Sabbath (4Q400–407, etc.), the Blessings (1QSb=1Q28b), the Benedictions (4Q280, 286–90) and other fragmentary manuscripts such as the Lamentations (4Q179, 501), the Words of the Heavenly Lights (4Q504–6), Daily Prayers (4Q503), and Prayers for festivals (4Q507–9) etc., or incorporated into various parts – particularly in the concluding hymn – of the Community Rule. Therefore it will be simpler and clearer to deal with the issues according to their subject matter rather than through discussing the individual literary sources.

Since worship and prayer are strictly arranged in a temporal framework, we must first learn something about the sect's calendar. The Community Rule emphasizes the necessity that the sectaries must abide strictly by their God-given religious timetable:

They shall not depart from any command of God concerning their times; they shall be neither early nor late from any of their appointed times.

(1QS 1:14–15)

This calendar essentially differed from that of the priests of the Jerusalem Temple and played a significant role in creating the rift between the latter and the members of the Qumran Community. The peculiar sectarian definition of the year constitutes the foundation of the Qumran liturgy.

Contrary to the generally adopted time reckoning system of biblical and post-biblical Judaism, with a lunar year of 354 days approximately reconciled with the solar year by means of adding an extra month (called the second Adar) in every third year, the Dead Sea Community opted for a solar calendar of twelve months, each comprising thirty days. They then prefixed an extra day to each of the four seasons. In counting 364 days in a year, they followed the Book of Jubilees, as is implied in the Damascus Document:

As for the exact determination of their times to which Israel turns a blind eye, behold it is strictly defined in the Book of the Division of the Times into their Jubilees and Weeks.

(CD 16:2–4)

This computation, which is still short of one and a quarter days of the astronomical year, had in the eyes of the sectaries the advantage of absolute regularity. Not only did their year consist precisely of fifty-two weeks, but also each of the four seasons – of thirteen weeks' duration – started on the same day of the week. This day was Wednesday according to the sectarian calendar since the time of the creation. Genesis tells us that the sun and the moon, the two great heavenly bodies ruling over the day and the night, were set on their course by God on the fourth day (Wednesday) of the first week (Genesis 1:14–19). To put it bluntly, in conformity with the divine law, time began on a Wednesday. As a consequence, the vernal or spring New Year (1 Nisan), the first day of the first month in the religious calendar of Israel, was always a Wednesday, and so was Passover, two weeks later, on the fifteenth day of the first month. In this system of perfect regularity, the Feast of Weeks (15 Sivan in the third month), coinciding with the renewal of the Covenant, always fell on a Sunday and the day of Atonement (10 Tishri, in the seventh month) on a Friday. This absolute uniformity, so different from the continuously changing mobile feasts of the calendar used in the Temple, was the proof in the eyes of the sectaries of the heavenly nature of their way of reckoning, mirroring 'the certain law from the mouth of God' (1QH 20:9). The Temple Scroll mentions further festivals of agricultural character at seven weeks' intervals: the Feast of the First Wheat on Sunday, the fifteenth day of the third month, the Feast of the First Wine on Sunday, the third day of the fifth month, and the Feast of the First Oil on Sunday, the twenty-second day of the sixth month. On the following day began the Feast of Wood Offering, supplying fuel to the Sanctuary for burnt sacrifices. The appended table will allow a quick grasp of this chronological harmony.

The days and months of the year

	I, IV, VII, X	II, V, VIII, XI	III, VI, IX, XII
Wed	1 8 15 22 29	6 13 20 27	4 11 18 25
Thu	2 9 16 23 30	7 14 21 28	5 12 19 26
Fri	3 10 17 24	1 8 15 22 29	6 13 20 27
Sab	4 11 18 25	2 9 16 23 30	7 14 21 28
Sun	5 12 19 26	3 10 17 24	1 8 15 22 29
Mon	6 13 20 27	4 11 18 25	2 9 16 23 30
Tue	7 14 21 28	5 12 19 26	3 10 17 24 31

Anyone familiar with the mentality of closed religious groups will realize that a clash on the calendar, resulting in a feast day for one group being an ordinary day for another, can deeply affect the relationship between opposing factions. At the end of the first century CE, the Jewish Patriarch Rabban Gamaliel II, disagreeing with the renowned Rabbi Joshua ben Hananiah on the date of the day of Atonement, publicly humiliated his opponent by ordering him to perform various acts (such as carrying a staff or a purse) forbidden on that day:

I charge you that you come to me with your staff and your money on the Day of Atonement according to your reckoning.
(Mishnah Rosh ha-Shanah 2:9)

Moving to the Qumran domain, the Wicked Priest, the Jewish high priest hostile to the founder of the Community, visited with his followers the Teacher of Righteousness and his company on *their* day of Atonement, which differed from his, to surprise and confuse them and put pressure on them (1QHabakkuk Commentary 11:4–8). In a Christian context, Pope Victor (189–198 CE) threatened to excommunicate the whole eastern half of the Church for celebrating Easter on the day of the Jewish Passover (15 Nisan) rather than on the following Sunday as the western Church did. Closer to our time, the calendar reform introduced by Pope Gregory XIII in 1582 was resisted by the English Church until 1752 and by the Eastern Orthodox Churches until as late as 1924.

The daily, weekly, monthly, seasonal and annual prayer times of the Community as well as the celebration of the seven-year (sabbatical cycle) and fifty-year (jubilee cycle) periods had to be observed with the greatest accuracy because if earthly worship did not coincide exactly with the heavenly cult of the angels, cacophony was expected to ensue in celestial-terrestrial liturgy. These prayer times are specified in a hymn attached to the Community Rule:

He shall bless Him [with the offering] of the lips
At the times ordained by Him.
At the beginning of the dominion of light,
And at its end when it retires to its appointed place;
At the beginning of the watches of darkness,
When He unlocks their storehouse and spreads them out
And also at their end, when they retire before the light . . .
At the beginning of the months of the (yearly) seasons
And on the holy day appointed for remembrance . . .
At the beginning of the years and at the end of their
    seasons,
When their appointed time is fulfilled, on the day decreed
    by Him
That they should pass from one to the other:
The season of early harvest to summer time,
The season of sowing to the season of grass,
The seasons of years to their weeks (of years)
And at the beginning of their weeks for the season of
    Jubilee.

(1QS 9:26–10:8)

A large number of individual and communal prayers and priestly blessings, listed at the beginning of this section, have survived more or less well preserved. Before turning to two ritual ceremonies, one performed daily and the other annually, an extract from the heavenly liturgy of the Songs of the Holocaust of the Sabbath, inspired by the vision of the heavenly chariot or *Merkabah* (Ezekiel chapter 1), deserves to be cited as an example of high-quality cultic poetry. (The 'gods' mentioned are heavenly beings attached to the throne-chariot.)

[Song of the holocaust of] the twelfth [S]abbath [on the twenty-first day of the third month]. . . :

The [cheru]bim prostrate themselves before Him and bless. As they rise, a whispered divine voice [is heard], and there is a roar of praise. When they drop their wings there is a [whispere]d divine voice. The cherubim bless the image of the divine throne-chariot above the firmament, [and] they praise the [majes]ty of the luminous firmament beneath His seat of glory. When the wheels advance, angels of holiness come and go. From between his glorious wheels, there is as it were a fiery vision of most holy spirits. About them, the appearance of rivulets of fire in the likeness of gleaming brass, and a work of . . . radiance in many-coloured glory, marvellous pigments, clearly mingled. The spirits of the living 'gods' move perpetually with the glory of the marvellous chariot. The whispered voice of blessing accompanies the roar of their advance, And they praise the Holy One on their way of return. When they ascend, they ascend marvellously and when they settle, they stand still. The sound of joyful praise is silenced and there is a whispered praise of the 'gods' in all the camps of God.

(4Q405 20–22)

Two particular ceremonies remain to be described to complete the sketch of the liturgical life of the Qumran sect. The daily common meal was probably taken in the evening, and the yearly ceremony of entry into, and renewal of, the Covenant was celebrated in the third month on the Feast of Weeks (Sunday, 15 Sivan), when all the Jews remembered God's granting of the Law (the *mattan Torah*) through Moses on Mount Sinai.

In regard to the meals, whether members of the married sect regularly ate in common is nowhere attested and is a priori doubtful, but they probably did so on solemn occasions such as the Renewal of the Covenant. By contrast, the units of the celibate groups of the sect, portrayed in the Community Rule, regularly shared a common table. The meal itself is outlined in 1QS and 1QSa and in both it follows a council meeting. In the council and at the meal everything is formal and organized hierarchically. The Community Rule first deals with the assembly of ten.

Wherever there are ten men of the council of the community, there shall not lack a priest among them. And they shall all sit before him according to their rank and shall be asked their counsel in all things in that order.

(1QS 6:3–4)

Next comes the rubric relative to the common table:

And when the table has been prepared for eating and the wine (*tirosh*) for drinking, the priest shall be the first to stretch out his hand to bless the firstfruits of the bread and wine.

(1QS 6:4–6)

Jewish custom conferred on the priests the privilege to recite grace before a meal. The mention of bread and wine does not necessarily mean that nothing else was served: bread can stand for solid food and wine for drink. The word used for the latter is not the ordinary term for wine (*yayin*), but a less common one (*tirosh*), which in rabbinic Hebrew also designates any kind of unfermented fruit juice, including grape juice. It is conceivable therefore, though by no means certain, that the sectaries abstained from alcoholic drink. From the regulation dealing with the training of candidates, we know that 'novices' were not allowed to partake in the solemn sectarian meals. These

149

were reserved only for the fully initiated members who had not been temporarily excluded from the common table.

The Rule of the Congregation sets out a similar directive for the council meeting and the formal supper in the messianic age, foreseeing the participation of 'the Priest' (Messiah) and the royal Messiah of Israel.

[This shall be the ass]embly of the men of renown [called] to the meeting of the council of the community.

When God engenders (the Priest) Messiah, he shall come with them at the head of the whole congregation of Israel with all [his brethren, the sons of] Aaron the priests, [those called] to the assembly, the men of renown; and they shall sit [before him, each man] in the order of his dignity. And then [the Messiah of Israel] shall [come], and the chiefs of the [clans of Israel] shall sit before him, [each] in the order of his dignity, according to [his place] in their camps and marches. And before them shall sit the heads of [family of the congreg]ation, and the wise men of [the holy congregation,] each in the order of his dignity.

And when they shall gather for the common table to eat and [to drink] wine, and when the common table shall be set for eating and the wine [poured] for drinking, let no man extend his hand over the firstfruits of the bread and wine before the Priest, for [it is he] who shall bless the firstfruits of bread and wine, and shall be the first [to extend] his hand over the bread. Thereafter the Messiah of Israel shall extend his hand over the bread, and all the congregation of the community [shall utter a] blessing, [each man in order] of his dignity.

It is according to this statute that they shall proceed at every meal at which at least ten men are gathered together.

(1QSa 2:11–22)

The precedence of the Priest Messiah is asserted at the messianic gathering and meal, too. He is to pronounce the blessing and help himself first, before the King Messiah. The mention of a series of blessings pronounced by each participant is missing from the ritual of the ordinary common meal given in the Community Rule. This absence contradicts to some extent the rule at the end of 1QSa, according to which the daily meal should follow the directives regulating the messianic banquet. The ordinary daily meal is conceived as inversely parallel to the Christian Eucharist. The Eucharist is believed to commemorate Jesus' Last Supper, whereas the Qumran community meal prefigures the common table rite of the messianic age.

In parenthesis, it is worth noting that the Rule of the Congregation is also attested by hundreds of tiny scraps of papyrus from Cave 4, written in a cryptic script. As the Cave 1 copy is not treated as especially secret, the production of this encrypted specimen in an arcane code has no rational justification. Was it the work of a mentally disturbed scribe?

Reference to the messianic banquet provides an opening for a mention of another appendix to the complete manuscript of the Community Rule, known as the Blessings (1QSb). As it ends with a benediction of the final Prince of the Congregation (the royal Messiah), it logically follows that all the other benedictions also refer to the messianic age and that the high priest is in fact the priestly Messiah. The words of blessing pronounced on him run:

May the Lord lift His countenance towards you; [May
    He delight in the] sweet odour [of your sacrifices]!
. . .
May He place upon your head [a diadem] . . . in

    [everlasting] glory; may He sanctify your seed in glory
    without end!
    May He grant you everlasting [peace] . . .

(1QSb 3:1–6)

The Prince of the Congregation is blessed by the Master in the following terms:

May the Lord raise you up to everlasting heights, and as a
    fortified tower upon a high wall!
[May you smite the peoples] with the might of your hand and
    ravage the earth with your sceptre; may you bring death to
    the ungodly with the breath of your lips . . .
May He make your horns of iron and your hooves of bronze;
    may you toss like a young bull . . . like the mire of the
    streets . . .
He shall strengthen you with His holy Name and you shall be
    as a [lion] . . .

(1QSb 5:23–9)

Among the annual festivals of the Community the most important was that of the Renewal of the Covenant celebrated on the Feast of Weeks. On that day, the 'novices' who had passed muster and the children born into the married branch of the Community who had reached the age of twenty years were enrolled into the sect by swearing an oath to return to the Law of Moses and observe it as interpreted by the Zadokite priests. Together with the newly professed, the existing members reiterated their commitment in the course of a solemn ceremony which entailed a 'baptism' or ritual purificatory immersion. The same festival witnessed the annual re-ranking of the sectaries in conformity with their spiritual performance during the preceding twelve months. The sad event of the occasion was the expulsion of members who had seriously failed to live up to the onerous moral and ritual demands of the Community.

The first section of the Cave 1 version of the Community Rule (1QS 1:1–3:12) focuses on this ritual. It begins by setting out the aim of the sect:

that they may seek God with a whole heart and soul, and do what is good and right before Him as He has commanded by the hand of Moses and all His servants the prophets.

(1QS 1:1–3)

The newcomers and those who reiterated their previous commitment are portrayed as men freely devoting themselves to the observance of the divine precepts by refraining from following 'a sinful heart and lustful eyes' and accepting all the revelations concerning the sect's 'appointed times'. Entry into the Covenant began with the recitation by the priests and Levites of a benediction of God, which was concluded by a double amen uttered by all. Next, the priests recounted God's loving kindness towards the biblical Israel and the Levites detailed the sins committed by the people in the past, leading to a public confession by all the participants:

We have strayed! We have [disobeyed!] We and our fathers before us have sinned and acted wickedly ... But He has bestowed His bountiful mercy on us from everlasting to everlasting.

(1QS 1:24–2:1)

The confession is followed by a priestly blessing of the lot of God in the form of a paraphrase of Numbers 6:24–5:

May He bless you with all good and preserve you from all evil!
May He lighten your heart with life-giving wisdom and grant
you eternal knowledge!
May He raise His merciful face towards you for everlasting
bliss!

(1QS 2:2–4)

It was then the turn of the choir of the Levites to curse
the lot of Satan, or Belial as he was called at Qumran, and
those who entered the Covenant confirmed the blessings
and the curses by saying 'Amen, amen'. The priests and
the Levites went on jointly to pronounce a malediction on
any dishonest member of the Community whose repentance did not come from the heart. They were told they
would be cut off from among the sons of light. 'Amen,
amen', approved the sectaries. This cursing seems to
amount to a formal expulsion of members who had trans-
gressed the rules in serious matters or broken any single
commandment of the Law of Moses. A parallel passage in
one of the Cave 4 manuscripts of the Damascus Document
lays down: 'And all the inhabitants of the camps shall
assemble in the third month and curse him who turns
aside, to the right [or to the left, from the] law' (4Q266,
fr. 11).

After the curses and the eventual banishments, all those
remaining formed themselves into a procession to enter
into, or to renew, the Covenant, first the priests, second
the Levites and third the people, each one in the place
allotted to him according to his spiritual progress, a place
they would keep until the reclassification due twelve
months later.

All the old and new members were to descend into
purifying waters and undergo a baptism, which was be-

lieved to wash away all uncleanness through the spirit of holiness, uprightness and humility from those who were motivated by a humble submission of their soul to all the laws of God.

The ceremonial baptism was accompanied by a doctrinal instruction by the Master (*maskil*), who delivered a sermon on the works of the two spirits, the spirit of light and the spirit of darkness. This is the oldest theological tractate that has survived in Jewish literature (1QS 3:13–4:26). This was followed by the reading out of all the sectarian regulations (1QS 5:1–9:25). The account recalls the renewal of the Covenant and the reading of the Law by the priest Ezra in early post-exilic times (458 or 398 BC), as recorded in the Book of Nehemiah 8:1–8. Ezra's ritual seems to be the prototype of the Qumran festival. The Community Rule ends with a splendid and uplifting long poem from which the following extract is taken:

As for me, my justification is with God.
In His hand are the perfection of my way
And the uprightness of my heart.
He will wipe out my transgression through his righteousness.
For my light has sprung from the source of His knowledge,
My eyes have beheld His marvellous deeds,
and the light of my heart the mystery to come.
He that is everlasting is the support of my hand;
The way of my steps is over stout rock which nothing can
    shake.
For the rock of my steps is the truth of God
And His might is the support of my right hand.

From the source of His righteousness is my justification,
And from His marvellous mysteries is the light of my heart.

My eyes have gazed on that which is eternal,
On wisdom concealed from men,
On knowledge and wise design (hidden) from the sons of men;
On a fountain of righteousness and a storehouse of power,
On a spring of glory (hidden) from the assembly of flesh.
God has given them to His chosen ones as an everlasting
    possession,
And has caused them to inherit the lot of the Holy Ones.
He has joined their assembly to the Sons of Heaven
To be a council of the community,
a foundation of the building of holiness,
an eternal plantation throughout the ages to come.

                                                    (1QS 11:2–9)

Besides communal liturgies, the Qumran library has also yielded prayers written for individual use. The best preserved of these are the Thanksgiving Hymns contained in a scroll from Cave 1 and supplemented by fragments from Cave 4 (1QH, 1Q36, 4Q427–32). They are all more or less well-inspired imitations of the biblical Psalter. The poet almost always speaks in the first person singular, the I-form rather than the we-form. Some of the psalms appear to voice the life and sentiments of a controversial Community leader. Hence their not altogether convincing attribution to the Teacher of Righteousness, recounting his conflict with ungrateful members of his Community and a hostile high priest, who forced him into exile (1QH 4, 10–11; Habakkuk Commentary 11:4–8). However, most of the poems may be applied to anyone. Profound humility and limitless gratitude towards a benevolent God characterize them. Two leading ideas run through the corpus: election and knowledge. A frail human being, a 'creature of clay', is chosen by the Almighty and graciously elevated to the company of the angels to sing God's praises in unison with the heavenly choirs.

Clay and dust that I am, what can I devise unless You wish it,
    and what can I contrive unless You desire it?
What strength shall I have unless You keep me upright
And how shall I understand unless by (the spirit) You have
    shaped for me?
What can I say unless You open my mouth
And how can I answer unless You enlighten me?
Behold, You are the Prince of gods and the King of majesties,
Lord of the spirits and Ruler of creatures;
Nothing is done without You, and nothing is known without
    Your will.
Beside You, there is nothing, nothing can compare with You
    in strength.
In the presence of Your glory there is nothing, Your might is
    priceless.
Who among Your great and marvellous creatures can stand
    before Your glory?
How can then he who returns to dust?
For Your glory's sake alone have you made all these things.

                                   (1QH 18:5–10)

As for the second theme, heavenly knowledge, the sectary, using the words of the poet, constantly seeks to express his thanks for being the beneficiary of the divine mysteries revealed to the Teacher of Righteousness and the spiritual masters of his community.

I [thank You, O Lord],
for You have enlightened me through Your truth.

In Your marvellous mysteries and loving-kindness to a man
  [of vanity
And] in the greatness of Your mercy to a perverse heart
You have granted me knowledge.

(1QH 15:26–7)

C. HISTORY AND BIBLE INTERPRETATION

No historical document in the strict sense has emerged from the Qumran caves. A very fragmentary calendar (4Q331–3), mentioning known personalities like the Priest John (probably John Hyrcanus I, 135–103 BCE) and Shelamzion or Queen Salome Alexandra (76–67 BCE), widow of the high priest Alexander Jannaeus (102–76 BCE), and a poem alluding to 'king Jonathan' (4Q448) of disputed identity (the same Jannaeus or Jonathan Maccabaeus, 153/2–143/2 BCE) usefully set the historical framework. Our best sources for the reconstruction of the origins of the Qumran Community are the Exhortation at the beginning of the Damascus Document (CD 1–8), a kind of sermon sketching the appearance of the Teacher of Righteousness and the early history of the sect, and commentaries or *pesharim* attached to the biblical books of Habakkuk, Nahum and the Psalter (Psalm 37), in which the interpreters assert that ancient predictions point at persons and events in the history of the Qumran sect and that these persons and events, divinely chosen and arranged, constitute the fulfilment and supply the meaning of scriptural prophecies.

1. The Exhortation of the Damascus Document

To start with the Damascus Document, the initial scene refers to the 'age of wrath', a period of political and religious turmoil, occurring 390 years after the conquest of Jerusalem by Nebuchadnezzar, king of Babylon, in 586 BCE, according to our chronological reckoning. The preacher of the Exhortation, relying on the scriptural concept of the 'righteous remnant', that is to say, a small group of God-fearing people providentially saved from the cataclysm, speaks of the root of a new plant springing to life out of Jewry, literally out of Aaron and Israel, to form a little society, full of good intention, but not knowing where to go and what to do. They 'groped for the way' in darkness like blind men for a time. After twenty years God took pity on them and sent for them a leader, the Teacher of Righteousness, to guide them towards the light. The career of the Teacher did not proceed smoothly. Opposition arose within the community, motivated by doctrinal and legal disagreements. The mischief-maker is variously nicknamed the 'Scoffer', the 'Liar' or the 'Spouter of lies'. He and his followers contrived to force the Teacher and his faithful followers into exile to the 'land of Damascus', probably a sobriquet for Qumran (CD 1:4–21; 8:21; 20:12). There the Teacher launched a new Covenant based on the correct interpretation of divine revelation. The details of his career are unknown and all we are told about his end is that he was 'gathered in', that is, he died, presumably in exile. His opponents were to reap their just deserts when God's revenge was meted out to them by the hand of 'the chief of the kings of *Greece*'. Another chronological detail alludes to a final forty-year period separating the death of the Teacher from the violent destruction of his enemies, depicted as 'the men of war who had deserted to the Liar' (CD B2:13–14), the leader who rose against the Teacher from within the ranks of the community. The historical and chronological analysis and identification of these and other allusions will be presented in chapter VIII.

2. Bible Interpretation and the Historically Linked *Pesher*

The Qumran caves have preserved documents containing various works of scriptural exegesis. The simplest of these figure in specimens of straight Bible translation: a small fragment of Leviticus (4Q156) and a mutilated scroll of Job (11Q10; 4Q157) have survived in Aramaic, and remains of Exodus (7Q1), Leviticus (4Q119–20), Numbers (4Q121), Deuteronomy (4Q122) and the Epistle of Jeremiah (7Q2) in Greek. Some further tiny Greek papyrus fragments from Cave 7, mistakenly identified first by José O'Callaghan and later by Carsten Peter Thiede as representing New Testament extracts, are more likely relics of the Greek version of the Book of Enoch.

The examples, not of translation, but of the actual exposition of Scripture oscillate between occasional paraphrases inserted into a biblical book, as in the Reworked Pentateuch (4Q158; 4Q364–7), and continuous and substantial interpretative passages cleverly woven into the text of the books of the Bible, prefiguring Josephus' reformulation of the Scripture narrative in his *Jewish Antiquities* and the midrashic enlargements built into the Palestinian paraphrastic Targums (Fragmentary Targum, Pseudo-Jonathan and Neophyti). The Genesis Apocryphon from

Cave 1 offers excellent illustrations. For instance, instead of the prosaic statement that on Sarah's arrival in Egypt, Pharaoh's princes reported her prettiness to their master (Genesis 12:14–15), the writer of the Apocryphon inserts a poem in which they enthusiastically sing the praises of the lady's stunning beauty:

... and how beautiful her face?
How ... fine is the hair of her head and how lovely are her
   eyes!
How desirable is her nose and all the radiance of her
   countenance!
...
How fair are her breasts and how beautiful all their whiteness!
How pleasing are her arms and how perfect her hands
And how[desirable] the appearance of her hands!
How fair are her palms and how long and slender are her
   fingers!
How comely are her feet and how perfect her thighs!
No virginal bride led into the marriage chamber is prettier
   than she,
She is fairer than all other women; truly her beauty is greater
   than theirs!
Yet together with all this grace goes abundant wisdom
So that whatever she does is perfect!

(1Qap Gen 20:2–8)

In another type of commentary on Genesis, the interpreter seeks to adjust the biblical chronology of the flood of Noah to the solar calendar of the Qumran sect and expressly associates the 'men of the Community' with the future 'Messiah of Righteousness, Branch of David' (4Q252).

The most important among the exegetical works attached to a distinct biblical book are the so-called *pesharim* (singular, *pesher*). The term simply means 'interpretation', but is used for a special kind of exegesis in which a biblical prophecy is explained through its realization in an event or in a person within the history of the Qumran Community. This type of exposition of the Bible, though characteristic of the Dead Sea Scrolls, is attested also in the numerous New Testament examples where biblical prophecies are claimed to have been realized in Jesus and, less frequently, in the midrashic literature of rabbinic Judaism where, for instance, the leader of the second Jewish rebellion against Rome, nicknamed Bar Kokhba or Son of the Star is seen as the fulfilment of the scriptural prediction, 'A star shall come out of Jacob' (Num. 24:17). It is not impossible and is even likely that this interpretative technique was borrowed from the Qumran Community by the evangelists, Paul and the later rabbis.

In the Scrolls the continuous *pesher* accompanied some of the prophetic books as well as the Psalms, the latter also being considered by the sect as 'uttered through prophecy' (11QPsalms 27:11). *Pesher*-type exegesis is attached to the biblical books of Isaiah (4Q162–5), Hosea (4Q166–7), Micah (1Q14), Nahum (4Q169), Habakkuk (1QpHab), Zephaniah (1Q15; 4Q170), Malachi (4Q253a) and Psalms (1Q16; 4Q171, 173). The Habakkuk Commentary, covering the first two chapters of the prophet, has been preserved in a nearly complete form covering thirteen columns. The Nahum *pesher* survives in several largish fragments as do those commenting on Isaiah and Psalm 37. The others are more scrappy.

As far as the history of the Dead Sea Community is concerned, the *pesharim* tell the story which has already been anticipated in lesser detail in the Exhortation of the Damascus Document. The synopsis is primarily based on the Habakkuk Commentary which offers the fullest picture. In it, we are faced on the one hand with the 'Teacher of Righteousness', a priestly leader having enjoyed special divine revelations. He was surrounded by disciples who formed his community. Within the group arose a rebellious leader who disagreed with the Teacher on various points of doctrine, and from outside came the 'Wicked Priest', a high priest endowed with political power ('he ruled over Israel'), who was at first well-meaning, but subsequently went astray, corrupted by might and money. The Teacher and his party were forced into exile, where they proclaimed themselves the spiritual replacement of the Jerusalem Temple. The fate of the Teacher of Righteousness is not disclosed – he probably died in exile – but that of the Wicked Priest is clearly stated: he was captured by unspeci-fied enemies called 'the violent of the nations' (Commen-tary on Psalms 37, 4Q171, 4:9–10), and his later successors were removed from power by the new world conquerors, the Kittim, who acted as God's chosen instrument in executing vengeance on 'the last priests of Jerusalem'. The historical perspective of the Habakkuk Commentary ends with the arrival of a ruler of the Kittim (Romans) in the capital of Judaea, no doubt Pompey the Great in 63 BCE.

The Commentaries on Hosea, Nahum and the Psalms mention two further political-religious parties distinct from and in conflict with the Qumran Community and meta-phorically designate them as 'Ephraim' and 'Manasseh', the two symbolical ancestors of the northern tribes of the biblical Israel who separated from the southern tribes of Judah and Benjamin. The Nahum and Hosea Commen-taries further refer to a bloodthirsty priest, nicknamed the 'furious young lion', who struck Ephraim (Commentary on Hosea) and 'hanged alive' (crucified) some of them (Commentary on Nahum), applying the penalty prescribed in the Temple Scroll for traitors of the Jewish nation (11QTemple 64:7–8). If the story is inspired by the crucifixion of 800 Pharisees by the Hasmonean priest-king Alexander Jannaeus (Josephus, *Jewish War* I:97), one would have reason to deduce that Ephraim stands for the Pharisees, Alexander's enemies, and consequently Manasseh would refer to the Sadducees, his supporters.

One of the Commentaries on Isaiah (4Q161) takes us to the final age by which time the Kittim, not yet inimical to the community in the Habakkuk Commentary, become – as in the War Scroll and the Book of War – the ultimate foe of the sons of light and are destined for annihilation by their royal Messiah, referred to as the Branch of David.

The deliberately obscure historical allusions of the Damascus Document and the Qumran *pesharim* will be subjected to a detailed interpretation in the light of the data furnished by archaeology and the writings of Flavius Josephus in the final section of chapter IX.

Beside *pesharim*, the Qumran Bible exegetes also produced thematic interpretative works based on selected scriptural extracts such as the so-called Florilegium (4Q174) which mentions the coming of two messianic figures, the 'Interpreter of the Law' (priestly Messiah) and the 'Branch of David' (the messianic king) and the Testimonia or Messianic Anthology (4Q175) which ends with an historical interpretation of Joshua 6:26 (see also 4Q379), announcing the coming of two brothers who would be 'instruments of violence'. Other thematic exegetical compositions reinterpret biblical law (4Q159, 513–14), weave together citations relating to the Heavenly Prince,

Melchizedek, identified with the archangel Michael, and mentioning his counterpart, Melkiresha or Belial/Satan (11Q13). To these should be added excerpts concerning divine consolation (*Tanhumim*, 4Q176) from which, unfortunately, most of the original sectarian interpretation has disappeared, and a collection (Catena/Chain) of biblical quotes referring to the last days (4Q177, 182).

D. WISDOM LITERATURE

Only a restricted amount of sapiential composition have been found at Qumran. Of these, eight manuscripts of a Wisdom work entitled *Instructions* form the bulk, but apart from fairly rare verbal similarities, like a reference to the 'mystery to come', they contain hardly anything that can be qualified as strictly sectarian. Their message concerns common piety and correct behaviour towards one's wife, children and neighbours. If they have any sectarian connection, it would be with the married community members of the 'Damascus' Covenant. It is best to assume that the *Sapiential Works* or Instructions (4Q415–18), *Bless, my soul* (4Q434–8) as well as *The Seductress* (4Q184), *The Songs of the Sage* (4Q510–11) and *The Beatitudes* (4Q525) existed before the foundation of the Dead Sea Community and were inherited by its members. Much of the counsel the sage hands out in the *Instructions* is sensible everyday practical wisdom.

Do not strike him who is without your strength
lest you stumble and your shame increase greatly.
[Do not s]ell yourself for wealth
it is better for you to be a slave in spirit.

And serve your master freely
And do not sell your glory for a price.
Do not give money in pledge for your inheritance
lest it impoverish your body.
Do not satiate yourself with bread while there is no clothing.
Do not drink wine while there is no food.
Do not seek luxury when you lack bread.
Do not glorify yourself in your need if you are poor
lest you degrade your life.
Also do not treat with contempt the vessel of your bosom
  (wife) . . .

                                      (4Q416 2:16–21)

Gospel parallels have secured some notoriety for the *Beatitudes*, as New Testament scholars sought to discover in it pointers to account for the differences between the Beatitudes of Luke 6:20–26 and Matthew 5:3–12. Yet whereas partial similarities between Matthew and 4Q525 are undeniable, the discrepancies in form and inspiration are considerable. The eschatological intensity of Matthew is greater and the units are structured differently: in Matthew each virtue is accompanied by its reward ('Blessed is the poor in spirit, for theirs is the Kingdom of God'), while the Qumran Beatitudes append an antithetic parallelism to the blessing (blessed is he who does this and abstains from doing that). In a way the negative aspect of the Qumran Beatitudes recalls the Woes which follow Jesus' blessings as described by Luke: 'Blessed are you poor, for yours is the Kingdom' – 'Woe to you that are rich, for you have received your consolation' (Luke 6:20; 6:24).

[Blessed is] . . . with a pure heart
and does not slander with his tongue.

Blessed are those who hold to her (Wisdom's) precepts
and do not hold to the ways of iniquity.
Blessed are those who rejoice in her,
and do not burst forth in ways of folly.
Blessed are those who seek her with pure hands,
and do not pursue her with a treacherous heart.
Blessed is the man who has attained Wisdom,
and walks in the Law of the Most High.

(4Q525 fr. 2, 2:1–4)

APPENDIX:
MISCELLANEOUS TEXTS

A document found by Roland de Vaux's team in Qumran Cave 3 and two inscribed potsherds accidentally discovered forty years later by an American archaeologist in the perimeter wall dividing the Qumran ruins from the cemetery do not fit into any of the previous pigeonholes. The first of these is the Copper Scroll (3Q15), preserved in two parts. It was first published independently by J. M. Allegro in 1960 as *The Treasure of the Copper Scroll*, and officially by J. T. Milik in 1962 in *DJD*, III. (Seemingly still hankering after the long defunct 'closed shop' era, Émile Puech refers – more than forty years after its publication – to Allegro's book as a 'pirated edition'.)

In 2006, the Copper Scroll was given a lavish new facelift, subsidized by the Foundation of Électricité de France. Scientifically reexamined by Daniel Brizemeure and Noël Lacoudre and retranslated by Émile Puech, it was reissued under the title, *Le Rouleau de cuivre de la grotte 3 de Qumrân (3Q15): Expertise – Restauration – Épigraphie I–II* (Leiden, Brill, 2006).

The Copper Scroll has always been an enigma. It consists of twelve columns of Hebrew text embossed on copper and listing sixty-four hiding places in Jerusalem, its neighbourhood and other locations in the Holy Land where a colossal quantity of silver, gold and Temple offerings were concealed. Cryptic instructions are given for the discovery of the treasures, but in hiding place no. 64 the lucky treasure hunter is promised 'a copy of this writing and its explanation and the measurements and the details of each item'. Allegro tried his hand in 1960 at uncovering the treasures, but with no luck.

No agreed view exists on the nature of the Copper Scroll. Those who argue in favour of real deposits of gold and silver surmise that the source of the coins and precious metals is either the Temple or the treasury of the Qumran sect. Neither opinion is without serious difficulties. No doubt, the Jerusalem sanctuary was extremely rich and could conceivably account for the enormous sums to which the deposits add up. But how can one account for a record (indeed, two records) of the Temple treasure being hidden, together with their other writings, by people from Qumran who were on hostile terms with the Temple authorities? Also, according to Josephus, who wrote his *Jewish War* only a few years after the destruction of Jerusalem probably between 75 and 79 CE, the 'vast sums of money' belonging to the Temple were still in the treasure chambers when the sanctuary was set on fire in 70 CE (*Jewish War* VI:282).

According to Puech's latest count, the various deposits amounted to 1,672 talents of silver, 362 talents of gold and 1,504 talents of unspecified precious material, plus a large unmeasured quantity of gold and silver. There are also 165 ingots of gold, 19 bars of silver, etc. Could this gigantic wealth have belonged, as Puech, Dupont-Sommer and others suggest, to an ascetic sect which called itself the Community of the Poor? Are the figures exaggerated or was the talent of the Scroll smaller than the Jewish *kikkar*, estimated to weigh 35 kilograms? Those who argue that the Copper Scroll speaks of real treasure are confronted with an apparently insoluble problem.

On the other hand, the theory, first advanced by J. T. Milik, the official editor of the Copper Scroll, that the document recounts a story about a legendary hidden treasure, runs into equally serious difficulties. Only an unbalanced mind would laboriously engrave on copper in language of utmost seriousness and realism, a twelve-column-long complicated list of sixty-four purely fictional caches. In short, with the Copper Scroll we are still at square one.

The two ostraca found by Professor James F. Strange from the University of South Florida in 1996 on the Qumran site itself are also a puzzle. The text on the second sherd is badly damaged and is without significance. The first is very difficult to decipher and two completely different interpretations have been offered. According to the 'official' editors, Frank Moore Cross and Esther Eshel, the potsherd contains the draft of a deed of gift in which a certain Honi, in fulfilment of his oath to the Qumran Community, handed over to Eleazar, son of Nahmani (the Bursar of the sect?) a slave called Hisday of Holon, as well as a house and an orchard. If this reading and interpretation are correct, we have the first external documentary evidence, discovered on the Qumran site itself, regarding a sectarian practice, that of a 'novice' handing over his property to an official of the sect (*DJD*, XXXVI, pp. 497–508).

However, another renowned palaeographer, Dr Ada

Yardeni of the Hebrew University, arrived at an entirely different decipherment and explanation. Instead of the name, Hisday of Holon, she reads 'these sackcloths', and 'when he fulfilled his oath to the community' becomes 'and every other tree'. Here, with no allusion to the sect, we have a pathetically prosaic donation by Honi to Eleazar of sackcloths, a house, fig trees and olive trees (*Israel Exploration Journal*, 47 (1997), pp. 233–7).

Both interpretations are problematic. One needs a substantial amount of good will or creative imagination to recognize with Cross and Eshel the crucial term 'Community' (*yahad*) on the ostracon. On the other hand, one would hardly expect a list of valuable gifts, a house and fruit trees to open with the unexciting item of sackcloths. I am afraid we have not yet heard the last word about this humble potsherd, which may or may not hold the key to the identity of the Qumran sect.

This is the summary account of the non-biblical sectarian Dead Sea Scrolls. The three main questions it still leaves open regarding the archaeological evidence, the identity and the history of the Qumran Community will be reinvestigated in the next chapter.

VIII

Unfinished Business:
Archaeology – Group Identity – History

Having reported directly and, I trust, fairly the story of the Qumran discoveries, followed up by an evaluation of the message of the non-sectarian and sectarian Dead Sea Scrolls, I still owe the reader a reconsideration of three major areas of the Qumran complex on which scholarly consensus has not yet been reached. I refer to the interpretation of the archaeological finds, the identification of the Qumran Community and a final attempt to outline the history of the Dead Sea sect. In the case of archaeology, the lack of agreement is partly due to the incompleteness of the available evidence and to the – in my view – mistaken unwillingness of some writers to include the Dead Sea Scrolls themselves among the archaeological data. The two other controversial topics, the identity of the ancient residents at Qumran (in particular whether they were the Essenes of Philo, Josephus and Pliny) and their history demand further treatment because of the necessarily hypothetical character of any conclusion one may reach. None of the texts attaches an easily recognizable label to the Dead Sea community, nor do we find a single clear pointer to a known historical fact. Despite six decades of unceasing intellectual struggle, Qumran archaeology, group identity and history still constitute 'unfinished business'.

1. Fresh Approaches to Archaeology

As a result of Roland de Vaux's happy-go-lucky way of conducting his excavations of the site of Qumran, its cemetery and the farm at Ain Feshkha, archaeology is the most unfinished of all the unfinished aspects of Scrolls research. Hardly more than 5 per cent of the graves have been opened and investigated; a good number of the hundreds of coins found in the various strata of the site are not only unpublished, but many of them have apparently gone missing. The thirteen years separating the final dig in 1958 from his death in 1971 were not enough for de Vaux to start, let alone complete, the writing of the official report he was duty-bound to issue about the Qumran excavations. As I once put it, if the slow-motion publication of the Dead Sea manuscripts was the academic scandal of the twentieth century, the miserable handling by de Vaux and his successors of the archaeological finds has stretched the scandal well into the third millennium. And the end of the tunnel is still nowhere in sight.

Archaeological research is meant to play a twofold role vis-à-vis the Qumran material. Its primary aim is to determine and explain the purpose and nature of the ruins and of the objects they contain, as well as to establish the chronology of this ancient settlement and the identity of its original occupants. Since none of the manuscripts, apart from two inscribed potsherds, was discovered among the ruins, archaeology's second task is to define the relationship, if any, between the inhabitants of Qumran during the time of its occupation in antiquity and the manuscripts discovered in the various caves in the area. Roland de Vaux and his team, whose interpretation of the site as the home of a Jewish religious community was first alluded to in chapter II (p. 39), automatically took for granted that there was a link between the establishment and the Scrolls, and came to adopt almost immediately the identification of the Qumran Community with the Jewish religious organization of the Essenes that flourished during the last two centuries before the destruction of the Temple of Jerusalem in 70 CE. Adopting the theory first proposed by Eleazar Lipa Sukenik and André Dupont-Sommer, in 1948 and 1950 respectively, de Vaux and his colleagues felt free to mix the information gathered from the Scrolls with that found in the classical Greek and Latin accounts (Philo, Josephus, Pliny) for the interpretation of the data supplied by archaeology.

In this, they may have been ultimately correct, but they proceeded in a somewhat hasty manner. If we discount the two inscribed potsherds accidentally discovered in the 1990s, which in any case were unknown to de Vaux, not a single manuscript was found on the site itself. Therefore it is *theoretically* conceivable that the deposit of written material had nothing to do with the inhabitants of the establishment, let alone with their Essene identity. Rightly or wrongly, remove from the equation the religious character of the settlement, and at once the Qumran ruins will be open to a variety of explanations as the history of the research has demonstrated since 1980.

The first broadside against the theory of Qumran as the home of the quasi-monastic congregation of the Essenes was delivered by Professor Norman Golb of Chicago University in various publications between 1980 and 1995. In his view, Scrolls and ruins formed two discrete categories which had strictly nothing to do with one another. In Golb's view, the manuscripts originated from Jerusalem (from one or several libraries) and came to be hidden in caves in the Dead Sea area during the Roman siege of the Holy City some time between 67 and 70 CE by people *unconnected* with the Qumranites. Having thus smoothly separated the Scrolls from the establishment, Golb proposed to see in the building complex of Qumran and in particular in its tower, a military establishment, a small rural fort, and in the adjacent cemetery the burial place of well over 1,000 fallen defenders of the post.

The second new theory also ignores the Scrolls and treats the Qumran buildings as a country residence constructed in the centre of an agricultural estate by rich landowners from Jerusalem. The Belgian archaeologist couple behind this thesis, Robert Donceel and Pauline Donceel-Voûte (1992, 1994), turned the plaster tables of de Vaux's *scriptorium* or manuscript copying room into a dining hall (*triclinium*). The tables were not used for writing; in fact, they were not tables at all, but couches on which the participants of many a splendid dinner reclined.

In 1994 another fresh idea was launched by Professor Alan Crown and his student Lena Cansdale of the University of Sydney. They saw in Qumran a hostelry for merchants, a kind of caravanserai, lying at a major crossroads on the way from Transjordan via a boat trip by the Dead Sea to Jerusalem. Once again the Scrolls have been left out of consideration.

In the same year (1994), the Dominican Father Jean-Baptist Humbert, the man who inherited the task of producing the final archaeological report on the excavations of Qumran that de Vaux had neglected to write, came up with a compromise solution. He abandoned the thesis of de Vaux in part and sided with the Donceels, accepting that Qumran was first a country villa, similar to other such estates in the region. However, he claimed that around the middle of the first century BCE, it passed to a religious group, possibly after the earthquake which hit the region in 31 BCE. At this juncture, Humbert reverted to de Vaux and to the mainstream interpretation of the Qumran ruins as a religious establishment.

The most comprehensive and determined attack on de Vaux's idea of an Essene Qumran was launched in 2004 by the recently deceased Hebrew University professor Yizhar Hirschfeld in a fashionably entitled monograph, *Qumran in Context: Reassessing the Archaeological Evidence.* (Nowadays to be with it, one must treat everything 'in context'.) Leaving aside the relics dating to the pre-exilic era, Hirschfeld allocates the archaeological finds to three periods. In the Hasmonean era, from the late second century to the mid-first century BCE, Qumran was a small fort and served exclusively military purposes. In the Herodian period, from *c.* 40 BCE to 68 CE, both Qumran and Ain Feshkha formed a rural estate belonging to a well-to-do Jewish family. Hirschfeld, like the Donceels before him, identified de Vaux's *scriptorium* as a *triclinium* or dining hall, and as far as industries are concerned, saw the production of balsam, for which Jericho and Engedi were world-famous in antiquity, as the distinctive speciality of the Qumran estate. This theory is primarily based on the discovery in a cave, not in close proximity to Qumran (about 3 km to the north), of a small bottle that *may* have contained balsam according to the 'very cautious' suggestion of J. Patrich and B. Arubas (*Eretz-Israel*, 20 (1989), p. 206*). Here again the Scrolls have no role to play. In Hirschfeld's view, the only possible connection between the inhabitants of the site and the Scrolls was that they may have assisted Jerusalem Jews, seeking to save their manuscript treasures, in advising them about suitable hiding places in the cliffs. Yizhar Hirschfeld proudly described himself as the champion of a *secular* Qumran which he had liberated 'from the burden of religious significance'!

Finally, in an electronic publication issued in 2007, Yitzhak Magen and Yuval Peleg, two archaeologists working for the Israel Antiquities Authority, rejected all the previous theories and in the light of their excavation of the site, conducted between 1993 and 2003, concluded that Qumran was an industrial centre primarily devoted to pottery production.

So was Qumran a military establishment (Golb)? A *villa rustica* or country estate (the Donceels and Humbert)? A luxurious inn for travelling merchants (Crown and Cansdale)? A pottery workshop (Magen and Peleg)? Was it first a fort, then an agricultural settlement and then finally turned into a balsam factory (Hirschfeld)? Or was an original fortress converted in time to become the residence of a Jewish religious group (Humbert)? Or was it, as mainstream scholarship in the footsteps of de Vaux has always held, the centre of a religious community?

Before tackling the revisionist ideas, let me confront their common underlying presupposition, namely that the Dead Sea Scrolls have nothing to do directly with the people who lived at Qumran at the turn of the era. It is true, let it be repeated, that no scroll, not even the minutest manuscript fragment, has turned up in the ruins themselves. It is also conceivable – even if unlikely – that the more distant natural caves (1–3, 11) may have served as specially chosen hiding places by people who did not live in the area. But the man-made caves (4–10) in the marl terrace within a stone's throw from the eastern edge of the building complex can hardly be imagined as *unconnected* with Qumran. Among these caves figures Cave 4, a library or manuscript depository, originally with wooden shelves, containing about two-thirds of over 900 Dead Sea Scrolls. Scholars who ignore these *archaeological facts* in their attempt to interpret the Qumran settlement do so at their own risk. But even the manuscripts deposited in the more distant caves do not lack an indirect, but significant, *archaeological* link with the Qumran site. Untypical cylindrical scrolls jars found in Cave 1, but almost unattested and definitely uncommon elsewhere, have been discovered both on the Qumran site and in neighbouring caves. In short, not only the great closeness of the majority of the discovered manuscripts to the Qumran establishment, but the presence of the peculiar Qumran-type pottery in Scrolls caves, make it a priori methodologically unsound to consider the manuscripts as unrelated to the nearby habitation.

Moreover, the unexamined theory, first mooted by Norman Golb and unhesitatingly adopted by Yizhar Hirschfeld and others, regarding the provenance of the Scrolls from Jerusalem, runs into a twofold difficulty. Imagine that the manuscripts discovered in the Dead Sea region of the Judaean desert actually had belonged to a Jerusalem institution, even perhaps to the library of the Temple, and their owners or guardians decided to take them to a safe place in a time of danger, why on earth should they have risked carrying large numbers of precious manuscripts to a God-forsaken spot like the faraway Qumran caves when equally good hiding places could have easily been found closer to home? Also, looking at it from a down-to-earth point of view, would the authorities which failed to put the Temple treasure in a safe location (see chapter VII, p. 168), have taken all that trouble to transport to relatively distant Qumran a collection of manuscripts?

A second serious argument militates against the Jerusalem library theory, namely the nature of a notable proportion of the texts. The reason for asserting the Jerusalem origin of the Scrolls is to combat the mainstream opinion that they came from the Essene sect resident at neighbouring Qumran. Yet many of the manuscripts found in the caves are definitely *sectarian*. Take, for instance, the liturgical calendars as an example. We number fifteen of these among the Scrolls. They all attest an unofficial sectarian calendar and not a single one comprises the time reckoning according to which the priests in Jerusalem regulated their worship. Examined from close quarters, the revisionist historians' endeavour to 'secularize' Qumran by 'liberating' it from the Scrolls falls flat. It would even become ludicrous if, in order to combat the theory that the Dead Sea Scrolls were manuscripts deposited by the Qumran Essenes in nearby caves, the revisionists had to fall back on the suggestion that the texts were concealed by Jerusalem Essenes in the Qumran area with which they had no prior connection! To strengthen my sarcasm, let me point out that Josephus' mention of an 'Essene gate' in the Holy City (*Jewish War* III:145) implies the likely existence of an Essene congregation in Jerusalem.

But even without their deliberate ignoring of the Dead Sea Scrolls, the revisionist theories stand up badly to scrutiny. The only argument in favour of Qumran being a fortress (Golb, Humbert, Hirschfeld) is that it has a reinforced tower, although some of the reinforcement should probably be attributed to repair work after the earthquake which hit Judaea in 31 BCE. But it is well known that towers were not necessarily linked to strongholds; they existed also in orchards and agricultural estates as observation points and even as protection against marauding gangs of brigands. Furthermore, the idea of a military establishment at Qumran is hardly consonant with the thin and shabby perimeter walls and the unsecured water supply. As for the adjacent cemetery consisting of 1,200 individual military graves, this hardly makes sense. If for hygienic reasons the victors had decided to bury the corpses of the fallen enemy, they would surely have thrown them, as Magen Broshi has remarked, into a shallow mass grave and not in neatly arranged individual resting places.

If the idea of a fortress does not fare well, neither does that of a rural mansion in the midst of an agricultural estate (Donceels, Hirschfeld). The arid land of the Dead Sea shore cannot be compared to the fertile oasis of the area of Jericho or Engedi, and Hirschfeld's assertion that the climate was more favourable to agriculture 2,000 years ago is an unascertainable supposition. The Qumran buildings, devoid of decorative features, do not resemble the structure of a typical *villa rustica*, and the idea of a *triclinium* for luxury banquets has been blown sky-high by Ronny Reich when he pointed out that the Qumran couch or divan is only 50 centimetres wide, too narrow to allow a person to recline in comfort. The only other plaster furniture of this sort discovered in Judaea and dating to the same period is 1.8 metres wide (*Journal of Jewish Studies*, 46 (1995), pp. 157–60).

The hostelry surmise (Crown, Cansdale) is the weakest of a set of ill-founded theories. For Qumran to be seen as a caravanserai for merchants travelling from Transjordan to Jerusalem, we must suppose that it lay close to busy roads. But there is no evidence that this was the case. There are no signs of nearby harbour installations either, nor do the ruins reveal remains of international commercial activity. Once I ironically referred to the Crown–Cansdale thesis as the Qumran Hilton theory, an installation providing comfort with swimming pools and a large library to rich salt merchants who sought relaxation in the study of religious literature. As for the unexpectedly large graveyard, attached to a place without regular inhabitants, it would be best explained by the hypothesis of successive outbreaks of salmonella poisoning.

A final word about the Magen–Peleg theory: two working kilns are scarcely enough for the establishment of a pottery manufacturing centre in the middle of nowhere.

The long and the short of the re-examination of the revisionist attempts is that they all lack the strength to undermine the mainstream interpretation of Qumran archaeology. Roland de Vaux's thesis that Qumran was the home of a Jewish religious community, which in some way was associated with the Dead Sea Scrolls, has stood the test by fire. This flattering conclusion does not mean, however, that the original excavator has said the last word on the subject. The understanding of the material objects found at Qumran has moved ahead during the last half century, and now is the moment to catch up with progress.

Over the years, and especially during the last two decades, both field archaeology and further study of the already available evidence have improved the commonly held views but have also questioned some of de Vaux's interpretations without affecting his generally accepted conclusions. A clear, even magisterial account of the current state of research has been available since 2002 in *The Archaeology of Qumran and the Dead Sea Scrolls* by Professor Jodi Magness. She has added much valuable information on pottery, water installations, ritual purification, etc. but her most notable innovation concerns de Vaux's chronology of the site. She is not convinced that de Vaux's earliest phase (Period Ia) of the communal occupation of Qumran (130–100 BCE) really existed, as the sect, in her opinion, did not settle in the area before 100 BCE. Magness's opening phase is de Vaux's Period Ib (100–31 BCE) ending with the earthquake. But as she – like a number of other historians, myself included – does not follow de Vaux's hypothesis about the devastated site being left unoccupied during the remaining years of king Herod's reign, her first period of sectarian occupation is dated between *c.* 100 and Herod's death in 4 BCE.

All the main propositions of de Vaux's concerning the communal and religious nature of the settlement still stand. They are testified to by the large assembly hall/dining room and the adjacent pantry with remains of a large quantity of tableware, pots and pans, as well as by ten out of the sixteen pools, some of them with steps leading to the water, which prove that ritual purification was an important part of the life of the ancient occupants of Qumran. Apropos of purity, one must not forget the latrine in Room 51 of the site, situated close to a pool of ritual purification, already referred to by de Vaux and discussed in full detail by Jodi Magness (see pp. 105–113 of her book).

Where did the inhabitants of Qumran sleep? The question of residential accommodation is still debated. It is possible that some rooms on the collapsed second floor served for living quarters. Estimates vary from 10 to 70 persons housed in the buildings. The rest of the population of the site (possibly 150 to 200 in total, judging from the size of the cemetery, according to Magen Broshi) slept in caves, huts and tents. The hypothesis is supported by the discovery by Broshi and Hanan Eshel of relics of tent equipment in the neighbourhood, and domestic utensils in 'residential' caves where no scrolls were found (*DSD*, 6 (1999), pp. 328–48).

A final comment on the fascinating question whether women lived at Qumran: the archaeological evidence implies only a sporadic and insignificant female presence and it should be recalled that most of the women and all the children buried in the southern extension of the cemetery are now identified by Joe Zias as recent Bedouin burials (see chapter II, p. 40). If we approach the problem from the vantage point of a hypothetical male celibate community, we are left to explain the presence of a couple of female skeletons in the western cemetery, together with one spindle whorl and four beads in the sectarian settlement (Magness (2002), p. 178). Whatever these prove, it is not a regular occupation of the establishment by female inhabitants in any way proportionate to the number of male members.

In conclusion, since the communal religious interpretation of the Qumran establishment and the contents of the sectarian Dead Sea Scrolls mutually confirm one another, it is now reasonably safe to move to the next question and seek to attach a name to the people who occupied the Qumran site some time between the turn of the second century BCE and 68 CE.

2. Identifying the Qumran Community

Having set out the aim, the organizational structure and the hierarchy of the membership of the Jewish groups described in chapter VII, let us now move a step forward and try to identify the Qumran sect with one of the known Jewish religious parties flourishing in Palestine in the pre-70 CE era. Before proceeding, it will be useful to rehearse succinctly the information relative to the structure and the religious ideas of the two types of congregation that the six Dead Sea rules have revealed.

To begin with the married group, attested in the 'Damascus' writing (CD) and all the other documents except the Community Rule (S), this new miniature biblical 'Israel', with its priests and its laity symbolically divided into twelve tribes and smaller traditional units, is represented as living in towns and 'camps' (rural settlements) all over Judaea in the midst of the bulk of the population, Jewish and Gentile, but in self-imposed separation from them. These families, distinguished from the other Jews by their more rigorous sexual mores, ritual observances and the specific education they gave to their children during the first twenty years of their lives, were engaged in farming and practised commerce – among themselves, and with other Jews and, within the framework of restrictive regulations, even with non-Jews. They worshipped in their own 'appointed times', but seem to have maintained some contact with the Temple, sending their offerings, and observing, while in Jerusalem, their special rigorous laws concerning ritual purity which required abstinence from marital sex.

The government of the married 'Damascus' sect was in the hands of learned Zadokite priests, but in the absence of a qualified priest, a well-trained Levite, member of the lower class of the priestly tribe, could be put in charge. The priest in command of each unit was known as the Guardian, who was acting on his own, without a council. His task was to instruct, exercise pastoral care and oversee the contact between his subjects and the outside world. He was entrusted with the training of the adult Jewish candidates for membership. No doubt he also played a part, together with the parents, in the religious education of the children of the members of his community until they attained the age of enrolment.

Ten elected judges administered justice in accordance with biblical law and communal regulations. They could, apparently, order the execution of persons found guilty of grave offences, and impose lesser penalties on the law-breakers and those who disobeyed the rules. On the whole, the Community's precepts were more stringent than those of Scripture – with one exception. The death penalty imposed by the Bible on a person who desecrated the Sabbath is downgraded to a seven-year prison sentence (CD 12:4–6). The rigorousness of the sectarian law may be illustrated by the possibility of 'fornication' between a husband and his own wife, a sin that incurred the penalty of expulsion from the group (4Q270). What constituted this 'fornication' is not specified. It may have been inter-course with a menstruating wife, or possibly sex with a pre-pubescent, pregnant or post-menopausal spouse if the sect, like the marrying Essenes of Josephus, believed that intercourse was legitimate only for the propagation of mankind.

Contact with non-Jews was envisaged as possible, but subject to special regulations. Gentiles were protected by the law: Community members were forbidden to steal from them or kill them. On the other hand, sectaries were not allowed to sell clean animals or birds to Gentiles for fear that they might sacrifice them to their gods. It was also prohibited, contrary to the custom followed in the Jerusalem Temple, to accept from a Gentile an offering for the sanctuary (MMT, 4Q394, fr. 4–7). Nor were members of the community permitted to sell them a servant who had been a slave prior to being made a proselyte and thus converting to Judaism.

Communal funds were administered jointly by the Guardian and the judges. Members of the Community, who kept the right to handle their property and earnings, were obliged to pay into the common kitty a sum equivalent to two days' wages per month, which were to be employed for charitable purposes.

The Guardian presided over the periodic assembly of the camp and the overall superior, the Guardian of all the camps, chaired the general assembly of all members once a year on the Feast of Weeks, on which occasion the Covenant was renewed, new members were initiated and unworthy old members excluded.

With the exception of the rules relating to matrimony and ownership of property, the doctrines and beliefs of the married Community, including their expectation of a Messiah of Aaron and a Messiah of Israel, may be presumed to have been essentially the same as those of the celibate sect.

The association described in the Community Rule is also a symbolical Israel in a nutshell, split into priests and laymen and bearing the title of the 'Community' (*yahad*), the 'council of the Community', the 'men of the Law', the 'men of holiness' and even the 'men of perfect holiness'. The members are described as cut off from the unrighteous. In explicit fulfilment of the prophecy of Isaiah, 'In the wilderness prepare the way of the Lord' (Isa. 40:3 quoted in 1QS 8:14), they chose to withdraw to the desert for the study of the divine Law as well as the ways of the spirit of truth and the spirit of falsehood, and committed themselves to the practice of all the virtues prescribed in the Torah. The Community was governed by, and followed the teaching of, the priests, Sons of Zadok.

Three characteristic traits distinguish the sect of the Community Rule from the 'Damascus' society: they renounced private ownership of property, having progressively handed over all their belongings to the Community in the course of a two- to three-year-long initiation; they lived a life of strict obedience to superiors and elders; and they practised male celibacy. The last point is never explicitly stated, but appears as a logical necessity in the total absence of legislation relative to anything connected with marriage.

A Guardian stood at the head of each unit of the celibate Community too, a priest who was aided by a Bursar, who administered the common property and was in charge of the material well-being of all the members. The supreme council of the Community comprised three priests and twelve laymen. The religious communism which the sectaries had embraced entailed free exchange among members of the sect, but no exchange of goods with outsiders except after payment.

Initiation was long – lasting over two years – and progressive, allowing the candidates to have an increasing share in the life of the Community. At the end, the 'novices' gained full membership and voting rights. The daily communal activity entailed at least one meal, blessed by the priestly superior, and a prayer and study meeting at night. The communal meal was expected to continue even after the onset of the messianic age (1QSa 2:17–22).

The sectaries were subjected to strict discipline with set punishments imposed on transgressors in conformity with their penal code, going from a penalty of ten days to irrevocable dismissal. Every member had his allotted place in the hierarchical order of the Community, an order that underwent yearly reassessment at the Feast of the Renewal of the Covenant in the light of the spiritual progress, or the absence of progress, achieved by each sectary.

As an aide-memoire for the annual re-ranking of the members, the Guardian kept a record of the transgressions committed by the sectaries. A damaged list, fascinating and pathetic, has preserved for posterity the names of three misbehaving sectaries together with their recorded wrong-doings (4Q477). A Yohanan son of—was short-tempered; Hananiah Notos either overindulged himself or showed favouritism to his family; another Hananiah loved ... (something he should not have done). No doubt, they were reprimanded and downgraded. Those convicted of more serious offences were cursed and expelled from the Community at the annual Renewal of the Covenant with no chance to return.

A brief synopsis of the religious thought and practice of both branches of the Qumran sect is needed before we can attempt an identification. Both types of sectaries claimed to be part of a 'new Covenant' (CD 8:21, 35; 1QpHab 2:3), concluded by the Teacher of Righteousness and maintained by the Zadokite priestly leaders of the Community. The members believed they had been granted revealed knowledge and divine grace. Their prayer and worship, performed in conformity with their calendar given by God, coincided with the successive acts of the liturgy performed in heaven by the choir of the angels. Biblical laws concerning ritual purity were sternly inter-preted and applied, and ablutions, including a special 'baptism' or immersion associated with the entry into the Covenant, were faithfully observed. External acts of wor-ship were qualified empty gestures unless they were accom-panied by corresponding inward spiritual attitudes.

Sectarian stance towards the Jerusalem Temple varied.

The Damascus Document and the Temple Scroll legislate on cultic matters as everyday realities, insinuating that the members of the married branch continued some kind of contact with the sanctuary in Jerusalem. However, the ascetic branch under the guidance of the Sons of Zadok held that the Jerusalem priests followed the wrong rules and observed the wrong appointed times. Misled by their unholy calendar, they turned the Temple into a place of pollution. In their view, the community in its wilderness exile was the true place of worship, where prayer and ascetic life replaced the Temple sacrifices. This interim arrangement would continue until the liberation of Jerusalem and the reorganization of the cult by the members of the Community in the seventh year of the victorious eschatological war fought by the sect's Sons of Light against the allied Jewish and Gentile foe of the Sons of Darkness (1QM 2).

The final age was to be inaugurated by the arrival of a messianic-eschatological prophet (1QS 9:11) and two redeemer figures, the priestly Messiah of Aaron, also called the Interpreter of the Law (CD 7:18–20; 4Q171 1:11), and the lay Messiah of Israel (CD 12:23–13:1), also known as the Branch of David or the Prince of the congregation (1QSb 5:20; 4Q285). Belief and hope in an afterlife is sporadically attested without firm indication whether it was seen as bodily resurrection or just as spiritual survival.

How do these pictures of the two varieties of the Qumran Community relate to the Jewish separatist religious bodies that existed during the last centuries preceding the destruction of Jerusalem in 70 CE? No doubt a good many small religious parties flourished among the Jews at the turn of the era, but apart from the 6,000-strong Pharisees, the unspecified number of Sadducees and

Zealots-Sicarii, the 4,000 Essenes, the Egyptian Essene-like Therapeutai of Philo, plus the freshly arisen Jewish-Christians of the New Testament (probably not exceeding a few thousand), there is no group sufficiently well known to allow a meaningful comparison.

Of the sufficiently well-described religious parties, let us first discard the Sadducees, notwithstanding the fact that some of their legal teachings are occasionally echoed in the Scrolls (for example in MMT). The lavish lifestyle of the aristocratic Sadducees is irreconcilable with the mode of existence of either branch of the Qumran Community. Besides, the Sadducees apparently did not believe in angels or in afterlife of any sort, while the Scrolls are full of angels and are not opposed to the idea of some kind of renewed existence after death, probably more in the form of spiritual survival than bodily resurrection.

Similarities with the Pharisees are also noticeable, but only on the general level. Both were pious, devoted to the study and interpretation of Scripture and deeply concerned with legal observance and ritual cleanliness. On the other hand, the Qumran Community recognized the overall doctrinal supremacy of the priests, whereas Pharisaism was essentially a lay movement considering learning as superior to social class. Furthermore, the Pharisees were outward-looking whereas the Qumran sect was closed to the external world, both Jewish and Gentile, and we cannot find a single record attesting Pharisee insistence on common ownership of property.

The Zealot-Sicarii theory was first proposed half a century ago by two scholars from the city of 'the dreaming spires', Professor Sir Godfrey Driver and my Oxford predecessor, Dr Cecil Roth. Subsequently it went out of fashion until it was recalled from its otherworldly somnolence by Professor Robert Eisenman in the 1980s. He gave to the thesis an odd Christian twist by turning the Zealots into followers – not of Jesus, but of his brother James. The two main arguments he marshalled in favour of his thesis are derived from the general gist of the War Scroll in which the Kittim-Romans, governed by a king (between 27 BCE and 66–70 CE) are the chief enemies of the community, and from the archaeological discovery of a Qumran Scroll (the Songs of the Sabbath Sacrifice) in the Zealot stronghold of Masada. But the War Scroll cannot be taken as a historical document. The armed conflict it describes is fictional, with its stages chronologically fixed in advance to fit a forty-year scheme, and the battles directed not by generals, but by priests and Levites, and ultimately won by angels (see chapter VII, pp. 134–5). As for the presence of a single Qumran manuscript at Masada, it could be attributed to the adoption by individual sectaries of the nationalist cause or even to a Zealot occupation of the Qumran site with – or more likely without – the consent of the Community previously residing there.

Neither did the laborious attempts to link the Qumran sect with Jewish Christianity make any genuine headway apart from whipping up interest in the popular media. The trend started in England between 1950 and 1954 with Jacob Teicher, the first of my predecessors in the editorial chair of the *Journal of Jewish Studies*, and John Allegro of 'Sacred Mushroom' fame, both identifying the Teacher of Righteousness with Jesus. It continued in Australia with Dr Barbara Thiering, who made John the Baptist the Teacher, and ended in California, where Robert Eisenman landed James, the brother of Jesus, with the sectarian lead part of Teacher of Righteousness. The villain of the show, the Wicked Priest, is St Paul according to Teicher and

Eisenman, but unexpectedly none other than Jesus in Thiering's rather idiosyncratic exegesis. Her Jesus, as one might easily have guessed, first marries Mary of Magdala and fathers a daughter and two sons, and after the Magdalene has turned her back on him, Jesus takes another woman by the name of Lydia from Asia Minor (Acts 16:14) and has another son from her. These theories are read into the New Testament text. They fail the basic credibility test, being foisted on, rather than springing from, the evidence. Thus the New Testament words that the Lord opened Lydia's heart are taken to mean that Jesus made her pregnant. Also, in order to claim credibility, the Judaeo-Christian theory must deny the pre-Christian date of some of the essential Qumran source material, such as the Habakkuk Commentary, despite the results of the carbon 14 tests performed in two of the world's leading laboratories in 1990–91 and 1994 (see chapter II, p. 31). The Habakkuk Commentary was carbon-dated to between 110 and 5 BCE. The positive aspects of the comparison between the Scrolls and the New Testament will be shown in chapter IX.

That leaves us with the Essene hypothesis that has been the front-runner ever since Eleazar Lipa Sukenik first advanced it sixty years ago. To assess its value, we must set against our synopsis of the archaeological and literary evidence derived from Qumran the testimony of the classical Greek and Latin sources relating to the mysterious community portrayed by two Jewish writers and a Roman first-century CE writer. Philo's Therapeutai, described in his book *On the Contemplative Life*, do not need to be taken into consideration despite the many similarities they display, as they are located by the Alexandrian author exclusively in the delta of the Nile, close to the Mareotic

Lake, and not in Palestine, the homeland of the Essenes. There are some later sources too, but they contain nothing significantly different, so the examination of the older writings will suffice.

The Jewish authors, Philo and Flavius Josephus, have left two accounts each, one long and detailed (Philo, *Every Good Man Is Free*, 75–91; Josephus, *Jewish War* II:119–61), and one short (Philo, *Apology for the Jews*, quoted in Eusebius, *Praeparatio evangelica* VIII:6–7; Josephus, *Jewish Antiquities* XVIII:18–22). However, the *Antiquities* passage of Josephus may not be an independent witness, as it appears to be based on Philo's *Apology*. Finally, Pliny the Elder has produced a brief, but splendidly written rich notice in *Natural History* 5:17, 4 (73). Noteworthy is the claim of Josephus that when he was sixteen years old, he had first-hand experience of Essenism as well as in the Pharisaic and Sadducean ways of life (*Life*, 10–11), although the few months he spent with them were clearly not enough for him to become an Essene, and in any case he tells us that at the end he joined the ranks of the Pharisees.

The etymology and the meaning of the name (*Essaioi* or *Essenoi* in Greek and *Esseni* in Latin) is still debated. Philo derives it from the Greek term, 'the holy' (*hosioi*). A good number of modern scholars tentatively link *hosioi* with the Syriac *hase*, meaning 'the pious'. I favour another possible etymology based on the Aramaic *'asen/'asayya* (healers), linked to Josephus's assertion that the Essenes, experts in the therapeutic qualities of plants and minerals, were concerned with the cure of the sick (*Jewish War* II:136) and on Philo's description of Essene-like Egyptian '*Therapeutai*', who owed their name to being healers of the body and the soul (Philo, *On the Contemplative Life*, 2). (All the relevant Greek and Latin texts with facing English translation are available in *The Essenes according to the Classical Sources*, edited by G. Vermes and M. Goodman (Sheffield, JSOT Press, 1989).)

Philo and Josephus give the number of the Essenes as just exceeding 4,000, comparable in size to the 6,000 Pharisees mentioned by Josephus during the reign of Herod the Great. Both writers make them reside in many towns of Judaea or even in every town of Palestine. Philo later contradicts himself and on doctrinal grounds declares that they shunned the cities because of urban immorality and places them in the spiritual countryside, which was obviously more to his liking. Pliny mentions only one Essene settlement, situated off the western shore of the Dead Sea somewhere between Jericho and Engedi.

Details concerning the sect can be garnered from all the sources. The local congregations, governed by superiors, dwelt in commonly owned and occupied houses. Candidates for membership (only grown-ups according to Philo and Pliny; adults as well as young men according to Josephus) had to wear a white robe and an apron, and had to carry a hatchet with the hygienic purpose of burying excrement. Father de Vaux believed he had found one such hatchet at Qumran (*Vetus Testamentum* 9 (1959), pp. 399–407). The 'novices' had to undergo instruction for one year before they were admitted to the ablutions of the Essene purity system. A two-year long initiation followed, at the end of which an oath of fidelity was sworn and table fellowship gained. Serious breaches of the rules were punished by expulsion, decided by a court of no fewer than 100 judges.

The Essenes practised religious communism or, as Pliny puts it more pungently, lived 'without money' (*sine pecunia*). Property and earnings were handed over to the superiors and all the needs of the members were catered for by a bursar. They were allowed to help the needy, but required special permission to support relatives. Their main occupation was agriculture. Philo asserts, possibly for his own philosophical reasons, that they were forbidden to manufacture weapons or to indulge in buying and selling as it could lead to cupidity. Josephus, on the other hand, concedes that they were allowed to carry weapons for self-protection against robbers. The commonly held idea of Essene pacifism is not borne out by the texts. A high-ranking commander of the Jewish rebels against Rome, John the Essene, was a member of the sect (see p. 211).

The Essenes rejected pleasure and sought to control passions. Their diet was frugal and they wore their garments until they fell to pieces. Among the Essene characteristics Philo and Josephus list rough appearance (they refused to anoint themselves), the wearing of white robes, frequent ritual baths, the avoidance of spitting and, on the Sabbath, of defecation. The sect's rejection of marriage is attributed to misogyny: living with a wife was judged incompatible with communal peace. Pliny bluntly asserts that they lived 'without women, renouncing sex altogether, having only palm trees for company' (*sine ulla femina, omni venere abdicata, socia palmarum*). The archaeologists have noted remains of palm trees at Qumran.

In an appendix to his longer notice on the Essenes, Josephus refers to a branch of the sect that allowed marriage. Only a regularly menstruating girl, who was presumed to be fertile, could become a bride. Since sex was permitted exclusively for the propagation of the human race, husbands were to keep away from pregnant (or post-menopausal?) wives. No doubt for ethical reasons, Philo stresses that the Essenes had no slaves: slave ownership would have clashed with his idea of love of freedom, which he also attributed to the Essenes.

The Essenes also disapproved of swearing an oath to prove the veracity of their words, declined participation in Temple sacrifices, and symbolically sacrificed among themselves instead. Nevertheless they sent offerings to Jerusalem. They may even have had an establishment in the Holy City somewhere in the area of the 'Essene gate' mentioned by Josephus (see p. 178). Their communal meals were prepared by priests following strict purity rules. They ate twice daily, taking a purificatory bath before each repast and every meal was preceded and followed by a grace recited by a priest.

As far as their religious convictions were concerned, the Essenes revered the Law and Moses the Lawgiver. Philo, once more attributing to them his own preferences, emphasizes their addiction to allegorical Bible interpretation. Fate, that is divine Providence, was held by them to be superior to human free will. Besides the teachings of Scripture, they also cherished the esoteric doctrines of their own secret books, open only to full members. They were venerated as prophets able to foretell the future infallibly and as expert healers with special knowledge of the medicinal plants and minerals.

Only Josephus reports on Essene eschatology. They believed, he tells us, in the survival of the soul after death, destined either for eternal joy or for everlasting torment. Bodily resurrection is nowhere alluded to, indeed it could hardly be conceived by people who considered the body as the prison of the enslaved soul, a soul that longed for liberation during earthly life and took its delight in freedom from matter after death.

In the light of the foregoing two portraits, can one assert

that the Qumran community and the Essene sect were one and the same institution? The answer is no and yes. If to identify the two, absolute accord on every single point is required between the Scrolls and the classical evidence, the answer must be negative. But bearing in mind the nature of the sources, is total unison conceivable? First, the documents are of fundamentally different character. The Dead Sea texts were written by members of an esoteric sect and were intended for the use of initiates only. Conversely, Philo and Pliny, and even Josephus, were outsiders and mostly addressed a non-Jewish readership in the Graeco-Roman world. For their benefit, Josephus vaguely compares the Essenes to the followers of Pythagoras (*Jewish Antiquities* XV:371) as he has declared the Pharisees similar to Stoics and the Sadducees to Epicureans. Moreover, both Philo and Josephus have produced two descriptions which are not altogether uniform. For these reasons we must allow some elasticity in the evaluation of the sources. After all, even the various Qumran rules indicate different types of organization and occasionally even clash with one another. The variations may be due to diverse causes among which evolving practices (such as penalties of various length given for the same transgression) may be the most likely.

Geographical, chronological and organizational arguments may be listed in favour of the identity of the Qumran Community and the Essenes. Whereas Philo and Josephus state that the Essenes lived in various places in Judaea, Pliny speaks of only one renowned Essene settlement at a short distance from the western shore of the Dead Sea where palm trees grow. The last town mentioned before the Essene notice was Jericho and the next two 'below' (*infra*) the Essenes were Engedi and the rock fortress of

Masada. Qumran would nicely fit this territorial setting if 'below' is interpreted, not as 'lower down', but as 'downstream' or 'further south' on the way to the southernmost site of Masada. The nature of the Qumran ruins (communal buildings, a huge quantity of crockery and many facilities for ritual bathing) strongly support the Essene theory. To lessen the probability of the identification of Pliny's location with Qumran, one would need a suitable site somewhere on the hills *above* Engedi. In the 1960s Israeli archaeologists, led by Benjamin Mazar, thoroughly investigated the area without finding any trace of the Essenes. By contrast, Yizhar Hirschfeld in the 1990s believed he had discovered above Engedi remains of wooden huts, but no pools or communal buildings. On the whole, the view that Qumran is Pliny's Essene village seems by far the most probable.

From the chronological point of view, Qumran was communally occupied from the late second century BCE, or on a more noticeable level at least from 100 BCE to 68 CE. If 100 BCE corresponds to the beginning of the first major architectural developments, the beginnings of the sectarian occupation are likely to date to the end of the second century BCE. This period, suggested by archaeology, matches the existence of the Essenes in Judaea as attested by Josephus. He first refers to them in the time of Jonathan Maccabaeus (mid-second century BCE) and their last mention in the *Jewish War* coincides with the great rebellion against Rome (66–70 CE) during which the Essenes had bravely resisted Roman tortures. With the destruction of Qumran, the Essenes disappear from the historical horizon.

The most important proofs of identity are the organizational correspondences. Thus initiation was by stages in both groups: a first probationary period was followed by two further years of training. The extremely unusual common ownership of property characterized the life of the Essenes and of the strictly ascetic Qumran group. The Essenes' renunciation of marriage, except in one of their branches according to Josephus, was equally uncommon. It matches the strict ascetics at Qumran, but not the 'Damascus' sect whose members, like Josephus' special branch of Essenes, approved of marriage. The Essenes were critical of the Jerusalem Temple and so were the celibate Qumran sectaries. Both considered their community as the place of worship approved by God. The meals, blessed by priests, were reserved only for full members both by the Essenes and by the strictly observant Qumran Community. Both opposed oaths, with the exception of the vow made at their entry into the association.

However, there are also some differences. The two major discrepancies – common or private ownership and celibate or married forms of life – resolve themselves once it is recognized that two separate branches of the same movement are attested by both the Scrolls and Josephus. Pliny's perfunctory statement that the Essenes lived without money (*sine pecunia*) does not tally with the numerous coins found at Qumran, but it may be explained by exaggerated 'poetic' licence and an artistic liking for a nice turn of phrase. Further conflicting features are that the Qumran candidates swore their oath to return to the Law of Moses at the beginning of their training, whereas the Essenes took a vow of allegiance to the Torah at the end. It may have happened on both occasions. Moreover, the 'Damascus' sectaries were allowed to have slaves while the Essenes, according to Philo and possibly according to Josephus, opposed this. But the reliability of the statement has already been queried (see pp. 194–5 above). Furthermore, the weighty role of the Zadokite priests and the subject of messianic expectation, well attested in the Scrolls, are lacking in the classical sources. But this silence can easily be assigned to the unwillingness of Philo and Josephus to burden their Gentile readers with complicated Jewish theological concepts. Let us further add the total absence in the Scrolls of the term 'Essene' or anything approaching it. Here the most likely reason for the Scrolls' silence is that the sectaries were described as Essenes only by outsiders; within the group they called themselves 'men of the Community', 'men of holiness' or 'men of the Law' in a somewhat similar way as members of the Catholic order of the Franciscans used to be commonly designated by outsiders as 'Grey Friars' and those of the nonconformist Society of Friends are usually called 'Quakers'. Set against all the weighty common traits the discrepancies appear insignificant.

Another kind of objection to the Essene identification, emphatically raised in 1995 by Professor Martin Goodman, is based on the incompleteness of our information concerning the religious profile of Judaism during the epoch in question. He reminds us that Josephus names only the Pharisees, Sadducees, Essenes and Zealots as existing religious parties ('A Note on the Qumran Sectarians, the Essenes and Josephus', *Journal of Jewish Studies* 46 (1995), pp. 161–6). Surely, Goodman claims, there were more than four dissenting religious factions among Jews at the turn of the era? The Talmud speaks of twenty-four sects of heretics. Hence, according to Goodman, the mainstream view that the Qumranites were Essenes is oversimplified: it stands on insecure and shaky foundations.

While this observation is not without value, neither does

it deal a fatal blow to the Essene theory. It merely means that if the Qumran sectaries were not Essenes in the absolute sense, they belonged to a company hardly distinguishable from the Essene sect. This reminds me of the scholar who was unwilling to accept that the land of Canaan was occupied by the biblical Joshua and preferred to ascribe the conquest of Palestine to a different military leader who lived in the same period, who acted in a similar fashion and who, according to questionable traditions, was also called Joshua. Joking apart, while the identification of the Dead Sea sect and the Essenes is not an established fact, it is a strongly argued and well-founded hypothesis which will remain tenable until Professor Goodman or someone else comes up with a more convincing alternative.

Rachel Elior's recent thesis claiming that the members of the Qumran community were not Essenes, because the Essenes never existed and were invented by Josephus, strikes me as an entertaining flight of fancy. As at the moment of writing these lines the theory is known only from press interviews released in March 2009; the interested public will have to await the appearance of the English edition of *Memory and Oblivion: The Secret of the Dead Sea Scrolls*, before her claim can be subjected to stringent scrutiny. Rachel Elior's much-vaunted discovery that the Dead Sea Scrolls were produced by a priestly group has in fact been common knowledge since the start of Qumran studies, but her assertion that this Community cannot be identified with the Essenes, because the Essenes of the classical sources do not appear in a priestly context, is mistaken. Josephus, although writing largely for a Graeco-Roman readership uninterested in Jewish peculiarities, still felt it necessary to underline the significant role of the priests in Essene life. He reported that the preparation of the sect's pure food was entrusted to priests and that their common table was presided over by a priest who recited the prayer before and after each meal (*Jewish Antiquities* XVIII:22; *Jewish War* II:131). As an indirect pointer, Josephus designated as a 'sacred robe' the white garment which constituted the Essene uniform (*Jewish War* II:131. He refers here to the ceremonial 'linen' or 'fine white linen' vestment prescribed for the priests by the Bible (Exod. 28:39–43; Ezek. 44:17–19) as well as the Qumran War Scroll (1QM 7:10–11).

Negatively, Elior deduces from the silence of the rabbis that the Essenes did not exist, but in doing so she does not bear in mind that by the time of the Mishnah and the Talmud (200–500 CE), the Essenes had already vanished and consequently there was no practical need for a debate about them. She further argues that the absence of the term 'Essenes' from the Scrolls proves that they had nothing to do with the Qumran texts. But such a statement overlooks the fact that the Semitic name 'Essenes' ('Saints' or 'Healers', see p. 192) was used only by outsiders like Philo, Josephus and the Roman Pliny. The initiates of the sect called themselves 'Men of the Community', 'Men of Holiness', 'Men of Supreme Holiness' or 'the Poor' in their writings. Such a linguistic phenomenon is quite common in the religious terminology of most languages. Members of the Catholic orders of St Francis of Assisi are officially called Friars Minor (Fratres Minores in Latin), but outsiders, as I have noted, call them 'Franciscans' or 'Greyfriars'. Likewise the members of the 'Society of Friends' are popularly known as 'Quakers'.

The main evidence used for the demonstration of the Essene identity of the Qumran sect consists in the unique features, unattested for any other Jewish group in antiquity, of common ownership of property and male celibacy, reinforced by Pliny's location of the Essenes on the western shore of the Dead Sea.

Against Professor Elior's contention that the Essenes were made up by Josephus, attention must be drawn to their very detailed portrayal in *Jewish War* and *Jewish Antiquities*, and to Josephus' numerous references to Essene individuals involved in Palestinian Jewish history from the mid-second century BCE to the war against Rome in 66–70 CE. Finally, in his autobiography Josephus states that he himself gained personal experience of Essenism when as a sixteen-year-old young man he joined the Essene community for a time. These concrete factual accounts, easily controllable by Josephus' contemporaries, do not strike one as the figment of someone's fertile imagination.

To return to weightier matters, we may need to adopt a fresh point of view in assessing the relationship between the married and the celibate communities. Josephus gives the impression that the non-marrying Essenes formed the main group and the marrying branch was an unimportant side shoot. The much more extensive Qumran evidence in favour of the married sect suggests the opposite view, namely that the 'Damascus' type sectaries represented the bulk of the movement, but that the fame of the celibate elite of Qumran reached the ends of the earth. 'Unbelievable though this may sound, for thousands of centuries a race has existed which is eternal yet into which no one is born,' Pliny tells us. Understandably, the Jewish apologists Philo and Josephus were only too glad to propagate this notion and present the Essenes as Jewish religious celebrities to their intellectually hungry Graeco-Roman readers.

3. The History of the Qumran-Essene Community

As is well known, the Qumran caves have not yielded one single strictly historical document. Hence any attempt at reconstructing the origin and development of the Dead Sea community must rely on an interpretation of theologically motivated data couched in cryptic language such as Teacher of Righteousness, Wicked Priest, Furious Young Lion, Kittim, etc. I will not be concerned here with the historical hypotheses which have already been shown to be unlikely or indeed unacceptable, like Zealotism or Jewish Christianity (see pp. 189–191). Leaving these out of consideration, what do the hints contained in the Scrolls add up to in regard to the history of the Qumran Community?

The Exhortation of the Damascus Document displays three chronological details of significance. The 'age of wrath', the political-religious upheaval corresponding to the first stages of the community, began *390* years after the conquest of Jerusalem by Nebuchadnezzar. The Teacher of Righteousness arrived *20* years later. Finally, about *40* years after the death of the Teacher of Righteousness, his opponents were punished by 'the head of the kings of Greece'. From the reference to the 'kings of Greece' we may conclude that the events have taken place in the Hellenistic period of Jewish history. The straightforward application of the three chronological figures (390, 20 and 40 years) points also to the second century BCE as the historical context of the birth and early development of the sect. Employing simple arithmetic, the onset of the 'age of wrath' 390 years after Nebuchadnezzar's victory in Judaea in 586 BCE brings us to 196 BCE, the beginning of the Syrian Greek (Seleucid) domination of Palestine which commenced with the Seleucid king Antiochus III, the Great's conquest of the Jewish homeland in 200 BCE, when he defeated the Egyptian-Greek Ptolemies at the battle of Panias. The changeover resulted in increasing Hellenistic influence on the Jews, which in turn provoked the formation of a group of tradition-loving pious men (the Hasidim), the presumed forefathers of the Qumran Community. The appearance, twenty years later, of the Teacher of Righteousness brings us close to the accession to the throne of Antiochus IV, Epiphanes (175–163 BCE), whose hostility to the Jewish religion marked the climax of a major upheaval, the Hellenistic crisis. The length of the career of the Teacher of Righteousness, which started in year 20 of the 'age of wrath', is not given. The lower end of the chronological perspective of the author of the Damascus Exhortation is about 40 years after the disappearance of the Teacher.

In mathematical terms: 390 + 20 + X (the Teacher's ministry) + *circa* 40 add up to 450 + X. In the early stages of Qumran research, scholars like Manchester University's Professor H. H. Rowley, took these figures at their face value. The 'age of wrath' started in 196 BCE (586–390) and with it the burgeoning community of the pious Hasidim of the pre-Maccabaean period came into being. The Teacher of Righteousness arose in *c.* 176 BCE and is identified with the martyr high priest Onias III, and the Wicked Priest with the Hellenizing pontiff Menelaus who in 171 BCE ordered the murder of Onias III (2 Macc. 4:34–5). The bottom line of the events is to be drawn somewhere in the second half of the second century BCE.

This solution of early Qumran history, plain at first sight, nevertheless runs into a double snag. The first arises from general historical considerations, the second from the Habakkuk Commentary. To take the figure 390 literally in a calculation of biblical chronology is unsound. No ancient Jewish writer had a correct notion of the length of the post-exilic era. In the third century BCE, the Jewish Hellenist chronographer Demetrius counted 573 years – 73 too many – between the Assyrian conquest of Samaria (722/1 BCE) and the start of the rule of Ptolemy IV in Egypt in 221 BCE. The reasonably careful Josephus was also guilty of several miscalculations. Figures relating to the same event can vary even between his *Jewish Antiquities* and the *Jewish War*. Thus he counted 481 (*Antiquities*) or 471 (*War*) years from the return from the Babylonian exile in 538 BCE to the death of the Hasmonean ruler Aristobulus I (103 BCE). The correct figure is 435 years. Again, Josephus made the Jewish temple built in Leontopolis in Egypt by Onias IV last 343 years, whereas the period between 160 BCE (the date of the construction of the temple) and 73 CE (the date of its overthrow) amounts only to 233 years. As for the rabbinic pseudo-historical work known as *Seder 'Olam Rabbah* or Great World Order, it allows 490 years to elapse between the first destruction of the Temple by Nebuchadnezzar in 586 BCE and the second by Titus in 70 CE. The true figure is 656 years. To accept therefore the 390 years of the Damascus Document for genuine chronology is risky, to say the least.

What stands definitely behind the Damascus Document's reckoning is the Book of Daniel's symbolical understanding of Jeremiah's prophecy concerning the 70 years of rule granted to Babylon (Jeremiah 29:10). According to Daniel, the implied meaning is 70 times seven or 490 years (Daniel 9:24). Without any doubt, this mystical number lurks in the background of the *Seder 'Olam Rabbah* and very likely of the Damascus Document. All we need is to assume that the ministry of the Teacher of Righteousness lasted the allegorical 40 years, like Moses' leadership of the Israelites in the Sinai desert, and we end up with 390 + 20 + 40 + 40 = 490, as the moment of the coming of the Messiah of Aaron and the Messiah of Israel.

Leaving aside this theological chronology, we may reasonably deduce from the cryptic allusions of the Damascus Exhortation that the origins of the Qumran community and the activity of its founder are to be placed in the second century BCE, say between 175 and 125 BCE, definitely during the Hellenistic era of Palestinian Jewish history. The Damascus Document itself is pre-Roman (pre-63 BCE), dated to the end of the second century BCE. To move further ahead, the various *pesharim* and other forms of exegetical material from Qumran enable the student to draw a neater contour for the historical canvas and fill it in with more colourful detail by providing, among other things, identifiable historical names. The Nahum Commentary and the Habakkuk *pesher* envisage Jerusalem and the surrounding lands as governed by two classes of rulers: the Greek (Seleucid) kings, Antiochus (Epiphanes) and Demetrius (Eukairos) on the one hand and the rulers of the Kittim who, like the Roman proconsuls, regularly changed. The Kittim-Romans, mentioned also in the fragmentary historical calendar, are portrayed as the ultimate conquerors of the world who later on, in the eschatological age, were to be governed by kings (= emperors). This extended historical horizon, for which the War Scroll (1 and 4QM) and the Book of War (4Q285) furnish additional information, covers sectarian history and eschatological expectation from 175 BCE to the end of the first century BCE, and probably well into the first century CE.

The badly preserved historical calendar provides further pieces for the completion of the puzzle. It mentions the priest John (probably John Hyrcanus I, 135–103 BCE); Shelamzion (Queen Salome Alexandra, 76–67 BCE); Hyrcanus (the high priest John Hyrcanus II, 63–40 BCE) and Aemilius (Marcus Aemilius Scaurus, governor of Syria, 65–62 BCE). To proceed further, the investigation must be focused on the Wicked Priest who, as high priestly ruler of the Jewish nation, is more likely to be identifiable thanks to the Books of the Maccabees and Josephus than the more shadowy leading characters of the sect. This Wicked Priest, being a contemporary and adversary of the Teacher of Righteousness, belongs to the opening phase of sectarian history in the second century BCE.

By the 1950s, in addition to H. H. Rowley's Hellenizing high priest Menelaus (171–62 BCE), two if not three Hasmonean high priests were proposed for the role of the Wicked Priest: Alexander Jannaeus (102–76 BCE), de Vaux's choice, and Aristobulus II (67–3 BCE) and Hyrcanus II (63–40 BCE), contemporaries of Pompey, jointly championed by Dupont-Sommer.

While the established scholars – de Vaux, Rowley and Dupont-Sommer – argued among themselves, a young man by the name of Geza Vermes, tucked away in Louvain (Belgium), had been working furiously since 1950 on what was to become in 1952 the world's first doctoral dissertation on Qumran. It was published in 1953. Poring over the evidence relating to the Wicked Priest, a remarkable passage of the Habakkuk Commentary, which had escaped the attention of his elders, caught his eyes:

This concerns the Wicked Priest who was called by the name of truth when he first arose. But when he ruled over Israel his heart became proud, and he forsake God ... for the sake of riches. He robbed and amassed the riches of the men of violence who rebelled against God, and he took the wealth of the peoples.

(1QpHab 8:8–12)

According to this text, two stages can be distinguished in the career of this Wicked Priest. At the beginning he was good – being called after the name of truth is definitely something positive – but after he had gained a position of power ('ruled over Israel'), he was corrupted by military success and money. Were there any Jewish high priests during the relevant period, say between 171 and 63 BCE, who corresponded to such a portrait? Of course, they all cherished power and wealth, but out of the ten or so possible candidates was there anyone who could have met with the sect's approval at the start of his activity?

Out of this puzzle arose the so-called Maccabaean theory of Qumran origins. Only the two Maccabee brothers, first and foremost Jonathan, but also the younger Simon, heroes of the war of liberation against Seleucid political and religious oppression, had at the start an immaculate pedigree. In addition to the Habakkuk Commentary, the positive attitude towards 'King Jonathan' in a poem from Cave 4 (4Q448) deserves quoting.

Holy city for king Jonathan
and for all the congregation of your people, Israel,
who are in the four corners of heaven.
May the peace of them all be on your kingdom.
May your name be blessed.

This poem should be interpreted as aiming at Jonathan Maccabaeus, as has been argued first by myself and then by Émile Puech (see *JJS* 44 (1993), pp. 294–300 and *RQ* 17 (1996), pp. 241–170) against the thesis of the official editors Hanan and Esther Eshel and Ada Yardeni, who favoured Alexander Jannaeus (*DJD*, XI, pp. 403–25). Also John Strugnell and Elisha Qimron, the editors of Some Observances of the Law (MMT) understand this document as a communication addressed by the Teacher of Righteousness and his colleagues to Jonathan whom they still thought they could persuade to change his mind and listen to them. Later Jonathan (and Simon) compromised themselves in the eyes of the leaders of the Community by usurping as non-Zadokites the high priestly function which by tradition was the preserve of the Zadokite pontifical family, to which the priests of the Qumran Community were linked. In 152 BCE, Alexander Balas, a usurper of the Seleucid throne, offered Jonathan the high priestly office, and although he had no genealogical entitlement, he illegally accepted the pontifical office and thus discredited himself in the eyes of the Dead Sea sectaries.

Simon, Jonathan's brother, shared with him the fame and glory of being treated as a saviour of the Jewish people, but in the judgement of the Qumranites he also followed Jonathan's downhill course when he consented to be proclaimed dynastic high priest and ruler over Israel (1 Macc. 14:41). Both brothers suffered violent deaths, but Jonathan's execution by a Syrian Greek general, Tryphon, in 142 BCE (1 Macc. 13:23), fits better the description given in the Commentary on Psalm 37 about the Wicked Priest, who was put to death by 'the violent of the nations', than Simon's demise. The latter, while drunk, was murdered by his son-in-law in 134 BCE in the fortress of Dok, not far from Jericho (1 Macc. 16:14–16).

The Maccabaean theory was first developed in my

Louvain thesis, *Les manuscrits du désert de Juda* (Tournai-Paris, 1953. English translation: *Discovery in the Judean Desert*, New York, 1956). It argues for a Maccabaean Wicked Priest. This interpretation was soon adopted by several leading Qumran experts (J. T. Milik, F. M. Cross, R. de Vaux) and has since become the mainstream view among Scrolls scholars. An over-complicated variation on the same theme, the oddly titled 'Groningen hypothesis', which envisaged Essene splinter groups and six successive Wicked Priests from Judas Maccabaeus to Alexander Jannaeus, is the product of A. S. van der Woude and Florentino García Martínez, two Qumran experts at the University of Groningen.

Combining the literary data with the archaeological evidence, the history of the Qumran Community may be summarized as follows. The movement began in the early second century BCE, close to the reign of Antiochus Epiphanes and the ensuing outbreak of the Hellenistic crisis. The ministry of the Teacher of Righteousness belonged to the middle years of the second century BCE, and small beginnings of a sectarian settlement at Qumran can be traced to the dying years of that same century. The Community flourished by the Dead Sea in the first century BCE from 100 BCE onwards, probably without interruption after the 31 BCE earthquake, and in the first century CE until its violent end almost certainly at the hands of the Romans in 68 CE.

So far the historical reconstruction has relied on the Dead Sea Scrolls, the archaeological evidence and the relevant information from the Books of the Maccabees and the writings of Flavius Josephus, but without the use of the classical notices concerning the Essenes. Assuming that the Essene identification of the Qumran sect is accepted, the following historical addenda may complete the picture.

1. Josephus first mentions the Essene sect, together with the Pharisees and the Sadducees, during the pontificate of Jonathan Maccabaeus (153/2–143/2 BCE) in *Jewish Antiquities* XIII:171.

2. The Essenes flourished under Herod the Great. They were popular with the king and were excused from taking an oath of allegiance (*Jewish Antiquities* XV:371–2).

3. Several individual Essenes are named by Josephus. The first, Judas, appears in the company of his disciples in Jerusalem during the rule of Aristobulus I (103–102 BCE). Judas had the reputation of being a prophet, able unfailingly to forecast the future. Among other things, he predicted the death of the brother of Aristobulus (*Jewish Antiquities* XIII:311–13). Another Essene prophet, Menahem, foretold that Herod would become king of the Jews (*Jewish Antiquities* XV:373–8). After the death of Herod in 4 BCE, the Essene Simon interpreted a dream of Herod's son Archelaus and predicted that he would rule as ethnarch for ten years (*Jewish Antiquities* XVII:345–8). We are also informed that at the age of sixteen, in 53 CE, Josephus himself sought instruction in Essene doctrine and practice (*Life*, 10–11). Finally, we learn from Josephus of an Essene, by the name of John, who was one of the commanders of the Jewish forces fighting against Rome during the first rebellion. He commanded the district of Thamna in Judaea and the cities of Lydda, Jaffa and Emmaus (*Jewish War* II:567). A 'man of first-rate prowess and ability', he fell in the battle of Ascalon (*Jewish War* III:11, 19). As Josephus was clearly not a full member, Judas, Menahem, Simon and John are the four Essenes whose names should be joined to those of the three guilty sectaries, Yohanan and

two Hananiahs, written in the bad book of one of the Guardians (4Q477), and just possibly Eleazar ben Nahmani and Honi, mentioned on Ostracon 1 from Qumran (see chapter VII, pp. 169–70).

With these supplements to the debate regarding archaeology, group identity and sectarian history, the unfinished business of Qumran has been settled as well as it is possible at this moment. All we need now is another look backwards and forwards to recapitulate the contribution of the Dead Sea Scrolls to our understanding of Judaism – biblical and post-biblical – and of nascent Christianity and a gaze into the crystal ball to forecast the future of Qumran studies.

IX

The Qumran Revolution in the Study of Biblical and Post-biblical Judaism and Early Christianity

The Dead Sea Scrolls (dating to *c.* 200 BCE–70 CE) belong to the post-biblical age and their relevance to the Hebrew Bible itself is limited to questions pertaining to the transmission of the text and to the canon of Scripture. As both topics have already been dealt with, only the salient points of the earlier findings will be recapitulated here. Nevertheless, all that the reader will find in the following pages will vindicate the claim made in the opening chapter that the Dead Sea Scrolls have completely 'revolutionized our approach to the Hebrew Scriptures and to the literature of the age that witnessed the birth of the New Testament'.

1. Judaism

Because no Hebrew biblical manuscripts have survived from pre-Christian times with the possible exception of the Nash papyrus (see chapter VI, p. 96), the contribution of the scriptural Scrolls from Qumran are unparalleled as far as our knowledge of the text of the Old Testament is concerned. What do we learn from them?

The Dead Sea finds partly confirm and partly question the reliability of the wording of the Bible handed down by Jewish tradition. On the one hand, as was shown in chapter VI, the Qumran Scripture is substantially identical with that passed on by the synagogue from the time of Jesus to the present age. On the other hand, the Dead Sea Scrolls furnish documentary proof of what has been surmised before, namely that, prior to the destruction of Jerusalem in 70 CE, unity was not yet achieved and different forms of the Hebrew text coexisted, showing verbal and stylistic variations, additions, omissions and changes in the order of the textual arrangement. Before the Qumran discoveries, we presumed that the Samaritan Bible (restricted to the five books of the Law of Moses), the form of the Hebrew Bible from which the ancient Greek version, known as the Septuagint, was translated, and the type of the text that was to evolve into the traditional (Masoretic) Hebrew Old Testament, existed side by side in different social groups. Qumran has corroborated this theory and has demonstrated that diversity could obtain in one and the same group. This phenomenon implies that the variant readings in the biblical text do not necessarily represent corruptions or deliberate alterations, but can just as well, if not better, echo earlier discrete written traditions. Unity, produced by Jewish religious authority, was usually sought in times of crisis, and was achieved by the selection of one of the existing text forms and the simultaneous rejection of all other competing versions. Such a deliberate unification is assumed to have been part of the general restructuring of Judaism by the rabbis during the years following the catastrophe of 70 CE, which entailed the loss of the Temple and the supreme council of the Sanhedrin as well as the replacement of the aristocratic high priestly leadership of Jewry by rabbis largely of plebeian origin.

The second, less stringent, conclusion that can be drawn from the Dead Sea biblical Scrolls relates to the canon of the Jewish Scriptures. Qumran unfortunately has not provided us with a register listing by name every book of the Bible. All we know is that, with the exception of the Book of Esther (missing also, as has been noted, from the list of the second century CE bishop, Melito of Sardis), some 215 original manuscripts have been retrieved from the eleven Qumran caves. They comprise fragments of more than seventy copies of the Law (the Torah), a dozen specimens of the Former Prophets (Joshua, Judges, Samuel, Kings), over forty copies of the Latter Prophets (Isaiah, Jeremiah, Ezekiel) and more than sixty copies of the Writings (among them thirty-six copies of the Psalms). Nothing specifically proves, however, that these texts belonged to a distinctive class of their own. Their privileged position may be deduced only from circumstantial evidence. For example, some of them (Genesis, Isaiah, several Minor Prophets and the Psalms) are furnished with commentaries. There is no evidence of a running interpretation attached to non-biblical documents at Qumran. Also, extracts from various books that tradition considers as Scripture serve as proof texts in the Community Rule, the Damascus Document and in other Qumran writings. However, the cogency of this argument is weakened if one recalls that a work attributed to Levi, son of Jacob (possibly an early version of the Testament of Levi), and the Book of Jubilees are also used in a similar fashion by the writer of the Damascus Document unless we agree with the authors of *The Dead Sea Scrolls Bible* that these works belonged to the Bible at Qumran (see chapter VI, p. 102). All we can safely deduce is a great likelihood that the writings held to be canonical in rabbinic Judaism enjoyed the same status in the Dead Sea community. This would imply that the list of authoritative books was established while Qumran was in existence, that is to say, before the year 70 CE at the latest, and not in the early decades of the second century CE, as is commonly held.

If so, the debate which gave an opportunity to Rabbi Akiba (martyred under Hadrian in 135 CE) to maintain the canonicity of the Song of Songs and Ecclesiastes simply shows that the status quo arrived at probably in the course of the first century BCE, concerning what constituted the Bible, was successfully restated by some rabbis after 100 CE against those other rabbis who sought to remove various disputed items from the traditional register of Scriptures. In this case, the creation of the Palestinian canon must have followed closely the entry into the Bible of the Book of Daniel, finally completed some time around 160 BCE. As Cave 4 fragments of this book, dating to the late second century BCE, prove, the text itself was already firmly fixed within half a century from the canonization of Daniel, and this includes even the switch in it from Hebrew to Aramaic in chapter 2:4 and again back to Hebrew in chapter 8.

In the domain of the Aramaic Bible translation, little novelty is available at Qumran. Two small Aramaic fragments of Leviticus and Job have emerged from Cave 4 with no variants worth mentioning. Cave 11 has yielded larger sections of the Book of Job with stylistic changes. However, the discrepancies should probably be attributed to the difficulties of the Hebrew language the translator of the book had to face rather than to textual variations.

The Aramaic Genesis Apocryphon, of which substantial sections have survived in Cave 1, prefigures the later rabbinic genre of the so-called Palestinian Targums in which the text of the Pentateuch rendered into Aramaic is amalgamated with a free and often extensive supplementary explanation, also in Aramaic. It demonstrates that this type of scriptural interpretation was not the creation of the rabbis in the third to the fifth century CE, as is generally thought, but came into existence probably as early as the second century BCE and consequently existed in New Testament times.

Greek Bible translations from Qumran are also few and far between and stay close to the traditional Septuagint with only minor verbal variations. A notable peculiarity appears in the Greek fragment of Leviticus 4:17 (4Q120) where the sacrosanct divine name 'YHWH' is phonetically transliterated as *Iao* instead of being replaced by the customary term, 'Lord' (*Kyrios*).

Works of Scripture interpretation, other than the so-called 'rewritten Bible' – already exemplified by the Book of Jubilees, a paraphrase of Genesis, the Book of Biblical Antiquities falsely attributed to Philo, and Flavius Josephus' *Jewish Antiquities*, retelling the story of the entire Old Testament – open a new chapter in post-biblical Jewish literature. At Qumran, the *Reworked Pentateuch* (4Q158, 364–7) represents this genre. There are also thematic collections of exegesis devoted to biblical laws (4Q159, 513–14) and interpretative documents on messianic or apocalyptic themes (4Q174–5). However, the principal fresh contribution of Qumran to post-biblical Jewish literature is furnished by continuous commentaries on Genesis, various prophetic books and the Psalms. Most of them aim at outlining and interpreting prophecy in its relation to the Qumran community's past, present and future history. They constitute the *pesher* class of the Dead Sea Scrolls (see chapter VII, pp. 162–4). Extracts from them are also occasionally quoted in Qumran writings of a doctrinal nature such as the Damascus Document (see CD 4:14).

Furthermore, the Dead Sea Scrolls have made a substantial contribution to a better grasp of the history of *halakhah*,

217

the rabbinic method of regulating Jewish religious conduct and morality. Indeed, the reinterpretation and adaptation of biblical law to evolving historical and social circumstances did not start after the destruction of the Temple of Jerusalem by the Romans in 70 CE. The Scrolls already contain examples of the formulation of new rules either through applied Bible exegesis, anticipating the literary genre of the rabbinic Midrash, or in the form of direct commands without scriptural support as attested in the Mishnah and the Talmud, works compiled between 200 and 500 CE.

The *midrashic* type of lawmaking is practised by the author of the Damascus Document (CD 5:1–2). He demonstrates through legal reasoning the compulsory character of the monogamous marriage by applying to every Jewish male person the law of Deuteronomy relative to the king who was forbidden to 'multiply wives' (Deut. 17:17), i.e. to have more than one spouse. The *mishnaic* genre, simple statement unsupported by Bible citation, is illustrated by the precepts included in MMT (4Q394–9) and the Statutes of the Damascus Document (CD 9–16).

The style of a legal document, organized into divisions according to subject matter like the tractates of the Mishnah and the Talmud, is explicitly exemplified in the Damascus Statutes where we find formal divisional headings such as 'Concerning the oath of a woman', 'Concerning the statute for free-will offering', 'Concerning purification by water', 'Concerning the Sabbath', etc., and less formally in MMT where, without express divisional titles, the laws are arranged as relating to the liturgical calendar, ritual purity, marriage and sundry decrees governing the entry into the sect.

Qumran's contribution to the domain of religious and

political sociology consists in revealing through literature and archaeology the detailed aspects of the life and structure of a Jewish sect that flourished between the latter part of the second century BCE and the first Jewish war against Rome (66–70 CE). Prior to the Scrolls, our main sources were Josephus, the New Testament, both dating to the first century CE, followed by the Mishnah and other rabbinic works recorded in writing from 200 to 500 CE. All of them mention subgroups within the Jewish body politic in Judaea and Galilee. Josephus, the most detailed of our informants, speaks of the religious parties of the Pharisees, the Sadducees and the Essenes, to which he adds 'the fourth philosophy' of the Zealots-Sicarii and, if the relevant part (*Jewish Antiquities* XVIII:64) of the *Testimonium Flavianum* is accepted as genuine, makes a fleeting reference to the Christians too. In addition to the early followers of Jesus, specially described in the Acts of the Apostles (2:43–7; 4:32; 5:1–11), the New Testament knows of the Pharisees and the Sadducees and includes an allusion to the Zealots, the adherents of Judas the Galilean (Acts 5:37). Rabbinic literature, although aware of the existence of the Zealots (*Qannaim*), representatives after 70 CE of the clandestine resistance to Roman power, is chiefly interested in the two rival groups of teachers, the Pharisees or Sages and the Sadducees, and distinguishes them from the 'people of the land', i.e. the bulk of the Jewish inhabitants of Palestine unaffiliated either to Pharisees, Sadducees or any other religious parties.

Of these five groups, three can hardly be designated as sects. The Zealots were essentially a political movement open to anyone opposed to Rome. The Sadducees, lay and priestly aristocracy attached to the high priestly families, formed the traditional ruling classes of Judaea under

Roman overlordship, whereas the Pharisees were the self-appointed doctrinal leaders competing with the priesthood, favoured by the urban bourgeoisie and, according to Josephus, by the women. No initiation was required to join the Pharisees or the Sadducees. Only the Essenes and the Jesus movement considered themselves so apart from the ordinary folk that full membership could be attained only after preliminary instruction and formal initiation. The Dead Sea Scrolls provide a remarkably full, rich and illuminating picture of the organization, aims and beliefs of the Qumran sect, and (if the two are identified) of the Essenes when their data are combined with the accounts of Philo, Josephus and Pliny.

The Dead Sea discoveries have also furnished us with a much firmer grasp of the historical dimensions of the Qumran-Essene movement than anything we possessed before 1947. Philo's description of the Essenes completely lacks historical perspective and Pliny's quite dreamily refers to them as an 'eternal race' that has existed for thousands of centuries. Only Josephus tries to connect the Essenes with Jewish history, first mentioning them under Jonathan Maccabaeus in mid-second century BCE; later reporting on their preferential treatment under the reign of Herod the Great, and finally he refers to them during the first Jewish war as heroically suffering Roman tortures while one of their leaders acted as a rebel general and fell on the battle-field. The Qumran manuscripts, especially the Damascus Document and the biblical commentaries, supply more concrete, though cryptographic, details about the Teacher of Righteousness, the founder of the sect, the Wicked Priest, his chief opponent, and the early history of the community from the Maccabaean age to Pompey's conquest of Judaea in 63 BCE. Other allusions seem to concern imperial Rome.

In sum, thanks to the Dead Sea Scrolls and the archaeological remains unearthed at Qumran we have gained a substantially refined knowledge of the religious history of the Jews during the last two centuries preceding the conquest and destruction of Jerusalem under Vespasian and Titus in 70 CE.

2. Christianity

Scholarly opinion concerning the impact of the Scrolls on the New Testament and early Christianity falls into two categories. To the first belong some writers, usually media-oriented, who directly associate Qumran with the nascent Church. They attempt to establish the association by seeking to discover a link between the personalities of the Dead Sea Community on the one hand, and on the other, Jesus, John the Baptist, James, the brother of the Lord, and St Paul. We should add to this category of Qumran scholars a few Greek papyrus experts who claim that a smattering of tiny manuscript fragments found in Qumran Cave 7 represent in reality New Testament documents (see pp. 223–5). By contrast, the large majority of scholars prefer to consider the Dead Sea sect and the primitive Church as two separate, independent but contemporaneous and parallel movements with the older Qumran group, possibly influencing here and there the younger Christian Church in matters of belief, doctrine and, most likely, religious organization and practice.

Let me rehearse briefly the theories amalgamating the Scrolls with the New Testament which have been dealt with in chapter VIII. The publication of the Cairo manuscripts of Zadokite Fragments by Solomon Schechter in

1910 already generated an attempt to view the Damascus Document as a Christian writing with specific Sadducean features. The protagonist of this thesis was G. Margoliouth, who argued without much impact, that for the Zadokites John the Baptist was the Messiah and Jesus the Teacher of Righteousness (*Expositor*, December 1911, pp. 499–517 and March 1912, pp. 212–35). The first Hebraist to renew this trend after the discovery of the Qumran Scrolls was Jacob Teicher of Cambridge in a series of articles between 1950 and 1954 in the then freshly founded *Journal of Jewish Studies*. He proposed to identify Jesus as the Teacher of Righteousness and St Paul as the Wicked Priest. His ideas were soon forgotten, but the cool reception Teicher's thesis met within scholarly circles did not discourage Robert Eisenman from reviving a similar theory some thirty years later with James, the brother of the Lord, replacing Jesus in the role of the Teacher of Righteousness, while St Paul maintained his position as the Wicked Priest, and the whole story was given a Zealot colouring (*Maccabees, Zadokites, Christians and Qumran* and *James the Just and the Habakkuk Pesher*, Leiden, Brill, 1983, 1986). At about the same time, Barbara Thiering issued a series of books, proclaiming John the Baptist as the Teacher of Righteousness and the married, divorced and remarried Jesus as the Wicked Priest (*The Qumran Origins of the Christian Church*, Sydney, Australian & New Zealand Studies of Theology and Religion, 1983; *Jesus the Man*, New York, Doubleday, 1992). As one might expect, these startling publications excited much press and TV interest, but being found short of solid foundation, they failed to affect scholarly attitudes towards the problem of the Dead Sea Scrolls (see chapter VIII, pp. 190–91).

Common sense is the first and foremost argument against identifying the Qumran Scrolls as Christian writings. Even a simple unsophisticated reading of these manuscripts clearly indicates that apart from some general themes, such as the proximity of the end, the final triumph of righteousness brought about by a messianic leader, the Scrolls and the New Testament fundamentally stand apart. The Qumran emphasis on the painstakingly exact observance of the Law of Moses is lacking from the Gospels, let alone from Paul, even though they, like Jesus, insist on the moral value of the adherence to the Torah. The little detail that is available regarding the priestly character of the Teacher of Righteousness does not tally with the portrait of Jesus in the Gospels which presents him instead as a Galilean charismatic healer and exorcist. Qumran, in fact, has no Galilean association whatsoever. Add to this the chronological difficulty: the Qumran texts most frequently cited as having a Christian association – the Damascus Document and the Habakkuk Commentary – are dated by the near-totality of experts to the pre-Christian era. Note that the Carbon-14 test performed on a fragment belonging to the Habakkuk Commentary in 1995 firmly set it before the start of the present era (between 110–15 BCE), although one must concede that such a small difference in the timescale of the radiocarbon evidence can not be judged decisive.

The second link between Qumran and Christianity is seen by a small number of New Testament papyrologists in minute Greek manuscript fragments discovered in Cave 7. The original editors, the French Dominicans, P. Benoit and M. E. Boismard, were able to identify only two of the 18 papyrus scraps and declared them as belonging to the Greek version of the Old Testament book of Exodus (7Q1) and of the Letter of Jeremiah (7Q2). The rest were published as unidentified pieces (*DJD*, III, 1962, pp. 142–5). Ten years later, the Spanish Jesuit textual critic, José O'Callaghan, caused worldwide sensation by alleging that six of the unclassified bits represented the New Testament: Mark 4:28 (7Q6,1); Mark 6:48 (7Q15); Mark 6:52–3 (7Q5); Mark 12:17 (7Q7); Acts 28:38 (7Q6,2); 1 Tim. 3:16, 4:1–3 (7Q4); James 1:23–4 (7Q8) and 2 Pet. 1:15 (7Q10). Bearing in mind that no one knew the length of the original lines, necessary for any hypothetical filling in of the gaping holes, C. H. Roberts, the greatest twentieth-century expert of New Testament papyri, and I immediately questioned O'Callaghan's theory in the Letters column of *The Times* in April 1972 and Roberts renewed his refutation in the *Journal of Theological Studies* (23 (1972), pp. 446–7). Even the pièce de résistance of O'Callaghan, the alleged Mark 6:52–3, consists of a mere seventeen fully or partly surviving letters, of which only nine are certain. They are distributed on four lines with both the beginning and the end of the lines missing, and with only a single three-letter word preserved complete in the text, the not very illuminating *kai* (= and). For a while the matter seemed to be settled, but twenty years later, in the 1990s, the New Testament theory was revived by C. P. Thiede and others, but was met with firm rebuttal from the weightiest textual authorities, Kurt Aland, M. E. Boismard, Émile Puech, etc.

By the way, even if miraculously some of the Cave 7 documents turned out to be New Testament passages, it still would not prove that the Qumran Community was Christian. As this cave yielded only Greek texts, quite unusual at Qumran – the only further Greek examples derive from Bible translations (4Q119–22) – it is not inconceivable that the 7Q deposit is separate and independent from the Dead Sea Scrolls proper, and was hidden there by fugitive Christians some time in the second century CE when the Qumran settlement was already abandoned and unoccupied.

Let us now turn to less fanciful matters. Even if we discard the idea that nascent Christianity is identical with, or derives from, the Qumran Community, we are still faced with some significant parallelisms which demand explanation. The issues to consider are the concept of the new Israel with a new ultimate leader, the idea of the new Temple replacing the Jerusalem sanctuary, the eschatological world view envisaging an imminent end or transformation of the ages, the role of the Bible in the life of the new association, similarities regarding the organization and the life of the two communities (ownership of property, government, marriage versus celibacy) and even some striking verbal similarities between the Scrolls and the New Testament.

(a) New Israel and new Temple

Both the Damascus Document and the Community Rule portray the Community as a miniature new Israel of the final age, symbolically divided into twelve tribes and led by twelve tribal chiefs (see chapter VII, pp. 123–3, 130). They and those who were to join them, would constitute the 'righteous remnant' of Isaiah 10:21, and form the true chosen people of God at the time of the arrival of the divine kingdom. The early Church envisaged itself along similar lines. The Gospel saying, put on the lips of Jesus, expresses the same idea:

When the Son of man shall sit on his glorious throne, you who have followed me will also sit on twelve thrones, judging the twelve tribes of Israel.

(Matt. 19:28)

*I assign you, as my Father assigned me, a kingdom, that you may
. . . sit on thrones judging the twelve tribes of Israel.*

(Luke 22:30)

Likewise, Paul considers the Church as the new 'Israel of
God' (Gal. 6:16) and the letter of James is addressed to
'the twelve tribes of the Dispersion' (Jas. 1:1).

In short, the budding Church was convinced, as had
been the Qumran sect before it, that its members alone
formed the elect of God. Also, just as the Dead Sea
Community saw itself as the sole legitimate substitute for
the Temple of Jerusalem, 'a sanctuary of men' where the
works of the law were offered to God 'without the flesh
of holocausts and the fat of sacrifices' as 'the smoke of
incense' or as 'a sweet fragrance' (1QS 8:8–9; 9:4–5;
1QpHab 12:3–4; 4Q174 i. 6–7), the Pauline Church, too,
believed that the bodies of the Christians counted as 'a
living sacrifice' within their 'spiritual worship' (Rom. 12:1).
This worship was offered in a symbolical Temple 'built
upon the foundation of the apostles and prophets, Christ
Jesus being the cornerstone' (Eph. 2:20).

(b) Eschatological world view

Another characteristic common to the Scrolls and the New
Testament is their eschatological world view, that is, the
conviction that their respective communities lived on the
doorstep of the kingdom of God, that divinely engineered
age in which all things would be renewed. In both litera-
tures, the founder – the Teacher of Righteousness or Jesus
– was believed to possess and to convey to his disciples
all the secrets surrounding the end of times. The Qumran
sectaries awaited the final age to be inaugurated by their

Teacher of Righteousness and when he died before achieving this aim, they expected the dawn of the messianic era to appear within forty years after his disappearance from among the living. Jesus, too, looked forward to the onset of the kingdom of God in the course of the lifetime of his generation and when the cross removed him from the scene of action, his followers, in the wake of St Paul, were convinced of his impending return still within their own days and enthusiastically longed for the *parousia*, the Second Coming.

The similarity between the two attitudes culminates in their reaction to the continued postponement of the end. The sectaries were encouraged to confront the delay with a blind, semi-fatalistic trust: 'All the ages of God reach their appointed end as he determines for them in the mysteries of his wisdom' (1QpHab 7:13–14). In their turn, mid-second century Christians, mirrored in the late document known as the second letter of Peter, comforted themselves with the thought that God's way of measuring time differs from that of men and that in any case the extension of the final age has the advantage of providing the faithful with additional opportunities for repentance (2 Pet. 3:3–9).

(c) The Bible

Another major factor, providing a fresh insight into Christian thought, is revealed by the respective stance of the Qumran Community and the early Church towards the Bible. The interpretation of Scripture as a source of behaviour and belief turns out to be of paramount importance in both groups. The Bible serves at Qumran as well as in the early Church to define correct conduct by means of applied interpretation and to explain history in the form of fulfilled prophecy. In regard to the former, the sectarian Scrolls – like later rabbinic literature – seek to derive from the words of the ancient Scripture rules determining the contemporary way of rightful action. This application exists, but is less frequent, in the New Testament too. Its paucity in the teaching attributable to Jesus is particularly noticeable. In fact, Bible quotations are employed by New Testament authors more for poetic, theological or rhetorical illustration than as proof texts.

There are, however, noteworthy examples pointing out the cases where the scriptural arguments used at Qumran and in the Gospels coincide. The most striking of these relates to marriage. Endeavouring to argue from the Bible that the doctrinal opponents of the sect are guilty of fornication when they take a second wife during the lifetime of the first, the author of the Damascus Document (4:20–21) cites 'Male and female created he them' (Gen. 1:17), meaning literally that God created one man and one woman. This is presented as the 'principle of the creation', implying that marriage is meant to involve only one husband and one wife. Although all the Bible quotations cited in the Damascus Document passage refer to monogamy, some Qumran interpreters seek also to derive from this same principle the prohibition of divorce, invoking the New Testament where Jesus is said to have used the same quote to outlaw absolutely or, according to Matthew, conditionally, the repudiation of a wife. To objectors who invoked the Bible in support of the right of a husband to dismiss his monogamous wife, Jesus retorted: 'For your hardness of heart (Moses) wrote you this commandment. But from the beginning of creation, God made them male and female' (Mark 10:5–6; Matt. 19:3–4).

Another, and perhaps the most important, Qumran contribution to the understanding of the New Testament is supplied by the specific Dead Sea Scroll interpretation of prophecy, known as the *pesher*. The *pesher*, as has been made clear (see chapter VII, pp. 162–4), expounds a scriptural prediction by indicating its realization in the history of the community. The best preserved of the *pesharim*, the Habakkuk Commentary, outlines various features of the Teacher of Righteousness and alludes to several episodes of his life, asserting that they constitute the fulfilment of predictions uttered by the prophet Habakkuk many centuries before the time of the Teacher: '*Write down the vision and make plain upon the tablets that he who reads may read it speedily*' (Hab. 2:1–2). God told Habakkuk to write down that which would happen to the final generation, but he did not make known to him when time would come to an end. And as for the saying, '*that he who reads may read it speedily*', interpreted it concerns the Teacher of Righteousness, to whom God made known all the mysteries of the words of his servants, the prophets (1QpHab 7:1–5).

Later, citing St Paul's favourite verse of Habakkuk (2:4), '*The righteous shall live by his faith*', the commentator adds: 'Interpreted, this (=*the righteous*) concerns all those who observe the law in the house of Judah, whom God will deliver from the house of judgement because of their suffering and because of their faith in the Teacher of Righteousness' (1QpHab 8:1–2).

Of all the surviving Jewish writings of the relevant period, the Gospels, especially Matthew, and the letters of Paul recall most closely the Qumran fulfilment interpretation of Old Testament prophecy. Matthew uses specific introductory formulae such as 'This took place to fulfil what the Lord has spoken by the prophet' (Matt. 1:22); 'So it is written by the prophet' (Matt. 2:5); or 'This is he who was spoken of by the prophet Isaiah' (Matt. 3:3). In his turn, Paul, anticipating the rabbis, regularly starts his citations with 'As it is written'. These expressions correspond to the phrases 'Interpreted', 'The interpretation of this saying concerns', etc., of the Qumran *pesher*. Naturally the events and personalities of the Qumran Community and of the Gospels, presented as implementation of biblical prophecy, further signify for the Qumran sectaries and the early followers of Jesus that their respective leaders and their history were predestined and prearranged by God. Although a similar use of the prophetic argument appears also from time to time in rabbinic literature (see chapter VII, p. 162), the massive occurrence of this type of evidence indicates that Qumran and early Christianity shared a common spiritual atmosphere, doctrinal heritage and religious outlook. In consequence, Qumran sheds here a particularly brilliant light on the beliefs and teachings of the primitive Church.

(d) Messianism

In doctrinal matters, the Dead Sea Scrolls display certain subjects in a much more colourful and nuanced manner than does the New Testament. Take, for example, the topic of Messianism. We encounter at Qumran the plain and traditional form of the Davidic Messiah, believed to be the ultimate military commander chosen and commissioned by God, ready to lead the army of the elect to final victory over the armies of Satan and his wicked Jewish and Gentile allies. This Messiah is described as the 'Branch of David' (4Q161, 285), the 'prince of the Congregation' (1QM 5:1; 4Q285), the 'Sceptre' (CD 7:20) or the 'Messiah of Israel' (1QSa 2:14, 20). However, in addition to the typical king Messiah, son of David, the Dead Sea Scrolls speak also of 'the Messiah of Aaron and Israel' in the singular and of 'the Messiahs of Aaron and Israel' (1QS 9:11), that is, an anointed leader descending from Israel and another one from Aaron. The New Testament, in turn, refers to a single royal Messiah. Nevertheless the letter to the Hebrews conceives of Jesus as the heavenly high priest (or priestly Messiah), and the Infancy Gospel of Luke, by describing Mary as the kinswoman of Elizabeth, wife of Zechariah, the priest, tacitly insinuates that Jesus descended from a combined Davidic and priestly ancestral line. Once more, Qumran and the New Testament indirectly testify to a joint ideological background.

(e) Organization

Another important aspect of the relationship between the Qumran sect and the early Church concerns their organization and communal life. After their respective leaders had ceased to be among them, the Qumran sect and the Jesus movement, the latter both in Palestine and in the Diaspora, established their own structure and adopted their peculiar way of life. The Dead Sea sectaries, whether the married or the celibate kind, obeyed single local leaders or Guardians and a superior general, the Guardian of all the units. The single heads were aided by other officers and advisers. The nascent Palestinian Christian sect was also headed by apostles and attended by charity workers or deacons, and the Pauline Churches outside Palestine by individual bishops or overseers like Timothy or Titus. Bishop (*episkopos*) is the Greek-Christian equivalent of the Qumran Guardian or Overseer (*mebaqqer*). Such a monarchic regime was unusual among Jews; their communities, both in the Holy Land and in the Diaspora, were governed by democratic councils of elders chaired by a president or *archisynagogos*. It is reasonable to surmise, therefore, that since the Qumran sect was older than the Christian community, the organizers of the latter could be tempted to imitate in setting up their local congregations the already well-established and tried systems flourishing elsewhere in their society, such as the Qumran-Essene congregations of Judaea.

The religious communism, or more precisely, the sharing of all private property, sanctioned by the apostles in the Jerusalem Church of the earliest period, strongly resembles, and possibly copies, the way of life of the 'monastic' Qumran brotherhood, though without being accompanied by compulsory celibacy.

And all who believed were together and had all things in common; and they sold their possessions and goods and distributed them to all, as any had need.

(Acts 2:44–5)

Now the company of those who believed were of one heart and soul, and no one said that any of the things which he possessed was his own, but they had everything in common.

(Acts 4:32)

Although the handing over to the community of privately owned property and money is nowhere said to be compulsory, as it was among the Qumranites who followed the Community Rule, the moral pressure on Church members to conform seems to have been enormous and could lead to deceitful pretence, as described in the anecdote of Ananias and Sapphira (Acts 5:1–11). After selling a plot of land, this couple let it be known that they had given the totality of the proceeds to the apostles, while secretly they kept part of the sum for themselves. Both husband and wife suddenly died one after the other and the tragedy was held to be heavenly punishment for lying to the Holy Spirit. The penalty inflicted on the guilty in the Christian community was incomparably heavier than that awaiting a sectary who 'lied in matters of property': the latter was merely excluded from common life for one year during which he was compelled to live on a reduced food ration (1QS 6:24–5). This is not the only example of greater severity in the Church's treatment of sinners compared to the practice prevailing at Qumran. Sectaries convicted of the greatest sins (rebellion, apostasy, etc.) were simply excommunicated, whereas St Paul condemned the immoral Corinthian Christian, who scandalized everyone by sharing the bed of his father's wife, to be delivered to Satan 'for the destruction of the flesh' (1 Cor. 5:1–5).

(f) Celibacy

A final comparison will be aimed at the practice of celibacy in the 'monastic' branch of the Qumran sect and in the teaching of Jesus and Paul. It is generally agreed that, despite the absence of a positive commandment prohibiting marriage, the internal logic of the Community Rule implies that members of the brotherhood subjected themselves to a compulsory and long-lasting celibate existence. On the other hand, since celibacy is nowhere presented positively as a rule, let alone a universal rule, it is not surprising that the Scrolls furnish no explanation or justification for it. Inspired by the customary Jewish male chauvinism, Philo and Josephus attribute Essene renunciation of marriage to the unsuitability of women for communal life, a form of existence, an old-fashioned club life, cherished only by men. It is more likely, however, that the concept of the Community being a spiritual Temple which demanded a constant state of ritual purity on the part of the members was thought to be irreconcilable with a society of married people. If, furthermore, the 'monastic' Qumran Community is held to be identical with the Essenes, a sect particularly famous according to Josephus for its practice of prophecy (the forecasting of the future possibly by means of Bible interpretation), abstinence from sex would have been the condition for permanent receptivity to divine communication. According to a Jewish tradition recorded by Philo of Alexandria, Moses, in order to make himself constantly ready for hearing God's message, had to purge himself of 'all calls of mortal nature', including 'intercourse with women' (*Life of Moses* II: 68–9).

In the context of the New Testament, celibacy is nowhere institutionally imposed. Nor is it associated with ritual purity, a subject never considered as of primary importance by Jesus and the Church. As far as Jesus is concerned, he is nowhere said to have had a wife at any time. His bachelor state may be ascribed to his prophetic vocation as well as to the general view that having a wife and children during the end-time hindered total devotion to the cause of the kingdom of God. In the days of the great ultimate tribulation, it was held to be preferable to be without family responsibilities: 'Alas for those who are with child and for those who give suck in those days' (Mark 13:17). St Paul, in his lively expectation of the return of Christ, while not actually condemning marriage, advises single Christians to protect their freedom by remaining unattached, thus following his own example. 'Do we not' Paul asks, 'have the right to be accompanied by a wife, as the other apostles, and the brothers of the Lord and Cephas (=Peter)?' (1 Cor. 9:5). Peter's wife is not actually mentioned, but her existence is revealed by Jesus healing Simon Peter's mother-in-law in Capernaum (Mark 1:30–31). In his turn, Paul recommends that, if possible, a man should not touch a woman and wishes they all were 'as I myself am', clearly implying bachelorhood (1 Cor. 7:1, 7). However, until the start of Christian monasticism in the fourth century, the Church did not advocate formally regulated celibate life. In this respect, the Qumran-Essenes were trailblazers. Apart from them and the Therapeutai, their Jewish imitators in Egypt with separate communities recruited from both sexes (see Philo, *Contemplative Life*), only hermits pursuing a solitary existence in the desert, like Josephus' temporary teacher, Bannus, and no doubt John the Baptist, opted for the unmarried way of life among Jews in the days of Qumran and the New Testament.

To end this survey with the billion dollar question, if the older Qumran sect influenced the Palestinian Jesus movement in some way, at what level did this influence penetrate the Church? Through John the Baptist? Through Jesus? Through the later Church?

John the Baptist has often been singled out as the most likely link between the Dead Sea Community and Christianity. His ascetic life in the wilderness and his preaching of a baptism of repentance to prepare for the arrival of God's kingdom neatly place him between sect and Church. If Luke's Infancy Gospel can be believed, he, like the members of the leading class of Qumran, was of priestly descent. Moreover, both John and the Dead Sea sect were seen as fulfilling the prediction of Isaiah 40:3.

The sectaries read the prophetic words as: 'A voice cries, In the wilderness prepare the way of the Lord', corresponding to a demand for withdrawal to the desert of Judaea for spiritual renewal. The evangelists, in turn, interpreted it as 'A voice cries in the wilderness, Prepare the way of the Lord', by which they portrayed John as the herald of Jesus, preaching in the desert of the Jordan valley the imminence of the kingdom of God.

Nevertheless, to someone familiar with the thought of the Dead Sea sect, the similarity between John and Qumran appears superficial and partial. A sectary, who conformed to the basic rules of the Community, would not have been allowed to proclaim his message indiscriminately to Jewish society at large as John did, and would have been restricted to passing on his teaching to the select few of the chosen. If the Baptist was ever a full member of the Qumran-Essene Community, we must suppose that by the time of his public ministry, reported in the Gospels, he was no longer one of them.

Was, then, Jesus the door through which Qumran influence entered Christianity? Despite a few common doctrinal themes, this seems to be most unlikely. The law-centred religion of Qumran is very far from the paramountly eschatological and ethical turn of mind of Jesus. Besides, the prophet from Nazareth who spent most of his active life in Galilee had few opportunities to encounter members of the Qumran sect whose presence in the northern province is nowhere attested.

John the Baptist and Jesus being discounted, the apostolic Church remains the likeliest candidate for borrowing Qumran ideas and introducing them into evolving Christianity. Logically it would make sense for a budding movement to look around and see how similar societies function, especially when the traditions relating to Jesus do not comprise traits that might account for the given features. Thus, since Jesus did not hand over a blueprint for a future Church – the notion of 'Church' (*ekklesia*) with the exception of two inauthentic passages in Matthew (16:18 and 18:17), is characteristically not to be found anywhere in the sayings attributed to Jesus – the system introduced into the life of the early Jerusalem community may have been inspired by the tried and successful Qumran model. The same can be said about the authoritative single-person leadership, say, for example, James, the brother of Jesus in Jerusalem, Paul and his appointees in the Diaspora Churches, that suited the infant communities better than the more flexible and argumentative councils of elders of the Palestinian Jewish communities and the Diaspora synagogues. On the level of religious thought, the Qumran vision of a small 'remnant' led to the final realm of God by the Teacher of Righteousness, himself the intermediary of all necessary revelations, was an excellent pattern for Christianity to be copied by the followers of Jesus. As for the Qumran *pesher*, it pointed the way towards the type of fulfilment exegesis that we find in the works of the evangelists and Paul.

Back in the late 1940s, scholars enthusiastically prophesied that the newly discovered Dead Sea Scrolls would transform beyond all recognition our approach to the Hebrew Bible and the New Testament, as well as our understanding of both Judaism and Christianity. In the light of six decades of intense research, study and thought, the prophecy seems to have come true. Thanks to the manuscripts discovered at Qumran, the study of ancient Judaism and early Christianity has made a giant step forward and has laid solid foundations for future scholarly work in generations to come. We have advanced a great deal, yet in a sense we are just at the beginning of integrating the contribution of the Scrolls to the general canvas of Judaism and Christianity. In an odd way, our task will be finished only when Qumran ceases to be a separate subject, having lost its distinctness in the process of becoming a recognized integral part of the Judaeo-Christian culture.

X

Epilogue

In the first chapter of this book, in the 'Portrait of the story-teller', I outlined how I initially got involved with the Scrolls. The rest of the volume offers snippets of my further participation in the Qumran saga and its vast contribution to the historical, cultural and religious knowledge of Judaism and Christianity. I feel enormously privileged and am humbly grateful for the part I have been allowed to play in it. This volume has gone to the printers in 2009, the year which eventually saw the completion of the publication of all the Dead Sea Scrolls, with the final volume of the series, *Discoveries in the Judaean Desert*. It also marks the sixtieth anniversary of my first essay on the Scrolls in the long-defunct Parisian periodical, *Cahiers Sioniens* (vol. 3, August 1949, pp. 224–33), 'Nouvelles lumières sur la Bible et le Judaïsme' (New lights on the Bible and Judaism). The next landmark – let us hope – will come in 2012, the golden jubilee of *The Dead Sea Scrolls in English*, born in 1962 with a Qumran manuscript on its front cover – printed upside down.

To continue on a lighthearted, cheerful but still personal note, let me end the volume by quoting from the conclusion of a lecture entitled 'Living with the Dead Sea Scrolls', which I delivered in the British Museum in 2004.

It records three memorable and amusing anecdotes of my life as a Qumran scholar.

Shortly after the publication of *The Dead Sea Scrolls in English* in 1962, I was asked at a conference in London by an elderly cleric, 'Young man, are you a *relation* of the Vermes who writes on the Dead Sea Scrolls?'

Some twenty years later, at a party in Oxford, an Israeli lady who acted as a part-time tourist guide at Qumran, exclaimed when she realized who I was: 'But I thought Vermes was just a *text book*!'

Finally, the third episode took place in California in the 1990s. My wife and I were guests at a dinner in the Huntington Library in Pasadena, and we left five-year-old Ian with the daughter of William Moffett, the director of the Library and chief liberator of the Scrolls. Next morning she smilingly reported a conversation she had overheard between her son and Ian, two boys of similar age. 'My grandad *found* the Dead Sea Scrolls,' boasted the Moffett offspring. 'Oh yeah,' retorted Ian Vermes, 'but my daddy *wrote* them.'

Referring, equally lightheartedly, to this last episode on the occasion of my eightieth birthday, Professor Philip Alexander, formerly a student, later a colleague and collaborator, and always a dear friend of mine, flatteringly remarked: 'It may be an exaggeration to claim that Geza Vermes *wrote* the Scrolls (unless, unknown to us, he is a reincarnation of the Teacher of Righteousness), but for tens of thousands around the world, both lay and academic, who have been enlightened by his translations of the texts, he is indisputably the man who wrote the Dead Sea Scrolls *in English*.'

Bibliography

Chapter I

Portrait of the Story-teller

Geza Vermes, *Providential Accidents: An Autobiography* (London, SCM Press; Lanham, MD, Rowman & Littlefield, 1998)

Biblical studies

P. R. Ackroyd et al. (eds), *Cambridge History of the Bible*, vols I–III (Cambridge, Cambridge University Press, 1963–70)

R. Morgan and J. Barton, *Biblical Interpretation* (Oxford, Oxford University Press, 1988)

Roman Catholic biblical studies

Pontifical Biblical Commission, *The Interpretation of the Bible in the Church* (1994)

—— *The Jewish People and their Sacred Scriptures in the Christian Bible* (2001)

Chapters II–V

General studies

G. R. Driver, *The Hebrew Scrolls from the Neighbourhood of Jericho* (Oxford, Oxford University Press, 1951)

A. Dupont-Sommer, *The Jewish Sect of Qumran and the Essenes: New Studies on the Dead Sea Scrolls* (London, Valentine, Mitchell, 1954)

M. Burrows, *The Dead Sea Scrolls* (New York, Viking, 1955)

G. Vermes, *Discovery in the Judean Desert* (New York, Desclée, 1956); *Les manuscrits du désert de Juda* (Paris, Desclée, 1953)

J. M. Allegro, *The Dead Sea Scrolls* (London, Penguin, 1956)

M. Burrows, *More Light on the Dead Sea Scrolls* (New York, Viking, 1958)

F. M. Cross, *The Ancient Library of Qumran and Modern Biblical Studies* (London, Duckworth, 1958; Sheffield, Sheffield University Press, 1996)

J. T. Milik, *Ten Years of Discovery in the Wilderness of Judaea* (London, SCM Press, 1959)

A. Dupont-Sommer, *The Essene Writings from Qumran* (Oxford, Blackwell, 1961)

F. M Cross, 'The Development of Jewish Script', in G. E. Wright (ed.), in *The Bible and the Ancient Near East* (New York, Doubleday, 1961)

J. M. Allegro, *The Shapira Affair* (London, W. H. Allen, 1965)

E. Wilson, *The Dead Sea Scrolls 1947–1969* (London, Penguin, 1969)

J. M. Allegro, *The Sacred Mushroom and the Cross* (London, Hodder & Stoughton, 1970)

R. de Vaux, *Archaeology and the Dead Sea Scrolls* (Oxford, Oxford University Press, 1973)

G. Vermes, *The Dead Sea Scrolls: Qumran in Perspective* (London, Collins, 1977)

G. Boniani et al., 'Radiocarbon Dating of the Dead Sea Scrolls', *Atiqot*, 20 (1991)

J. C. VanderKam, *The Dead Sea Scrolls Today* (Grand Rapids, Eerdmans; London, SPCK, 1994)

L. H. Schiffman, *Reclaiming the Dead Sea Scrolls* (Philadelphia, Jewish Publication Society, 1994)

A. J. T. Jull et al., 'Radiocarbon Dating of Scrolls and Linen Fragments from the Judean Desert', *Radiocarbon*, 37 (1995)

J. G. Campbell, *Deciphering the Dead Sea Scrolls* (London, Fontana Press, 1996)

H. Shanks, *The Mystery and Meaning of the Dead Sea Scrolls* (New York, Random House, 1998)

H. Stegemann, *The Library of Qumran* (Grand Rapids, Eerdmans, 1998)

G. Vermes, *Providential Accidents* (London, SCM Press, 1998), chapters 8, 9 and 16.

G. Vermes, *Introduction to the Complete Dead Sea Scrolls* (London, SCM Press, 1999)

L. H. Schiffman et al. (eds), *Encyclopedia of the Dead Sea Scrolls* (New York, Oxford University Press, 2000)

L. H. Schiffman et al. (eds), *The Dead Sea Scrolls Fifty Years after their Discovery 1947–1997* (Jerusalem, Israel Exploration Society, 2000)

T. H. Lim et al. (eds), *On Scrolls, Artefacts and Intellectual Property* (Sheffield, JSOT Press, 2001)

P. R. Davies et al. (eds), *The Complete World of the Dead Sea Scrolls* (London, Thames & Hudson, 2002)

J. Gascoigne et al. (eds), *Dead Sea Scrolls Special Issue, Journal of Religious History*, 26 February 2002

T. H. Lim, *The Dead Sea Scrolls: A Very Short Introduction* (Oxford, Oxford University Press, 2005)

E. M. Schuller, *The Dead Sea Scrolls: What Have We Learned 50 Years On?* (London, SCM, 2006)

M. T. Davis and B. A. Strawn, *Qumran Studies: New Approaches, New Questions* (Grand Rapids, Eerdmans, 2007)

J. A. Fitzmyer, *A Guide to the Dead Sea Scrolls and Related Literature* (Grand Rapids, Eerdmans, 2008)

Chapter VI

Official editions of the Dead Sea Scrolls

Discoveries in the Judaean Desert, vols I–XL (Oxford, Oxford University Press, 1955–2009)

Y. Yadin, *The Temple Scroll*, vols I–III (Jerusalem, Israel Exploration Society, 1983)

M. Broshi, *The Damascus Document Reconsidered* (Jerusalem, Israel Exploration Society, 1992)

T. H. Lim (ed.), *The Dead Sea Scroll Electronic Reference Library* (Leiden, Brill, 1997)

Concordance

M. G. Abegg, *The Dead Sea Scrolls Concordance*, vols I–II (Leiden, Brill, 2003)

Original text and English translation

F. García Martínez and E. J. C. Tigchelaar, *The Dead Sea Scrolls*, vols I–II (Leiden, Brill, 1997–8)

English translations

G. Vermes, *The Complete Dead Sea Scrolls in English* (London, Penguin, 2004)

M. Wise, M. Abegg and E. Cook, *The Dead Sea Scrolls: A New Translation* (New York, HarperCollins, 2005)

General bibliography

E. Schürer, G. Vermes, F. Millar, M. Goodman, *The History of the Jewish People in the Age of Jesus Christ*, vols II–III (Edinburgh, T. & T. Clark, 1979, 1986)

G. Vermes, *The Dead Sea Scrolls Forty Years On* (Oxford, Oxford Centre for Postgraduate Hebrew Studies, 1987)

J. H. Charlesworth (ed.), *The Old Testament Pseudepigrapha*, vols I–II (New York, Doubleday, 1983, 1985)

D. J. Harrington, *Invitation to the Apocrypha* (Grand Rapids, Eerdmans, 1999)

E. Ulrich, *The Dead Sea Scrolls and the Origins of the Bible* (Grand Rapids, Eerdmans, 1999)

P. W. Flint (ed.), *The Bible at Qumran: Text, Shape and Interpretation* (Grand Rapids, Eerdmans, 2001)

E. D. Herbert and E. Tov (eds), *The Bible as Book: The Hebrew Bible and the Judaean Desert Discoveries* (London, British Library, 2002)

E. Tov, *Scribal Practices and Approaches reflected in the Texts found in the Judean Desert* (Leiden, Brill, 2004)

G. Vermes, *The Complete Dead Sea Scrolls in English* (London, Penguin, 2004)

J. H. Charlesworth (ed), *The Bible and the Dead Sea Scrolls*, vol. I, *Scripture and the Scrolls* (Waco, Baylor University Press, 2006)

Chapter VII

E. Schürer, G. Vermes, F. Millar and M. Goodman, *The History of the Jewish People in the Age of Jesus Christ*, vol. II (Edinburgh, T. & T. Clark, 1986)

J. O'Callaghan, *Los papiros griegos de la cueva 7 de Qumrân* (Madrid, Editorial Católica, 1974)

M. P. Horgan, *Pesharim: Qumran Interpretation of Biblical Books* (Washington, DC, Catholic Biblical Association of America, 1979)

L. H. Schiffman, *The Eschatological Community of the Dead Sea Scrolls: A Study of the Rule of the Congregation* (Atlanta, Scholars Press, 1989)

R. Eisenman and M. Wise, *The Dead Sea Scrolls Uncovered* (Shaftesbury, Element, 1992)

D. J. Harrington, *Wisdom Texts from Qumran* (London and New York, Routledge, 1996)

G. Vermes, 'The Leadership of the Qumran Community: Sons of Zadok, Priests, Congregation', *Martin Hengel Festschrift*, I (Tübingen, Mohr Siebeck, 1996), pp. 375–84

J. J. Collins, *Apocalypticism in the Dead Sea Scrolls* (London and New York, Routledge, 1997)

Charlotte Hempel, *The Laws of the Damascus Document* (Leiden, Brill, 1998)

Charlotte Hempel, *The Damascus Texts* (London and New York, Continuum, 2000)

S. White Crawford, *The Temple Scroll and Related Texts* (London and New York, Continuum, 2000)

J. R. Davila, *Liturgical Works* (Grand Rapids, Eerdmans, 2000)

J. K. Lefkovits, *The Copper Scroll (3Q15): A Reevaluation* (Leiden, Brill, 2000)

G. L. Doudna, *4Q Pesher Nahum: A Critical Edition* (Sheffield, Sheffield Academic Press, 2001)

E. J. C. Tigchelaar, *To Increase Learning for the Understanding Ones: Reading and Reconstructing the Fragmentary Early Jewish Sapiential Text 4Q Instruction* (Leiden, Brill, 2001)

T. H. Lim, *Pesharim* (Sheffield: Sheffield Academic Press, 2002)

G. Vermes, *The Complete Dead Sea Scrolls in English* (London, Penguin, 2004)

P. Alexander, *Mystical Texts: Songs of the Sabbath Sacrifice and Related Manuscripts* (London and New York, T. & T. Clark, 2006)

J. G. Campbell, *Exegetical Texts* (London and New York, T. & T. Clark, 2006)

J. Duhaime, *War Texts: 1QM and Related Manuscripts* (London and New York, T. & T. Clark, 2006)

É. Puech et al., *Le Rouleau de cuivre de la grotte 3 de Qumrân (3Q15): Expertise – Restauration – Epigraphie, vols I–II* (Leiden, Brill, 2006)

S. Metso, *The Serekh Texts* (London and New York, T. & T. Clark, 2007)

M. Popovic, *Reading the Human Body: Physiognomics and Astrology in the Dead Sea Scrolls and Hellenistic-Early Roman Period of Judaism* (Leiden, Brill, 2007)

I. C. Werrett, *Ritual Purity and the Dead Sea Texts* (Leiden, Brill, 2007)

S. W. Crawford, *Rewriting Scripture in Second Temple Times* (Grand Rapids, Eerdmans, 2008)

Chapter VIII

C. Roth, *The Historical Background of the Dead Sea Scrolls* (Oxford, Blackwell, 1958)

A. Dupont-Sommer, *The Essene Writings from Qumran* (Oxford, Blackwell, 1961)

G. R. Driver, *The Judaean Scrolls: The Problem and a Solution* (Oxford, Blackwell, 1965)

R. de Vaux, *Archaeology and the Dead Sea Scrolls* (Oxford, Oxford University Press, 1973)

G. Vermes, *The Dead Sea Scrolls: Qumran in Perspective* (London, Collins, 1977)

E. Schürer, G. Vermes, F. Millar, M. Black, *The History of the Jewish People in the Age of Jesus Christ*, vol. II (Edinburgh, T. & T. Clark, 1979)

R. Eisenman, *James the Just and the Habakkuk Pesher* (Leiden, Brill, 1986)

P. R. Callaway, *The History of the Qumran Community* (Sheffield, JSOT Press, 1988)

Geza Vermes and Martin Goodman, *The Essenes according to the Classical Sources* (Sheffield, JSOT Press, 1989)

S. Talmon, *The World of Qumran from Within* (Jerusalem, Magnes Press, 1989)

B. Thiering, *Jesus the Man: A New Interpretation from the Dead Sea Scrolls* (New York, Doubleday, 1992)

C. P. Thiede, *The Earliest Gospel Manuscript?* (Torquay, Paternoster Press, 1992)

E. Ulrich and J. C. VanderKam (eds), *The Community of the Renewed Covenant* (Notre Dame, Notre Dame University Press, 1994)

R. Donceel and P. Donceel-Voûte, 'The Archaeology of Khirbet Qumran', in M. O. Wise et al. (eds), *Methods of Investigation of the Dead Sea Scrolls and the Khirbet Qumran Site* (New York, New York Academy of Sciences, 1994), pp. 1–38

J. B. Humbert, 'L'espace sacré à Qumrân', *Revue Biblique*, 101 (1994), pp. 161–214

J. B. Humbert and A. Chambon (eds), *Fouilles de Khirbet Qumran et de Ain Feshkha* (Fribourg, Editions Universitaires, 1994)

A. D. Crown and L. Cansdale, 'Qumran: Was it an Essene Settlement?', *Biblical Archaeology Review*, 20/5 (1994), pp. 24–35, 73–8

N. Golb, *Who Wrote the Dead Sea Scrolls?* (New York, Scribner, 1995)

M. Goodman, 'A Note on the Qumran Sectarians, the Essenes and Josephus', *Journal of Jewish Studies*, 46 (1995), pp. 161–6

C. P. Thiede and M. d'Ancona, *The Jesus Papyrus* (London, Weidenfeld, 1996)

E. M. Laperoussaz, *Qoumrân et les manuscrits de la Mer Morte: Un cinquantenaire* (Paris, Cerf, 1997)

L. Cansdale, *Qumran and the Essenes* (Tübingen, Mohr, 1997)

M. Broshi, *Bread, Wine, Walls and Scrolls* (Sheffield, Sheffield Academic Press, 2001)

Jodi Magness, *The Archaeology of Qumran and the Dead Sea Scrolls* (Grand Rapids, Eerdmans, 2002)

J. H. Charlesworth, *The Pesharim and Qumran History* (Grand Rapids, Eerdmans, 2002)

J.-B. Humbert and A. Chambon (eds), *The Excavations of Khirbet Qumran and Ain Feshkha: Synthesis of Roland de Vaux's Field Notes* (Fribourg, Fribourg Academic Press, 2003)

J.-B. Humbert and J. Gunneweg (eds), *Khirbet Qumrân et 'Ain Feshkha II: Études d'anthropologie, de physique et de chimie; Studies in Anthropology, Physics and Chemistry* (Fribourg, Fribourg Academic Press, 2003)

Yizhar Hirschfeld, *Qumran in Context: Reassessing the Archaeological Evidence* (New York, Hendrickson, 2004)

G. Vermes, *The Complete Dead Sea Scrolls in English* (London, Penguin, 2004)

J. H. Charlesworth (ed), *The Bible and the Dead Sea Scrolls*, vol. II: *The Dead Sea Scrolls and the Qumran Community* (Waco, Baylor University Press, 2006)

Edna Ullman-Margalit, *Out of the Cave: A Philosophical Inquiry into the Dead Sea Scrolls Research* (Jerusalem, Magnes, 2006)

Y. Magen and Y. Peleg, 'The Qumran Excavations 1993–2004' (Jerusalem, Judea and Samaria Publications 6, 2007)

G. Vermes, 'Historiographical Elements in the Qumran Writings: A Synopsis of the Textual Evidence', *Journal of Jewish Studies*, 58 (2007), pp. 121–39

J. Taylor, 'Qumran in Context: Reassessing the Archaeological Evidence', *Bulletin of the Anglo-Israel Archaeological Society*, 25 (2007), pp. 171–83

H. Eshel, *The Dead Sea Scrolls and the Hasmonean State* (Grand Rapids, Eerdmans, 2008)

S. Mason, 'Did the Essenes write the Dead Sea Scrolls? Don't rely on Josephus', *Biblical Archaeology Review*, 34, no. 6 (2008), pp. 61–5, 81

K. Atkinson, H. Eshel and J. Magness, 'Do Josephus's Writings support the Essene Hypothesis?', *Biblical Archaeology Review*, 35, no. 2 (2009), pp. 56–9

J. Taylor, 'Roots, Remedies and Properties of Stones: The Essenes, Qumran and Dead Sea Pharmacology', *Journal of Jewish Studies*, 60 (2009), pp. 226–44.

Chapter IX

M. Black (ed.), *The Scrolls and Christianity* (London, SPCK, 1969)

G. Vermes, *Jesus and the World of Judaism* (London, SCM Press, 1983)

H. Shanks, *Understanding the Dead Sea Scrolls* (New York, Random House, 1992)

J. H. Charlesworth (ed.), *Jesus and the Dead Sea Scrolls* (New York, Doubleday, 1992)

L. H. Schiffman, *Reclaiming the Dead Sea Scrolls* (Philadelphia, Jewish Publication Society, 1994)

S. E. Porter and C. A. Evans, *The Scrolls and the Scriptures: Qumran Fifty Years After* (Sheffield, Sheffield Academic Press, 1997)

C. A. Evans and P. W. Flint, *Eschatology, Messianism, and the Dead Sea Scrolls* (Grand Rapids, Eerdmans, 1997)

T. H. Lim, *Holy Scripture in the Qumran Commentaries and Pauline Letters* (Oxford, Clarendon Press, 1997)

F. H. Cryer and T. L. Thompson, *Qumran between the Old and the New Testaments* (Sheffield, Sheffield Academic Press, 1998)

G. Vermes, *Introduction to the Complete Dead Sea Scrolls* (London, SCM Press, 1999)

L. H. Schiffman et al. (eds), *The Dead Sea Scrolls Fifty Years after their Discovery 1947–1997* (Jerusalem, Israel Exploration Society, 2000)

J. A. Fitzmyer, *The Dead Sea Scrolls and Christian Origins* (Grand Rapids, Eerdmans, 2000)

T. H. Lim et al. (eds), *The Dead Sea Scrolls in their Historical Context* (Edinburgh, T. & T. Clark, 2000)

J. J. Collins and R. A. Kugler, *Religion in the Dead Sea Scrolls* (Grand Rapids, Eerdmans, 2000)

G. Vermes, *Jesus in his Jewish Context* (London, SCM Press, 2003)

S. Paul et al. (eds), *Emanuel: Studies in Hebrew Bible, Septuagint, and Dead Sea Scrolls in Honor of Emanuel Tov* (Leiden, Brill, 2003)

J. R. Davila (ed.), *The Dead Sea Scrolls as Background to Postbiblical Judaism and Early Christianity* (Leiden, Brill, 2003)

G. J. Brooke, *The Dead Sea Scrolls and the New Testament* (London, SPCK, 2005)

G. Vermes, *Scrolls, Scriptures and Early Christianity* (London, T. & T. Clark, 2005)

J. H. Charlesworth (ed.), *The Bible and the Dead Sea Scrolls*, vol. III, *The Scrolls and Christian Origins* (Waco, Baylor University Press, 2006)

J. J. Collins and C. A. Evans (eds), *Christian Beginnings and the Dead Sea Scrolls* (Grand Rapids, Baker, 2006)

Index